Mary Mc Ivor

April 2023

DIVIDED SCOTLAND

DIVIDED SCOTLAND

Ethnic Friction
and Christian Crisis

TOM GALLAGHER

ARGYLL ✠ PUBLISHING

© Tom Gallagher 2013

First published by
Argyll Publishing
Glendaruel
Argyll PA22 3AE
Scotland
www.argyllpublishing.co.uk

The author has asserted his moral rights.

British Library Cataloguing-in-Publication Data.
A catalogue record for this book in available from the British Library.

ISBN 978 1 908931 28 3 hardback
ISBN 978 1 908931 37 5 e-book

Printing: PB Print UK

For Professors Steve Bruce and Tom Devine,
and John Boothman, the news and current affairs chief of BBC
Scotland, whose handling of the politics of religion in Scotland
convinced me that another interpretation was overdue.

And especially for Bernard Aspinwall,
a much under-estimated historian of religion in modern
Scotland who will be widely missed, in many quarters.

Acknowledgements

I am grateful to the National Endowment for Democracy in the USA who, through a Fellowship in 2008, enabled me to ponder over both old and new sources of ethnic friction in the United Kingdom and ways of effectively responding to them. Several people looked over sections of the book, especially examining the role of football in Scottish society, and I am grateful for their helpful comments. This book benefited greatly from the publishing expertise of Derek Rodger who offered constructive advice and enabled space to be made for examination of fresh developments right up to the eve of printing. Thanks are also due to those who agreed to offer their perspectives on particular themes while research was being carried out in 2012-13. My partner Jim provided invaluable support, especially when the book reached the proof stage. Any mistakes contained in the book are solely my responsibility.

Tom Gallagher
May 2013

Contents

Introduction

SECTARIANISM has provided Scotland with several centuries of controversy. It refers to ideas, assumptions and myths about religious difference which enable judgments to be made about the behaviour and worth of individuals and the groups to which they adhere. Often organised rivalry and long-term suspicions result. Without the arrival in Scotland of large numbers of Roman Catholics from Ireland nearly 175 years ago, it is unlikely the term sectarianism would ever have acquired common currency. In the early twenty first century, it has been a commonplace expression used to describe factional disputes, often of a bloody nature, in parts of the Middle East between rival confessional groups and sometimes within large faith communities like Islam. But outside Northern Ireland, Scotland is the only other European country where the term assumes even a fraction of the prominence that it currently has in Iraq, Syria or the Lebanon.

It stemmed from rivalry, misunderstanding and low-level friction between mainly unskilled Catholic workers who formed a durable enclave in Protestant and industrial Scotland, and indigenous Scots. Many of the immigrants and their descendants defined themselves in ethnic and religious terms that were at variance with the Protestant and British values that shaped pubic life in Scotland. Today, this Protestant, British and industrial Scotland is slipping into history and secularism, economic prosperity and the severance of ties with Ireland have brought the ghetto walls tumbling down for most Catholics. But in changing times, sectarianism still manages to maintain a visible and occasionally deeply unsettling presence in Scotland.

At the level of popular culture, football rivalry provides an outlet for sectarianism. 'Into football is poured centuries of religious difference,' one journalist wrote in 1999.[1]

The football analyst Rob Marrs believes that as one of the few remaining catalysts for bringing people regularly together in large numbers, football is bound to be a lightning conductor for ugly pathologies in society:

> 'Sectarianism is a big deal in Scotland – a far bigger deal than most Scots acknowledge or care to admit – and therefore it is understandable that those involved in such conflict are likely to be attracted to entities that attracts large crowds, personify communities and clash regularly with "the other side".' [2]

It has persisted and indeed renewed itself (most notably in 2011) even as the protagonists have drawn ever-closer together in terms of the common culture that they share. It continues to find an outlet even as the two main footballing rivals, Celtic and Rangers have taken overt measures to discourage sectarianism (and it would be a brave person who would assert that its back has been broken simply by the relegation of Rangers to a minor league in 2012). Speaking in 2011, Neil Lennon, the high-profile manager of Celtic, claimed that the problem lay outside the stadiums: 'It starts in the home. It's passed down from generation to generation. . . You would like to think that in ten or fifteen years' time we won't have all this. But I'm ten years down the line and we're still talking about it.' [3]

The increased incidence of religiously mixed marriages began in the 1970s and has never slowed down since. It should conceivably have rendered a fatal blow to sectarianism if the marriage arrangements of thousands of Scots mocked such divisive categories. But if a healthier social climate has arisen, it has not been sufficient to prevent even some of the offspring of these mixed marriages getting caught up in the old group antagonisms.

Scotland has grown increasingly secular as organised religious has retreated steadily from the everyday lives of perhaps most of its people. Some might expect communal quarrels and suspicions to die with mass adherence to rival faiths. In 2004, the sociologist Michael Rosie wrote: 'sectarian is not a sustainable description of contemporary Scotland. Scotland is an increasingly secular society where religious differences are diminishing in social significance.' [4]

But holding such a view assumes that the staying power of sectarianism stemmed in some way from the integrity or intensity of intra-Christian rivalries. Those who are knowledgeable about poor communities where religion is clearly in retreat are often aware that identities can be crudely fabricated out of religious symbols. These fabricated identities are absolutely removed from faith and belief. But they still provide the munitions to prolong conflict and establish battle lines in fractured communities, ones where anger and alienation abound.

A report from the Church of Scotland in 2012 described a phenomenon of low-level intensity but one whose overall impact was still destructive:

> 'Sectarianism in Scotland today is seen and heard in the small asides which say little and reveal much. . .
>
> [It] is most publicly evident in behaviour associated with football matches but is by no means confined to this.
>
> [It] is maintained by the presence of exclusive organisations that perpetuate sectarian divisions.
>
> [It] is, thanks to changing patterns in society, less blatant than before.
>
> [It] is still, in its most extreme form, ugly, intimidating and murderous.
>
> [It]is still very much in the public eye, generating extensive media coverage and comment.
>
> [It] is capable of demonstrating itself throughout Scotland; it is not limited to cities and urban communities.
>
> [It] will continue to be pervasive unless we are willing to search our own consciences and to review our own language, attitudes and actions.' [5]

The Church of Scotland issued a formal apology earlier in the new century for the role it had played in fuelling the problem in the tense pre-1939 period by singling out Catholics of Irish descent for regular criticism. Since then, fresh controversy has been generated from perhaps a surprising source. Radical secularists, increasingly influential at the heart of the state and in the media, have criticised Christianity as harmful. Special attention has been devoted to the Catholic Church perhaps due to its continued outspokenness in arguing that Britain can only overcome mounting social problems if government policies are shaped by Christian ethical principles which champion a stable family life. Such an assertion is seen as a threat to a progressive secular order build around rationalist principles enabling people to make their own personal life choices without interference from traditional interests.

In 2010, it was not the Orange Order but these secularists who mounted the liveliest opposition to Pope Benedict XVI's visit to Scotland. In 2011, it was the supposedly ultra-modernist Scottish Green party which included in its manifesto the promise to abolish Catholic state schools.

Secularists and humanists view Catholicism as a backward belief system that should not be permitted to influence public life, nor mould the minds of children. The most influential proponent of this British anti-clericalism, the scientist Richard Dawkins enjoys the visibility that no exponent of anti-Popery ever enjoyed in modern Britain. His book *The God Delusion* never appears to have been out of the bestseller list since it was published in 2007.[6]

Sectarianism appears a less unusual hangover from the past if it is seen as a dramatic expression of a distrustful and factional spirit that still percolates across Scottish life. A grandmother of Niall Ferguson, arguably now the world's best-known historian, is described in a profile of him as expressing relief about the young Indian woman whom he brought for tea, remarking, 'She was very nice – at least she's not a Catholic'.[7] The biographer of Scotland's most high-profile Catholic prelate Thomas Winning recounts that once, when he was cardinal, 'he politely ushered a group of Protestant visitors out of his Clyde Street offices and as soon as the door was closed mimed the flute players of the Orange bands to indicate to a church employee who the group were.' [8]

Scotland has not been short of internecine disputes whose origins and staying power are hard to understand if viewed from afar. It is a poor country which geography has shaped into distinct regions whose interests have not always coincided. The harsh elements and poor soil meant that in most phases of its history it was often a grim struggle for most human beings to survive. These struggles gave rise to competition for limited resources that spilled over into conflicts over wealth, status and power. Rivalries, not just between different religious groups but different regions (Highland versus Lowland, Glasgow versus Edinburgh and different economic forces) cast a definite shadow over phases of Scottish history.

Internecine rivalries persisted even within religious blocs (such as Scottish Protestantism) which sapped their vitality and gave rivals (Scottish Catholicism obviously) a chance to hold out against them.

Detective Chief Superintendent John Carnochan, the Strathclyde policeman in charge his force's Violence Reduction Unit has innovative ideas for managing the problem, but he conceded in 2011:

> 'The violence we see here is of such intensity that it's almost unique in western Europe ... [It is] accepted as legitimate, a community norm, something that cannot be changed. The statistics are bad enough but much of what goes on never gets reported.'[9]

Religious or quasi-religious rivalry does not appear to be at the root of the gang culture that flourishes in some of Glasgow's districts. Many years of observing disputes in the educational sector and ones involving mobilised interest groups in Scotland's two largest cities, have convinced the educationalist and social commentator Walter Humes that Scotland's default position is that of a tribal society.[10] He sees myths of cultural solidarity, (ones that have sometimes beguiled the rest of the world into imagining a more compact and unified Scotland exists) as required so as to preserve at least a superficial level of unity for a country with sharp and enduring fault-lines. I think this is a tenable view to hold and it enables sectarianism to be seen less as a spectre from a bygone age and more as the outworking of tangled rivalries that rear their heads all too often in different corners of Scottish life (though usually in less overt and unsettling ways).

This book will therefore interpret sectarianism in a broad and not a narrow sense. It examines why inter-communal strife involving the use (and many would say mis-use) of religious and national symbols has enjoyed such an extended life. It analyses the new tensions that have erupted since 2010, and the response of the state, the media, churches, the soccer world and a range of civic groups. It argues that while Scotland has ceased to be overtly Protestant, anti-Catholicism remains an option that is acquiring respectability of the kind that it never had for almost a century. The Catholic Church's defence of traditional social values, and the state school system where it enjoys sway over the curriculum and

13

appointments, has placed it on a collision course with secular interests. Arguably these have filled the power vacuum in Scotland that opened up following the crumbling of a once-dominant Protestant order.

No answers appear to be in sight for running a modern society with a range of complex social problems, one which is facing the possibility of severing its British links and becoming fully self-governing perhaps in the near future. The book argues that the insolubility of problems that have given Scotland some of the lowest Western rankings for indicators denoting social well-being, has created a sense of complacency among its political and administrative leaders. They seem content to manage decline and displace problems that sap the vitality of the nation by devoting their time to alternative pursuits. These involve the age-old struggle for power and success involving mobilised interest groups.

More recently, the Scottish National Party has emerged as an electorally successful movement which sees a solution for acute policy failures in Scotland occurring by removing Scotland permanently from the British orbit. But on closer inspection, it is a movement, ambitious in rhetoric, that is very much bound up with the electoral cycle and perhaps therefore unavoidably short-term in its broad approach.

Like plenty of other parties, it is attentive to the needs of special interests that may help it to achieve its overriding constitutional goal but whose continued influence may also prevent any meaningful transform-ation of Scotland taking place. This may also mean a continued preference for quick-fix answers to deeper-seated problems as with the 2011 law to confront sectarianism that mainly confined itself to rigorously policing football chants and songs and internet communications. It is true that the SNP government formed a commission under Ulster academic Duncan Morrow to explore initiatives that might loosen the grip of sectarianism in different walks of life. But it is likely to confront widely different perspect-ives about the scope and influence of the phenomenon and whether any new state-led approaches are indeed necessary.

Dr. Michael Rosie, a member of the commission, has in the past disparaged the attention focussed on sectarianism. The composer, James MacMillan whose 1999 Edinburgh Festival speech briefly focussed national attention on the phenomenon, found himself compared with the 1930s firebrand John Cormack. Rosie believed that both were obsessed with the dangers posed by 'the Other' and thus allowed themselves to become captives of 'dead history'. It is interesting that Cormack's movement briefly enjoyed a much higher level of electoral success at the municipal level than any ever enjoyed by the conventional British far-right. But a bibliographical search reveals many hundreds of books on interwar British fascism while the published work on Cormack's Protestant Action is meagre even though he remained in electoral politics for nearly thirty years.[11]

Often it is academics who try to highlight concerns that have been overlooked (sometimes deliberately so) by important groups in society. But sectarianism has been played down by social scientists and historians in Scotland with a few shortlived interruptions and in Scotland it seems easier to get into print via an academic publisher with books that question the phenomenon. Ironically, it is religious institutions, previously at logger-heads, that have insisted on the need for the issue to be addressed by both state and society.

In 2001 Norman Shanks, then one of the best-known figures in the Church of Scotland, left no doubt about its importance: 'Sectarianism is a running sore within Scottish society whose insidious influence on our attitudes is so deep and damaging. We hope the voice of the church will be raised more strongly against sectarianism.'[12] Later in that decade, the Catholic church dropped its low-key attitude and became forthright about how the problem of sectarianism continued to affect it. Peter Kearney, its media spokesman spoke out forcefully and found himself subject to much the same scorn and ridicule that greeted MacMillan for his outspokenness. But anti-Catholicism, not sectarianism, was the term preferred by many of those Catholics drawing attention to communal friction and lingering discrimination. For the educationalist Michael Brady, sectarianism is an 'umbrella term that hinders tackling the problem of religious bigotry and racism in Scotland.'[13] For Dr. Joseph Bradley of Stirling University, it is 'a catch-all and evasive phrase' suggesting that both sides are equally to blame and that there is something problematic about 'an identity rooted in religion and/or ethnic background'. [14]

By contrast, I find the term an apt one for exploring the persistence first of religious and then quasi-religious rivalry and for trying to explain why new social movements have come forward to supplant Protestant voices and challenge Catholic moral claims and institutional forms of influence.

In surveying two hundred years of sectarianism, this book uses materials for the pre-1985 period from an earlier book *Glasgow the Uneasy Peace: Religious tension in Modern Scotland* (Manchester University Press 1987) which quickly went out of print; but over half the text is new, based on research, much of it carried out in 2011-2013 when unsettling incidents brought sectarianism once again into the public eye.

NOTES

1 Jack O'Sullivan, *Independent*, 4 June 1999.

2 Rob Marrs, 'Scotland's Gordian Knot' 23 April 2011,
www.leftbackinthechangingroom.com

3 Craig Brown and Stuart Bathgate, 'Lennon: 'We can't cure sectarianism',
Scotsman, 16 April 2011.

4 Michael Rosie, *The Sectarian Myth in Scotland: Of Bitter memory and Bigotry*, Palgrave, Houndsmill, 2004, p. 3.

5 Sectarianism, A Report for the Church of Scotland General Assembly, Church and Society Council, Edinburgh 2012, p.3.

6 See www.richarddawkins. net

7 'Niall Ferguson: admirable historian, or imperial mischief maker?' *Guardian*,18 June 2012

8 Stephen McGinty, *The Turbulent Priest: The Life of Cardinal Winning*, Harper-Collins, London 2001, p. 184.

9 Paola Tataro, 'Fear and loathing in a city of rage', *Sydney Morning Herald*, 11 June 2011

10 Walter Humes, 'Post-independence politics will be no different in tribal Scotland', *Scottish Review*, 8 September 2011.

11 For Rosie's comparison, see *The Sectarian Myth* p.p. 149-50. There is a chapter on Protestant Action by him in Martin J. Mitchell (ed), *New Perspectives on the Irish in Scotland*, John Donald, Edinburgh 2008.

12 *Herald*, 23 May 2001.

13 Michael Brady, 'Dropping the ball on Sectarianism', *Scottish Catholic Observer*, 20 May 2012.

14 Joseph M.Bradley, *Ethnic and Religious Identity in Modern Scotland: Culture, Politics and Football*, Aldershot, UK: Avebury, 1995, p.1.

CHAPTER 1

Protestant Scotland
and the arrival of the Irish

IMMIGRANTS from rural Ireland first began to arrive in Scotland in considerable numbers at the dawn of the nineteenth century. The industrial revolution was already gathering pace in lowland Scotland and, with it, a demand for low-cost labour needed to build the roads, canals and railways, and work in the mines, factories and mills that would transform the appearance of central Scotland in a few decades. With Lancashire in mind, Friedrich Engels claimed in 1843 that the industrial revolution would have been a much more gradual affair but for the human raw material provided by the immigrant Irish.[1] This may have been even more true of Scotland where, by 1851, 7.2% of the population was Irish compared with 2.9% in England and Wales.[2] But in no part of industrial Britain were the Catholic Irish welcomed or esteemed, and they in turn showed no anxiety to correspond to the customs and routine of their adopted communities.

In Scotland it could have been predicted in advance that the encounter between host and newcomer would be traumatic for both parties. In previous centuries a sharp cultural and developmental gulf had opened up between Ireland and Scotland which had not previously existed when both had lain outside England's political orbit. The catalysts were the Reformation, the Act of Union of 1707, and the industrial revolution, starting around 1760.

Scotland enthusiastically adopted the new reformed faith, more hesitantly entered into political union with England, and became one of the first nations to industrialise, as Ireland remained faithful to Rome, locked in colonial subjugation to Britain, and economically destitute but politically un-reconciled to the version of *Pax Britannica* imposed upon it.

Of course, this broad generalisation needs to take into account developments in the north of Ireland where, in the seventeenth century, a British settler community took hold whose links with the west of Scotland and with Lancashire, were bound to greatly complicate community relations in these two areas of heaviest immigration from Ireland. Otherwise Scotland moved closer to England even though it preserved important areas of autonomy through its legal, religious, and educational institutions, while Ireland drifted apart from the larger island, even though under absolute domination from London.

By the 1800s, when the first emigrant ships were docking at the Broomielaw in Glasgow, blood ties and a common heritage up to the end of the Middle Ages counted for little between the peoples of Scotland and Ireland. Bishop Gray explained to Henry Manning, the English prelate who visited Scotland in 1867, that there was little common ground between them:

> 'The Scotch are animated by a strong hereditary hatred of Catholic-
> ity. Nor is the feeling of the country favourable to Irish settlers . . .
> The religion, the history, the character and habits of the two peoples
> show many elements not of difference only but antagonism.' [3]

Manning spent a week in Scotland in order to draw up a report for the Vatican about strife within the church between Scottish and Irish clergy. Even the leadership of the church, drawn mainly from the Highlands, had been more than touched by the changes occurring in Scottish society so that it presented an alien face to many of the Irish. Acceptance of such conditioning may have been the price for its survival after the Reformation of the mid-sixteenth century.

The Scottish Reformation was so complete that, unlike other parts of northern Europe, no bloody civil war between Protestants and Catholic factions was necessary for the reformed faith to triumph. The old faith simply melted away except in the Gaelic-speaking West Highlands, some of the offshore Hebridean islands, and in Banffshire in the north-east. Scotland and avoided the horrific carnage of the Thirty Years War fought in central Europe between 1618 and 1648. Persecution of Roman Catholics in Scotland could not be described as systematic or savage. The only priest to be put to death in seventeenth century Scotland was St. John Ogilvie SJ, who was executed at Glasgow cross in 1615. [4]

Protestants were far more vindictive towards fellow Protestants as the bloody persecution of the Covenanters in the 1680s by the temporarily ascendant Episcopalians (who subscribed to the Anglican communion), showed. This was not the first nor would it be the last time that family quarrels in the reformed Christian church diverted attention from the 'Menace of Rome'. Protestant fundamentalists and radicals would always be more animated by anti-elitism or by religious deviationism within their own ranks than by the survival of some thousands of Scottish Catholics.[5] But their tiny church entered its most perilous phase in the year 1700 when the penal laws introduced throughout Great Britain and Ireland banned Catholics from practising their faith, prohibited them from teaching even their own children, and risked them losing their property to their nearest Protestant relatives. Between 1680 and 1800 the number of Catholics in Scotland may have dropped from 50,000 to 30,000.[6]

Catholic attachment to the Jacobite cause, which was vanquished in the rebellions of 1715 and 1745, increased the pressure of the state on them and thousands of Highland Catholics emigrated to north America in succeeding decades. But the penal laws were not applied as harshly as in Ireland; some powerful Catholic nobles existed who were able to protect tenant farmers and labourers from the worst rigours of persecution; the eighteenth century Enlightenment glowed strongly in Scotland, one of its cornerstones being religious toleration; and the Highland clan society disintegrated so rapidly after 1745 that the penal laws were increasingly allowed to lapse.

A growing spirit of toleration was confirmed by the 1793 Relief Act which abolished the most punitive anti-Catholic laws still on the statute books. By now the bishops and clergy of the Scottish mission (Rome relegated the Catholic church in Scotland to missionary status between 1603 and 1878) were ready to accept the new Hanoverian order and indeed had lost the taint of Jacobitism more quickly than the Episcopalians. George Hay, bishop of the lowland district, insisted that all clergy and laity pray for the Hanoverian monarch and, by the end of the eighteenth century, some Scottish priests were beginning to serve as chaplains in the British army.[7]

In the 1780s Scottish bishops were already making it clear to Rome that, although they desperately needed extra clergy, they would prefer not to have Irish priests, some of whom were willing to sanction resistance to British domination.[8] They remembered the anti-Catholic riot in Edinburgh during 1779 and the 'No Popery' scare of 1788, in which 12,000 Glaswegians vowed to suppress idolatory and managed to block a relief bill.[9] One nineteenth century historian claimed that in the 1790s, when Glasgow had no more than thirty-nine Catholics, there were forty-three anti-Catholic societies.[10]

Such hostility stemmed from a more general fear of Jacobitism in lowland Scotland. Any revival of Prince Charles Edward Stewart's cause would, it was feared, jeopardise the new-won prosperity of industrial Scotland and perhaps encourage a French invasion. So potential adherents of the pretender's cause were scarcely esteemed and the hostile atmosphere delayed by fourteen years a relief bill already law in Ireland and England by 1779.[11]

So the 1770s and 1780s demonstrated how deeply anti-Catholicism was embedded in the popular culture of Scotland. However, the death of the pretender in 1788 and the manner in which the French revolution produced an unlikely alliance between Britain and the Vatican broke down much upper-class religious prejudice in Britain. The exchequer even paid a grant to Catholic clergy from 1798 to 1804, since the revolutionary upheavals in Europe had closed off their main sources of financial support.[12]

But when Sir James Mackintosh, the rector of Glasgow University, made a favourable reference to the new cathedral, he was howled down by the students.[13] Toleration still had a long way to go and it could not simply be legislated into existence. This was demonstrated in 1829 with the stormy passage of the Catholic Emancipation Act which allowed Catholics to be elected to parliament. If allowed to express their opinion in a referendum, the majority of Scots would probably have voted no and the opposition intensified as one moved east to west and nearer to Glasgow.[14] By a large majority, the General Session of Glasgow (comprising ministers and elders of the Church of Scotland) rejected the act as did Glasgow University students. The town council voted against, although by a narrow majority, and the *Glasgow Herald* was hostile.[15]

Ordinary Glaswegians displayed particular hostility to the act for social as well as religious reasons. Workers and artisans were acutely aware how rapidly the city's Irish community was growing and what the consequences might be for their livelihoods:

> 'the lower orders in the west of Scotland were very naturally ever ready to do anything which, in their opinion, would press and keep back the Irish Catholics who pour in upon them almost with every tide, coming to compete with them successfully in all their occupations, and thereby materially lowering the rate of wages.' [16]

Hitherto immigrants had been mainly seasonal agricultural labourers who were often only temporary visitors hardly visible to most of the Scottish population. But a new type of immigrant appeared after 1775 when the Scottish canals began to be dug. They stayed for longer periods, some settled permanently in Scotland, and their growing numbers led to friction with indigenous Scottish labourers. They collided with Highland migrants for whom it had been hoped the building of the canals would relieve some of the acute distress in the north.

Few if any Irishmen settled in the Scottish countryside where work was usually only seasonal and which many Scots were themselves quitting for the towns. Many labourers needed to send money to dependents at home and often the reward for farm work was payment in kind.[17] So, like the immigrant Irish elsewhere, those in Scotland increasingly flocked to the populated centres. In a few years, the whole map of Scottish Catholicism was to be changed. By 1822, there were an estimated twelve hundred Catholics in Glenlivet, a Highland stronghold of the faith, compared to 15,000 in Glasgow;[18] by 1851, the Irish made up 7.2% of the Scottish population and 18.2% of that of the largest city, Glasgow.

Unlike later waves of migration, religion only lightly touched the first arrivals once in Glasgow the common culture of poverty.[19] By the 1840s, there were only half-a-dozen Scottish clergy to cope with the 70,000 Irish immigrants who were pouring into the west of Scotland as famine raged in Ireland, when over one hundred priests, preferably from the same society as the immigrants, would have been needed. In 1847 three of those Scottish priests, one in Greenock and two in Paisley, died of typhus fever while

21

ministering to destitute refugees in flight from mass starvation at home.[20] It has been reckoned that when Irish priests did begin to arrive, it was thirty years too late and wholesale apostasy had already taken place.[21]

Concentrated on the bottom rungs of the occupational ladder and huddled into their cramped quarters in the chief urban centres, the Irish constituted 'the most abject part of the population, prepared to tolerate a lower standard of life than all but the very poorest' of the workforce.[22] Many were unable to survive the very painful transition from a rough and simple peasant society to the far more brutal and alien industrial environment and they succumbed to disease, under-nourishment, or alcohol. The most accomplished writer to depict the hardship and uncertainty of the immigrant community was the Donegal-born Patrick MacGill (1891-1963) in books such as *Children of the Dead End* and *The Rat-Pit*.

The average life expectancy in Glasgow during the 1840s was thirty which is lower than in most big cities of the Third World today. On average, Scots drank five times as much spirits as the English so this shared weakness did not make the Irish nearly as conspicuous as they were in other centres of the diaspora where their fondness for alcohol became a key element of their stereotype.[23] But nevertheless the Irish were despised and feared because of their poverty and alien character and respected nineteenth century opinion moulders like Matthew Arnold and Thomas Carlyle did not hesitate to describe the Irish influx as a social disaster for Victorian Britain.

The priest was the only authority to whom Irish labourers readily showed any deference and he was *the* central figure in immigrant neighbourhoods.[24] Irish priests were not welcomed by the Scottish church which feared being colonised outright by the much larger church in Ireland. Alexander Cameron, bishop of the lowland distrist from 1805 to 1825, at the very time of maximum transition, was even reluctant to accept any sons of immigrants to train at the single Scottish seminary.[25] Scottish priests complained of the superstitious practices indulged in by the Irish and could be exasperated by the inconsistency of parishioners whose devotion could be disfigured by recourse to drink or to brawling.[26]

In their turn, the Irish sometimes felt that Scottish Catholics were little different from Protestants. Their clergy disliked the continental-style devotions, the religious images, and the elaborate ceremonial, all things the Irish cherished.[27] Immigrants did not readily forget the ways of the 'oul country' and would not be ready for many years to contemplate assimilation with even fellow Scottish Catholics. The animosity between the Irish and their Scottish clergy of the 1820s and 1830s spread to later waves of immigrants and would produce a full-scale crisis in the church during the 1860s.

The polarisation of the Catholic church in Scotland on straight ethnic lines demonstrated how completely out of step the immigrants were with the outlook and values of the host society. But it was the Irishman's readiness to toil longer, harder, and for less remuneration which elicited the bitterest response from Scottish and also English workers. During 1854, miners in Airdrie struck to expel the Irish from the coalfields.[28] As late as the 1880s, Keir Hardie could complain about the Irish collier who had 'a big shovel, a strong back and a weak brain', came straight from 'a peat bog or a tattie field' and produced 'coal enough for a man and a half'.[29]

Coal owners and iron masters did not hesitate to import Irish workers (and Highlanders) so as to break strikes. In 1831, Irish labour was used to break a strike in Coatbridge which became an important immigrant centre rivalling the adjacent and mainly indigenous mining town of Airdrie.[30]

Well into the nineteenth century, plenty of Irish were to be found in those parts of the Scottish coalfields where non-union labour predomin-ated.[31] Sometimes employers sponsored sectarian infighting by recruiting an Irish workforce composed of rival Protestant and Catholic ('Orange' and 'Green') segments and then setting them down in the same locality.[32] As a parliamentary candidate for Falkirk in 1851, Sir James Baird, the coal-owner included anti-Catholic statements in his manifesto even though he had sent agents to Ireland in order to recruit a workforce from among rural Catholics.[33]

Over 150 years later, the area's local Catholic bishop recounted:

> [there are] 'twenty matching pairs of villages [in Lanarkshire] where the population in one was very heavily Catholic and the population

23

in the other was quite the reverse. We also saw thus in terms of jobs
. . . the Catholics tended to go down the pits and the Protestants in
the steel works [had]. . . the better jobs. . . sectarianism was almost
inevitably a part of life at the time and it has never really gone
away.'[34]

In Glasgow, with its high ratio of skilled jobs, there was less economic
friction since the poorly educated immigrants, totally lacking local
connections, simply could not compete for them. Instead they dominated
the unskilled labour market in the city finding work as casual construction
or dock labourers, coal heavers, and as sweated labour in textiles, and in
the chemical and dyeing works which were polluting the city by the middle
of the century; here men, and especially women, toiled in truly appalling
conditions.[35]

Down the River Clyde in Greenock and in the adjacent town of Port
Glasgow, the labour market was far more fluid than in the nearby
metropolis of Glasgow. Here Catholic and Protestant workers from Ireland
worked in uneasy proximity in the sugar refineries and on the dockside
quays. Economic competiton was fierce and spilled over into communal
disorders, especially in the 1850s. Some employers in Greenock favoured
the Irish because they were more adaptable than Scottish workers.[36] In
Lanarkshire, the Irish secured work in the textile mills, from which they
had been barred in the north of England, because of the reluctance of Scots
to be drawn into the factory system on terms that the Irish accepted far
more willingly.[87]

If economic friction had been the only major source of division,
community relations would have begun to steadily improve, perhaps even
in the lifetimes of the first and second generation Irish resident in industrial
Scotland. However, the gulf between the Irish and nearly every section of
the host population was more of a cultural one which made it difficult for
misunderstandings and social antagonisms to be breached. A whole
bundle of distinguishing characteristics – race and accent, religion,
occupation, residence, and politics – set the Catholic Irish portion of
Glasgow's population apart from the rest.[38] Prejudice towards them came
not just from traditional religious or political foes but was endemic
throughout society. In 1847, when the anti-Catholic journal, *The Witness*,

associated Roman Catholicism with dependence and indigence, and Protestantism with vitality and progress, it was merely repeating a widely-held Victorian nostrum.[39] Some years later, the *Glasgow Herald* reacted bitterly against the starving Irish, much preferring that they choose north America as a permanent home, while pointing to the potential benefits for Britain in the recent famine:

> The Irish family grows on the other side of the Atlantic, and grows so prosperous that we could almost hope that the whole of their disconnected connections who have been left behind, will shortly follow them ... If the country continues to be thinned, as we believe it will be by the deportation of families left behind, we may yet have the power, so much desiderated, of establishing a British population in Ireland and rendering real the Union of the United Kingdom.[40]

In order to make themselves acceptable in Victorian Scotland, the Irish would have needed to make themselves invisible.'[41] Perhaps their most conspicuous distinguishing feature was their religion; certainly in Scotland it may have been the one which most delayed integration into the host society. Looking at Britain as a whole, it is not difficult to see why. The Victorian Age was one where much of the world was seen and understood in religious terms even by those who did not regularly practice a faith. This was no less true for the immigrants, but it made no difference since their religion was regarded as a menace to Protestant Britain and its liberties. The 1643 Westminster Confession of Faith was still a cornerstone of Scottish and English Protestantism. It called the Pope that 'anti-Christ, that man of sin, and son of perdition'. It rejected the Catholic belief in transubstantiation, i.e. that Christ was present body and blood in the Eucharist, and it affirmed that there are only two sacraments – baptism and communion – as against the seven proclaimed by Roman Catholicism.[42]

Note how the language Protestants used to each other, never mind towards Papists, could be deeply intolerant. When the Church of Scotland was split in two as a result of the Great Disruption of 1843, the churches of the established faith were soon being dubbed 'synagogues of Satan' by the disruptionists or Free Kirkers who were 'traducers of the Mother Kirk' to those who remained within the Church of Scotland.[43] So the invective reserved for Roman Catholics was bound to be even more scalding.

The supremacy claimed by Rome over the whole of the Christian church was angrily rejected by the national or voluntary Protestant churches of Britain. During the 1860s, the Vatican in Rome would re-affirm its claim for spiritual leadership over world Christianity, as *the* one true faith. The Doctrine of the Syllabus of Errors of 1864 condemned liberalism and socialism and was followed by the declaration of Papal infallibility in 1870. Its effect on Protestant sensibilities can be imagined when even a liberal reformer like Gladstone was finally driven to conclude that Roman Catholicism and modern civilisation were incompatible. [44]

'Popery' was the broad term coined for Roman pretensions. An elaborate mosaic of theological, moral, political, economic, and even sexual attitudes lay behind popular anti-Catholicism. The intolerance of the host society could sometimes be matched by a similar response from the leaders of the immigrant community whereby any contact or discourse with Scottish Protestants was thoroughly forbidden. In 1864 a correspondent in the newspaper of the immigrant community warned of the danger of association with Protestant Scotsmen: [they] 'will poison and corrupt our hearts, they will, by degrees, make us cold and indifferent about our religion and duty to God'.[45]

Priests and other community leaders encouraged what amounted to voluntary segregation in all the big areas of Irish settlement and in many of the smaller ones where the conditions existed for a distinct enclave community. The preservation of the faith and the need strangers in a strange land had for solidarity were strong incentives. Increasing numbers of clergy reinforced the distinctiveness of the immigrant community. Partly from its meagre resources the funds were largely scraped together for the impressive Gothic churches, elaborately decorated inside, which usually provided such a striking contrast to the mean dwellings in the rest of the neighbourhood. These handsome churches were the nerve-centre of the community and elicited reluctant admiration from some Protestants relieved to find that the results of the Irish influx were not all degradation and decay. But often such manifestations of Catholic revival were viewed with barely concealed hostility by less tolerant Victorians.

In 1850, the Scottish Reformation Society was founded at a time of mounting alarm that the Catholic church was rapidly ceasing to be the church of the immigrant poor and that it was attracting the well-born and the successful in growing numbers. By 1914, there were some thirty million Roman Catholics in the British Empire and their numbers were increasing.[46]

Defections were not as steep or as alarming in Scotland as in England. It was only in 1900 that two Church of Scotland clergymen, Henry Grey Graham and Robert Charleson, became the first ministers to defect to Rome since the Reformation.[47] But a grave shock had occurred in 1868 with the conversion of John Crichton-Stuart, 3rd Marquess of Bute... [then] the richest man in Britain. The *Glasgow Herald* described his decision as a 'perversion'. The tenants and estate workers on the island propped a portrait of their young laird against the wall and pelted it with stones. Unabashed, he horrified his Presbyterian neighbours. . . by erecting an enormous marble chapel on the island, complete with a replica of the tower of Saragossa cathedral.[48]

In the Scottish Borders town of Kelso, in 1856, a newly-built Catholic church endowed by the convert James Hope-Scott was burned to the ground, with the school-house and dwelling-house adjoining.[49] Priests were sometimes assaulted in public during tense periods. In 1850, the redoubtable Michael Condon was seriously beaten up at Hamilton in Lanarkshire 'by an Orange gang to whom the sight of a "Papist" priest was too much'.[50] Assessing a list of 50 disturbances in Lanarkshire, between the 1830s and the mid-1880s, involving Irishmen, the historian Calum Brown wrote, 'the frequency of recorded confrontations. . . suggests that the unrecorded cases represented an artery of hate operating throughout Scottish urban society.'[51]

The larger urban centres tended to be more peaceful than smaller densely-populated communities and even amidst the acrid atmosphere which much of lowland Scotland presented in the middle years of the last century, there were some signs of mutual regard. Thomas Chalmers (1780-1847), the best-known evangelical preacher in nineteenth century Scotland refrained from making anti-Catholic statements even though giving in to popular prejudice would no doubt have enhanced his reputation, at least in the short-term. Instead he backed Catholic emancipation, made provisions for the Catholic poor in his social work activities in Glasgow and preached sermons for religious tolerance in Ulster as well as in Scotland.[52] Chalmers was among those who welcomed the Irish priest Theobald Mathew when he came to Glasgow in August 1842 to preach total abstinence; in fact he received a tremendous welcome from Protestants and Catholics alike, brought together by a common concern about drunkenness.[53] Very occasionally, personal encounters smoothed the path of reconciliation. For instance, in Hamilton, the Free Church minister in 1851 preached a sermon appealing for the revival of the spirit of Cromwell to combat Catholicism. Shortly afterwards, the neighbouring priest, Fr. Michael Condon helped to save the manse (the home of a Presbyterian minister), when a chimney fire threatened to spread. After this contact, Condon recorded in his diary how 'the sword of the Puritan was no longer appealed to'.[54]

Although anti-Catholicism acquired its longest-lease of life on the British mainland in Scotland, it would be wrong to assume that the most concentrated inter-ethnic strife occurred here. Lancashire in fact witnessed the sharpest collision between Irish immigrants and British workers, in the period between 1848 and 1870. Well into the 1880s, it remained the case there that the larger the proportion of Irish immigrants, the greater the tendency to vote Conservative.[55] This was not nearly as true of the west of Scotland where Orangeism and populist Toryism revived around the same time as in Lancashire but without being able to influence voting habits, at least until much later. Founded in Ulster in 1795, Orangeism proved suitable for export because it blended well with certain ideals and prejudices that were widely shared in nineteenth century Britain. It came increasingly to stand for the maintenance of British power in Ireland and the defence of the Protestant constitution and liberties established by the Glorious Revolution of 1688 when their hero, King William of Orange, ascended the British throne. This victory for limited monarchy and the reformed faith was clinched by the defeat of the Catholic King James II at the Battle of the Boyne in Ireland on 12th July 1690. It is this date which Orangemen in different parts of Britain and Ireland have celebrated each 12 of July down to the present day (although in Scotland Orange marches take place on the previous weekend to enable Scottish Orangemen to travel to Ulster for the 12th, where it is a public holiday).[56]

The main reason for Orange progress in the west of Scotland was the proximity of Ulster, the birthplace and chief stronghold of Orangeism. Clydeside shipyard workers who had earlier gone to Belfast to teach workers how to build iron ships were returning to Glasgow at the end of the 1850s, just as the upturn was starting.[57] Belfast's shipyard workers were the most intensely Orange section of that city's proletariat and, by the 1870s, the same thing was being said about shipyard workers living in the Partick and Springburn districts of Glasgow. By the 1860s, Ulster Protestants made up 25% of all the Irish in Glasgow and they were also well established in Liverpool.[58] Many had prospered and close personal and social ties were forged with the citizens of Glasgow, whose religion and ancestry they shared. But the Ulster Protestants retained their specific identity and were well-organised in religious and other societies.[59]

The boom period for recruitment in Glasgow was the 1870s. By 1878, it was estimated that there were a hundred lodges in the city with a total membership of fourteen to fifteen thousand.[60]

The Orange Order was all-Protestant by statute and the Tories in Glasgow would be the same in practice until well into the twentieth century. These sharp religious distinctions ran through many other areas of Victorian life as immigrants often discovered if they tried to better themselves or collided with, or else became dependent on, the state. 'No Irish Need Apply' was a common warning in the employment columns of the press or on the walls of economic concerns looking for extra hands.

Inevitably, the reluctance of most citizens to treat the Irish as part of the mainstream community was reflected in their treatment at the hands of the authorities. There was little love lost between the police and the Irish in Victorian Scotland. Irish champions, like John Denvir, felt that the police approach towards the Irish was often one of straight victimisation.[61] Certainly they figured in Victorian crime statistics much more prominently than any other specific grouping. But, if broken down, the offences committed by immigrants often appear to have been of a comparatively minor kind – drunkenness, petty theft, vagrancy, and crimes committed against the person in mitigating circumstances.[62] Writing in 1904, Denvir offered an example of the type of offence which boosted the gaol statistics:

> 'A 'basket girl' or hawker might be sent to gaol, not having the money to pay the fine for simply 'obstructing' the pathway trying to sell her fish, or apples, or oranges. Nay, the same hawker might fall into the hands of the police a second or third time and be classified each time as a separate and distinct criminal in the year's returns.' [63]

Sometimes, when the Irish were in need of police assistance, it was withheld or only offered grudgingly. The *Glasgow Herald* of 24th July 1835, when reporting an anti-Catholic riot in Airdrie, wrote that 'the crowd seemed to have the tacit support of the local authorities. When the crowd attacked the home of a Protestant by mistake, the head of the Airdrie police merely pointed out the error to them but made no effort to dissuade them. One of the burgh magistrates was also reported to be in the midst of the mob. [64]

A man who attempted to take the life of a Catholic policeman with pistol and dagger, during similar violence in Greenock, in 1852, received a sentence of only sixty days. Finally, in January 1853, with violence continuing, the government intervened, to suspend the magistrates and the town clerk, and appoint in their place a stipendiary magistrate.[65]

Often priests found they were barred from entering the workhouse to provide religious comfort and instruction for Catholic children. Many of the middle-class guardians who administered the Poor Law in towns like Greenock, were hostile to Catholics. The Catholic Church frequently complained in the 1860s and 1870s about local Poor Law boards in which Catholic children were taught the Protestant catechism, refused permission to attend Mass on Sundays, and boarded out to Protestant families.[66]

In Greenock, the guardians insisted that orphans should be brought up according to the religion of the majority of ratepayers. Finally, in 1870, Catholics appealed to parliament for redress and, in that year, Fr. Bernard Tracey, later the first Roman Catholic elected to a school board in Scotland, submitted a report to the House of Commons on the proselytism of Catholic children in the care of local authorities.[67] Conditions gradually

improved but, in the 1880s, the Catholic *Glasgow Observer* was campaigning against the destitute children institute known as the Quarrier homes
which had been founded in 1876 by William Quarrier. A leader in the paper
on 20th June 1885, made the following accusation against the Quarrier
homes: 'that in the city of Glasgow, and within the short space of twelve
months, 800 destitute Catholic children should be shamelessly bribed to
become Protestants and then transported to Canada and other places
beyond the seas.' [68]

The trade unions were also hostile to Irish immigration. In the
nineteenth century, only certain craft trades were unionised in Britain.
The Irish who dominated the unskilled labour market in Glasgow were
not organised and in the second half of the nineteenth century, the outlook
of many Glasgow trade unionists towards them was 'racist'.[69] An example
of prevailing attitudes among Scottish workers comes from Aberdeen
where, in 1881, the trades council, listened to delegates complaining that
'in great measure, the chief obstacle to any material or satisfactory
improvements in the conditions of the people of Ireland lay in certain
natural defects incident to their race'.[70]

Anti-Irish prejudice had a longer lease of life in Scotland than in other
countries of the Irish diaspora and the immigrants were more isolated from
the host society than elsewhere, but nevertheless, the *violent* backlash
against the Irish was not as extreme in Scotland as in some other places.
There was no equivalent of the Know Nothing movement, which turned
anti-Irish sentiment into a strong political force on the north-eastern
seaboard of the USA during the early 1850s. Scotland was spared the savage
inter-communal violence which flared up sporadically in Liverpool during
the eighty years after the great famine. Irish immigration and its attendant
social consequences also affected the *politics* of lowland Scotland to a
lesser extent than for instance the eastern United States or Liverpool.

Why then was anti-Irish hostility pressed into a number of deep but
narrow channels which only rarely burst their banks to swamp society as
a whole? A number of tentative explanations can be offered:

1. High immigration occurred just at the time when the face of Scotland
   was being altered more rapidly than at any other moment in the nation's

history. So, at a time of maximum transition and great economic upheaval, the influx of the Irish was far less traumatic and dislocating than it would have been at other moments. Allied to this, the economy was buoyant in the 1840s and 1850s and able to absorb the extra numbers; in fact there was a demand for unskilled labour which could not be met from the local population and which prompted some Scottish capitalists to actually send their agents to Ireland in order to recruit labour for their expanding concerns.

2. Scotland already had an immigration culture that had grown up because her cultivated land, in recent centuries, had not been productive enough to sustain the settled population. This tradition may have made the arrival of the newcomers slightly less intolerable than otherwise might have been the case; the expansion of the British empire at the time of the Irish diaspora may also have acted to dampen down unrest in Scotland since it must have removed a number of energetic and restless people who might have fomented inter-communal strife if they had chosen to remain in Scotland.

3. The Irish were also pouring into Scotland just at the time when north British values seemed to be replacing Scottish ones as important symbols of identity. So although they were despised for their religious allegiances or lowly status, they were not treated as scapegoats by a nationalistic bourgeoisie as was already beginning to happen to their counterparts in the multi-national empires at the opposite end of Europe. Strangely enough, it was the third or fourth generation of Irish, more accurately described as the 'Scoto-Irish' who, in the 1920s and 1930s were victimised for their 'unScottishness' but this was a shortlived phenomenon that will be examined in a later chapter.

4. One of the upheavals which Scottish society was already experiencing as the Irish arrived was the civil war within the Presbyterian church which was known as the Church of Scotland by virtue of being the established faith of the country. In 1843, the year of the 'Great Disruption', the Church of Scotland split over the question of church patronage – whether a minister should be appointed by the elders of the congregation or whether local landowners should have an important say as permitted by the 1712 Patronage Act. Overall, the fact that Presbyterianism in all

its forms was more immune to Roman Catholicism than Anglicanism was, also made the religious environment more secure. There were fewer defectors to Rome and most Scottish Protestants had no reason to doubt Queen Victoria's belief that 'the Scottish Church is the real and true stronghold of Protestantism'.[71] Papal interference and Jesuit intriguing in international and British politics, which was staple fare in English anti-Catholicism, did not loom so large north of the border, possibly because Scotland no longer possessed a state of its own. A test of Protestant feelings came when the Scottish Catholic hierarchy was restored in 1878. Remembering the backlash which had greeted this development in England after the Catholic hierarchy there had been restored in 1850, the British government, through its agents in Rome, had been lobbying against a Scottish restoration throughout the 1860s, for fear of 'the disastrous effect in Scotland'.[72] But when the first act of the new Pope, Leo XIII was to restore the hierarchy on 13 March 1878 after a gap of 275 years, it passed off relatively peacefully.

In Liverpool, Pastor George Wise, triggered off serious rioting in the city in 1903 and 1909. Glasgow may have escaped communal violence on the same scale due to the determination of the city's authorities to keep provocative sectarian displays in check.[73] The self-restraint of opposing factions may also have made the policeman's lot easier in Glasgow than in Liverpool or Belfast. The leaders of Orange and Irish factions in Glasgow often emphasised in their followers the need for discipline. When trouble did arise it was not unknown for apologies to be offered to the offended community.[74] Such restraint may have been simple commonsense in a city where, by 1914, some 700,000 people lived in its three central square miles, the densest concentration of people anywhere in Europe.[75] The absence of space discouraged complete residential segregation on an ethnic or religious basis. So Glasgow avoided much of the polarisation which in Belfast and Liverpool stemmed from the creation of rival religious ghettoes. No districts were completely inhabited by members of one denomination and even Irish strongholds like the Calton, High Street, Bridgegate, the Gorbals, and Cowcaddens were partly mixed. These factors acted as an important safety-valve preventing a total collision between hosts and newcomers.

NOTES

1 Erich Strauss, *Irish Nationalism and Britsh Democracy*, Methuen, London 1951, p. 123.

2 Gerry Charles Gunnin, *John Wheatley, Catholic Socialism and Irish Labour in the West of Scotland*, Ph.D. thesis, University of Chicago, 1973, p.23.

3 Memoranda for Archbishop Manning drawn up by Bishop Gray, quoted by J. F. McCaffrey, 'Roman Catholics in Scotland in the nineteenth and twentieth centuries', *Records of the Scottish Church History Society*, 21, 2, 1983, pp. 283-4.

4 John Cooney, *Scotland and the Papacy*, Paul Harris, Edinburgh, 1982, p. 10.

5 Owen Dudley Edwards, 'Scots and the Pope', *Irish Times*, 26 February 1983.

6 James Darragh, 'Catholic population of Scotland in the twentieth century', *Glasgow Observer and Scottish Catholic Herald*, Scottish Survey 1978-1956, p.11

7 A. L. Drummond and J. Bulloch, *The Church in Victorian Scotland, 1843-1874*, St. Andrew Press, Edinburgh, 1974, p. 71; Cooney, Scotland and the Papacy,p. 14.

8 Drummond and Bulloch, *The Church in Victorian Scotland*, p. 71.

9 Cooney, p. 10.

10 See Colm Brogan, *The Glasgow Story*, Muller, London, 1954, p. 183.

11 Christine Johnson, *Developments in the Roman Catholic Church in Scotland*, John Donald, Edinburgh, p. 18.

12 Cooney, p. 13.

13 Brogan, *The Glasgow Story*, p. 13.

14 Ian A. Muirhead, 'Catholic emancipation: Scottish reactions in 1829', *Innes Review*, 24, 1, 1973, p. 41.

15 Muirhead, p.p. 26-8.

16 Sir M. S. Stewart, quoted in Muirhead, p. 31.

17 Colm Brogan, 'Catholics in changing social conditions', *Glasgow Observer and Scottish Catholic Herald*, Scottish Survey, p. 4.

18 Johnson, p. 36.

19 Sheridan Gilley, 'English attitudes to the Irish in England, 1780-1900', *Immigrants, Hosts, and Minorities in British Society*, (ed.) C. Lunn, Dawson, Folkestone, 1978, pp. 92-3.

20 Johnson, p. 139.

21 See Bernard Aspinwall, 'The ties that bind and loosen: the Catholic community in Galloway, 1800-1998', *Records of the Scottish Church History Society*, vol. 29, 1999, p.p. 96-7.

22 Neville Kirk, 'Ethnicity, class and popular Toryism, 1850-70', C. Lunn, *Immigrants and Minorities*, Dawson, Folkestone, 1980, p. 69.

23 Owen Dudley Edwards, 'The Irish in Scotland', in David Daiches (ed.), *A Companion to Scottish Culture*, Edward Arnold, London, 1981,p.185.

24 E. P. Thompson, *The Making of the English Working Class*, Pelican edition, London, 1968, p 479.

25 Johnson, p. 137.

26 V. A. McClelland, 'The Irish clergy and Archbishop Manning's apostolic visitation of the western district of Scotland, 1867', *Catholic Historical Review*, LIII, 1, 1967, p. 2.

27 McClelland, 'The Irish clergy, p. 2.

28 See Gordon M. Wilson, *Alexander McDonald, Leader of the Miners*, Aberdeen University Press, 1982, pp. 122, 168.

29 Quoted by David Howell, *British Workers and the Independent Labour Party, 1886-1906*, Manchester University Press, Manchester, 1983, p. 142.

30 Alan B. Campbell, *The Lanarkshire Miners, a Social History of their Trade Unions, 1775-1874*, John Donald, Edinburgh, 1979, p. 181.

31 Campbell, p. 237.

32 Sydney and Olive Checkland, *Industry and Ethos, Scotland 1832-1914*, Edward Arnold, London, 1984, pp. 88, 94.

33 James E. Handley, *The Irish in Modern Scotland*, Cork University Press, 1947, p. 138

34 Stephen McKinney, Catholic Schools in Scotland: Mapping the Contemporary Debate and their Continued Existence in the 21st century, Ph.D, University of Glasgow, 2007, Interview with Bishop Joseph Devine, p. 134.

35 Handley, p.p. 130-4.

36 R. D. Lobban, 'The Irish community in Greenock in the nineteenth century', *Irish Geography*, vi, 1971, pp. 273-4.

38 E. H. Hunt, *British Labour History, 1815-1914*, Weidenfeld & Nicolson, London, 1981, p. 165.

38 L G. C. Hutchinson, Politics and Society in Mid-Victorian Glasgow, 1846-86, Ph.D. thesis, University of Edinburgh, 1974, p. 475.

39 *The Witness*, 25 January 1847, quoted by Handley, p. 25.

40 *Glasgow Herald*, 7 July 1851, quoted by Handley, p. 32.

41 William Walker, *Juteopolis: Dundee and its Textile Workers, 1885-1923*, Scottish Academic Press, Edinburgh, 1979, p. 171.

42 Cooney, *Scotland and the Papacy*, p. 10.

43 James G. Kellas, *Modern Scotland, the National since 1870*, Pall Mall, London, 1968, p. 56.

44 E. R. Norman, *Anti-Catholicism in Victorian England*, Allen & Unwin, London, 1968, p. 21.

45 *Glasgow Free Press*, 2 January 1864.

46 See Anthony C. Rhodes, *The Power of Rome in the Twentieth Century, the Vatican in the Age of Liberal Democracies, 1873-1922*, Sidgwick & Jackson, London, 1983, p. 164.

47 Handley, p. 108.

48 Denis Sewell, *Catholics: Britain's Largest Minority*, London: Penguin, 2001, p.p. 17-18.

49 G. I. T. Machin, *Politics and the Churches in Great Britain, 1832 to 1868*, Clarendon Press, Oxford, 1977, p. 254.

50 Bernard J. Canning, *Irish-born Secular Priests in Scotland, 1829-1879*, Bookmag, Inverness, 1979, p. 50.

51 Calum Brown, *The People in the Pews: Religion and Society in Scotland since 1780*, Scottish Economic and Social History Society, 1993, p. 36.

52 J. F. McCaffrey, *Scottish Catholic Observer*, 29 October 1982.

53 Anthony Ross, OP, 'Development of the Scottish Catholic community, 1878-1978', *Modern Scottish Catholicism, 1878-1978*, David McRoberts (ed.), Burns, Glasgow, 1979, p.40.

54 McCaffrey, 'Roman Catholicism in Scotland', pp. 289-90.

55 Henry Pelling, *Social Geography of British Elections, 1885-1910*, Macmillan, London, 1967, p. 284.

56 For Orangeism in general, see Eric P. Kaufmann, *The Orange Order: A Contemporary Northern Irish History*, Oxford: Oxford Univesity Press, 2007; for Scotland, see William Marshall, *The Billy Boys*, Mercat Press, Glasgow 1996.

57 Hutchinson, thesis, p. 395.

58 Hutchinson, thesis, p.476-7.

59 Hugh McLeod, *Religion and the Working Class in Nineteenth Century Britain*, Macmillan, London, 1984, p. 31. Hutchinson, thesis, p.388.

60 Hutchinson, thesis, p.388.

61 John Denvir, *Glasgow Observer*, 19 March 1904.

62 Hunt, *British Labour History*, p.p. 162-3.

63 Denvir, *Glasgow Observer*, 19 March 1904.

64 Campbell, *The Lanarkshire Miners*, p. 202.

65 Handley, *The Irish in Modern Scotland*, p. 96.

66 Handley, p. 251.

67 Bernard J. Canning, *Adventure in Faith, St. Ninian's, Gourock, 1880-1980*, Burns, Glasgow, 1980, p. 19.

68 Handley, p. 258. An iconoclastic view, arguing that large-scale flight from the ghetto was often voluntary and not coerced, is provided by Bernard Aspinwall, 'Baptisms, marriages and Lithianians, or, Ghetto? What Ghetto?: some reflections on modern Catholic historical assumptions', *Innes Review*, Vol. 51, no 1, spring 2000, p.p. 45-68.

69 Checkland, *Industry and Ethos*, p. 90.

70 James G. Kellas, The Liberal Party in Scotland, 1885-1895, Ph.D, University College, London, 1961, p. 366.

71 Kellas, thesis, p. 204.

72 McClelland, 'A hierarchy for Scotland', p.483

73 McCaffrey, 'Roman Catholicism in Scotland', p. 291.

74 Hutchinson, thesis, p. 394.

75 Checkland, *Industry and Ethos*, p. 185.

CHAPTER 2

Strangers in a strange land: the immigrant Irish community

THROUGH their homogeneity and concentration in largely separate neighbourhoods, a distinct identity was being forged that would place the Irish at variance with different aspects of Scottish life. Second or third generation Irish who were counted as Scottish in the census returns, often retained the attitudes and traditions of their Irish parents or grandparents, even if outwardly, these heirs of the original settlers, seemed to have adopted the speech and ways of west central Scotland.

The survival of a double identity among the descendants of the immigrants caused confusion and could be exploited for partisan ends. Even well-meaning observers talked about 'the Irish in Scotland' well into the twentieth century when already, by the last quarter of the nineteenth century, a clear majority of west of Scotland Catholics were Scottish-born; to more sophisticated commentators, in the 1920s and 1930s, such as the Scottish Nationalists Oliver Brown and Hugh MacDiarmid, they had graduated to being the `Scoto-Irish'. But these were the decades when Tory, ultra-Protestant, and Nationalist zealots, identifying continued Irish immigration as the chief symptom of Scottish decline, demanded repatriation and sought to underline the gravity of the problem by indiscriminately branding the bulk of Glasgow's Catholics as 'the Irish'.

In the 1850s and 1860s friction occurred between the mainly Highland leadership of the church and Irish priests only one of whom was in charge of a parish by 1867.[8] Discontent about the lack of recognition for their labours burst into the open in January 1864 when twenty-two priests in the western district sent a memorial to their bishop setting out ten grievances, the most important of which were that: new bishops are always Scottish; appointments to missions are not made by merit and that priests are removed arbitrarily; the laity have no say in managing institutions like reformatories or orphanages which are mismanaged due to excessive clerical control; and no clergyman was ever furnished with a copy of the statutes of the mission.

Archbishop John Henry Manning of Westminster found himself an intermediary between the two quarrelling parties.[1] In his own London diocese, he had established excellent relations with the London Irish and, unlike most other English Catholics, became a supporter of Irish home rule, meeting frequently in the House of Commons with Irish MPs. His detachment stemmed from the fact that he was a convert who did not possess the hidebound attitudes of the 'recusants', or old English Catholics who had survived down the centuries often through preserving a studied anonymity and demonstrating an unswerving loyalty to the British state. A compromise occurred through the appointment as bishop of the western district in 1869 of a patrician Englishman from Yorkshire, Charles Eyre (1817-1902). By now plans for the restoration of the hierarchy, accomplished in 1878, were being made. Lord Bute, the chief Catholic layman in Scotland and the spokesman of the Catholic aristocracy, also favoured Scotland becoming a complete unit of the Catholic church once again and he lent his authority to the idea. Bute was an early Scottish home ruler who wrote in 1881 that 'if the Irish could manage their own affairs . . . I don't see why they shouldn't [have home rule] . . . but my impression is that they are incapable. No one would say the same thing about us. [2]

Bute ensured that the Scottish island his title derived from was placed in the diocese of Argyll and the Isles and not Glasgow. Edinburgh, and not Glasgow, was chosen as the metropolitan see or chief archdiocese. Lord Bute would have preferred St. Andrews, the centre richest in ecclesiastical traditions but it only had two dozen Catholics.[3] Although Manning, in his report, had assumed that Glasgow would have acquired metropolitan rank because it was the greatest centre of Catholic population as well as Scotland's largest city,[4] it was rejected, possibly because the troubles of the previous decade and the unassimilated nature of its Catholic faithful gave it an alien and discordant image. But care was taken to make Glasgow an archdiocese, directly subject to the Holy See and not to the province of St. Andrews and Edinburgh, under whose authority lay the other dioceses of Aberdeen, Argyll and the Isles, Dunkeld, and Galloway.[5]

Charles Eyre, Glasgow's first modern archbishop was an energetic and skilful administrator who pressed ahead with much needed expansion. In 1874, he founded a seminary into which he put part of his own fortune and other benefactors, such as Lord Bute were similarly generous with endowments.[6] The number of clergy rose from 134 in 1878 to 234 in 1902; the number of parishes increased from sixty to eighty-four and a total of forty-four new chapels and chapel-schools were built; in 1869, the number of baptisms was 8,519; in 1900 they totalled 13,414 and over the same period the Catholic population increased by around 100,000.[7]

The Victorian philosopher Thomas Carlyle scoffed at these signs of growth and consolidation. 'Popery can build new chapels. Let them. Popery cannot come back, any more than paganism can.[8] It would be many decades before Rome's detractors faced up to the fact that the Catholic church's identification with the poor was actually a source of strength rather than weakness. Catholic priests were the only clergy in Scotland to live on the standards of the nineteenth century working-classes.[9] They easily assumed the leadership of Catholic parishes where so many of the inhabitants not only sharing the same faith, race, and political outlook, but also sometimes coming from the one locality and, as James Handley says, 'held in unity through the difficulty of mixing freely with the native population'.[10]

Strong willed churchmen, emphasising ritual and devotion and having little time for independent thought were the norm. They blended well with the ethos of the immigrant communities. Acutely aware of how bleak and hazardous life could be, they yearned for certainty which was provided by many through their religious conviction. Even those who were indifferent towards attending mass and taking the sacraments, seldom lost their emotional loyalty to the Catholic church and the key dates of the life cycle (birth, marriage, death), were seldom commemorated without the church's involvement.[11] Throughout the areas of densest settlement, the Irish adamantly refused to follow the most effective route to assimilation which was intermarriage. Family and neighbourhood pressures and the implacable hostility of the priest were strong deterrents. These were reinforced by the Vatican's 1908 *Ne Temere* decree which made the conditions for marriage with a non-Catholic even more rigorous than before, all combining to keep the community Catholic and Irish in outlook.

The most detailed research on nineteenth century Catholic marriage patterns in Scotland has been made in Greenock, a classic area of Irish settlement. Irish Catholic migrants were joined in the town by Protestant Irish and Highlanders. Throughout the second half of the nineteenth century, the Catholic Irish had the greatest degree of inter-group marriage. In 1851, some 80% of the Irish men and women in Greenock had found partners from amongst their own number while, in 1891, the percentage figure was 72.4.[12]

A strong Scottish identity existed in the nineteenth century but it contained little that the Irish could draw inspiration from. As the immigrants became more politicised – behind the cause of nationalism in their former homeland – the rather synthetic Scottishness which had been usurped and even recast, by the royal family, the British army, and the English music hall, held little appeal. Without being aware of his words, many Home Rulers took their cue from Parnell whose opinion of the Scots is enshrined in the remark that 'Scotland has ceased to be a nation'. Much later, in the 1930s, the novelist Compton Mackenzie spelled out their feeling of alienation from Scotland in possibly exaggerated terms, not long after he had become a Catholic convert:

> 'The Irish who settled in Scotland settled in a country which seemed to them, to have surrendered what they had never surrendered – nationhood . . . They were not willing to suffer a comparable loss of status, and finding where they penetrated little peculiarly Scottish left except religious intolerance and sectarian hate, they preferred to remain expatriate Irish.'[13]

In the nineteenth century, it was difficult to preserve an Irish identity if one embarked upon the odyssey of self-improvement that was part of so-called 'Scottish Democracy'. One who managed it was Patrick O'Hare, the first Catholic elected to Glasgow town council. O'Hare graduated to the licensing trade from the Lanarkshire steelworks and he brought up his family in the lower middle-class suburb of Dennistoun. They were probably the first Catholic family in a locality which would put militant anti-Catholics into the council during the 1930s. Patrick O'Hare's grandson recalls that his own father and uncle had to fight their way to school at St. Mungo's academy practically every day.[14]

Against this background, it may have been easier for rising Catholics to quietly drop their religion completely if they made the transition out of the immigrant neighbourhood. Irishmen who became 'turncoats' got on faster than those who kept the faith because, outside the enclave, it was far easier to adopt an individualistic approach to life. Probably the best-known nineteenth-century Scottish lapsed Catholic was the Edinburgh-born novelist and creator of Sherlock Holmes, Arthur Conan Doyle (1859-1930).

Evangelical Protestant missionaries had comparatively little success in detaching Catholics from their faith.[15] Instead mixed marriages were viewed increasingly as a source of danger as the boundaries of the ghetto began to grow more elastic at the turn of the century. It is interesting that the best-known Scottish Catholics in the Communist Party, William Gallacher (1884-1966) and Harry McShane (1892-1988) were both products of mixed marriages where their Catholic fathers had gone out of the enclave to find marriage partners in the wider community. Once the infrastructure of the church-in urban Scotland began to take shape, priests sought to control the 'leakage'.

To counteract the external influences which weakened the solidarity of the Catholic community, church leaders, from about 1885 onwards, began to create a wide variety of organisations which were designed to absorb the energies and take up the leisure time of parishioners young and old. These bodies had distinct religious, recreational, charitable and social functions and in a parish where each of them was in place, it was felt that Catholics had no need to go further afield to look for companionship or to use up their leisure time. By the turn of the century, Catholics lived in 'a self-enclosed social world in which the Church had duplicated every movement of Protestant and secular social service and charity'.[16]

The proliferation of Catholic associations came after the successful efforts of evangelical Protestant,s to provide a religious dimension to ordinary life. The Young Men's Christian Association (1841) and the Boys

Brigade (1883) were both founded in Scotland and immigrant associations seeking to preserve ties with Ireland, were already in existence; these included the Gaelic Athletic Association which spread over much of the west of Scotland after the 1890s, to a lesser extent the Gaelic League, dedicated to the restoration of the Irish language, and numerous other associations devoted to the cultivation of Irish music and song, Irish debating and literary clubs, and informal and formal countrymen's association. St. Patrick's Day, 17 March usually saw the annual climax of their activities and was the most important day in the calendar for most Catholic immigrants.

The Society of St. Vincent de Paul which came to Scotland in 1845 and is still in existence today, tried to make a dent on appalling levels of poverty. The strength of piety was underscored by the visibility of the Catholic Truth Society founded by the Bishop of Salford in 1885. It contributed to the education of Catholics in all things pertaining to their faith and also sought to provide answers for or refute the calumnies of non-Catholics interested in the faith as the titles of just a few of its pamphlets make clear: 'Does the Pope Claim to be God?' 'What Catholics Do Not Believe', 'Why in Latin?' etc.[17] The CTS was backed up by religious associations such as the Sacred Heart and the Legion of Mary organised on a parish or parochial basis and known as confraternities. Their membership provided the dedicated worshippers who attended extra Catholic services, such as the Rosary, Sunday Benediction, weekly evening devotions, and the Stations of the Cross.

Most of these bodies were under clerical control but elections did occur in the Catholic Young Men's Society, which was an association open to all Catholic men in the parish and has been described by one member as an early working man's club.[18] The CYMS had three fundamental rules, Monthly Communion, the Chaplain's Veto, and No Party Politics.[19] Its branch at the main Catholic parish in Edinburgh, St. Patrick's, Cowgate was under the direction of an energetic Limerick priest, Canon Edward Hannan (1836-91). From St. Patrick's CYMS, Canon Hannan founded Hibernian football club in 1875 and became its first manager.[20] For the first sixteen years of its existence, its constitution laid down that its players had to be practising Catholics. Because of this Hibs has been dubbed as 'the first sectarian team in Scotland'.[21] The charge may not be an entirely fair one since the ruling may well have been enforced as much to keep out nominal or lapsed Catholics as to bar Protestants.

In Glasgow, Celtic FC emerged from similar origins but over a decade later in 1887. It was founded by Brother Walfrid from Sligo who, aged fifteen and then known as Andrew Kerins, took a coal boat to Glasgow in search of work. He attended night classes provided by the Marist teaching order and, aged 24, he decided his vocation was to join them.[22] The Marists had been at the forefront of bringing education and care to the malnourished and poverty-stricken Irish in the east end of the city. The idea behind the formation of Celtic was to raise money for free dinners, clothing, and other relief for the poor of the east end of Glasgow in the parishes of St. Mary's, St. Andrew's, and St. Alphonsus.[23] He stubbornly held out for the name Celtic against strong opposition from the aspirational Catholics who were planning the sporting venture with him.[24] On Monday, 28 May 1888, Celtic played its first match on its home ground, a friendly against Rangers.

Celtic opened its doors to all-comers and in 1897 moved away from its charitable origins when it became a limited liability company. Its new shareholders were largely drawn from the immigrant community and a perusal of the early membership of its committees and later board of directors gives a good indication of who were the rising figures in the community: John Glass, a joiner-builder did much to get Celtic off the ground in its earliest years; the Shaughnessy's were prominent in law and the priesthood; the McKillop's were big restauranteurs in Glasgow; and John McLaughlin was a publican from Hamilton.[25] Indeed, all but one of the first seven-man board of directors was a publican.

Members of the drink trade had been instrumental in forcing the changes which turned Celtic into a professional club. They were opposed by the *Glasgow Observer* (weekly paper of the immigrants after 1884) and its redoubtable editor, Charles Diamond, whose ally was the League of the Cross, the church temperance organisation. Archbishop Manning had founded the League in 1873. It spread to the west of Scotland in the late 1880s and by 1892, the Glasgow archdiocese had 128 branches and 30,000 members.[26] Many of these branches provided games rooms in which the main pastimes were billiards, dominoes, cards, and draughts. Usually located on church property, they were intended to act as counter-attractions to public-houses, shebeens, and street gambling. But after 1918 while the League of the Cross collapsed, apparently due to its failure to recruit among younger Catholics. Protestant temperance societies that, like the band of Hope, placed a greater emphasis on moral reform, enjoyed greater longevity.[27]

The licensing trade was one of the chief avenues of advancement for Catholics since entry could be secured with very little capital. But it produced tensions in Catholic homes and probably sapped the energy needed for worthwhile community initiatives. The clergy were not noted for encouraging sturdier enterprises such as co-operatives or savings associations which might have meant that, over time, rather fewer enterprising Catholics graduated to 'trades that ministered to the weaknesses of mankind'.[28] Once more, Canon Hannan of Edinburgh was exceptional in that he enrolled 1,500 into a Penny Savings Bank.[29] But an Irish co-operative society in Lanarkshire, where there was the density of numbers for it to be feasible, failed to get off the ground. In northern Italy and other parts of Europe such as Bavaria and the Low ccuntries, priests were encouraging Catholic co-operatives and savings societies at this time.[30] But, in urban Scotland, there was no educated professional elite and very few skilled artisans who could have provided the initial impetus for such schemes. The Catholic population was overwhelmingly proletarian and only a few priests may have had the expertise or the inclination to get such ventures off the ground. Nevertheless, some parishes, such as St. Patrick's in Dumbarton acquired a strong Catholic infrastructure. As early as 1912, it was organising annual local pilgrimages to Lourdes and from 1901 to 1950 Monsignor Hugh Kelly remained unchanged as its parish priest.

Glasgow was much slower than Liverpool and other centres of Irish immigration such as the USA and Australia in producing thriving businessmen and respected civic leaders. By 1900, 'it would have been possible to accommodate in a third-class carriage all the Catholic men who occupied positions of public prominence or trust'.[31] In Catholic education, there was just no equivalent of a school like Allen Glen's founded in 1853 to provide an education shaped by pure and applied science, technology, and craftsmanship.[32] Thus in a city whose prosperity was disproportionately based on heavy engineering and manufacturing industry, the sons and grandsons of Irish immigrants were automatically excluded from entering the areas of the local economy which conveyed prestige and acceptability.

In the USA, the openness of society and the faster rate of expansion enabled the Irish to surmount discrimination and social disadvantage far more quickly than in Britain. Their anti-British and non-royalist instincts made them feel far more at home in America than the Irish felt in Glasgow or Liverpool. They had a head start over other European migrants to the New World since they did not need to discard any remote language or culture so as to become acceptable in the eyes of the host community; 'their "intermediate ethnic status" between Yankees and continental Europeans gave them the role of imposing social control as priests, policemen, political leaders and trade union bosses'.[33]

In a community corresponding to 250,000 people in 1880, there were only six Catholics studying at Glasgow university, five in medicine and one in law.[34] Only in 1884 was it possible for a stable Catholic immigrant paper to be launched. This was the pugnacious and well-designed *Glasgow Observer.* In its twentieth anniversary special edition, it mentioned that, by common consent, the most prominent Catholic layman in the city was not a son of Erin, but Mr James Brand KCSG, a building contractor – and a convert.[35]

But already by the 1880s, a two-tier community was taking shape among the Glasgow Irish. Enterprising figures started out as hawkers, or second-hand dealers, for which little capital was needed. From this, they might move on to own pawnshops, lodging houses, public houses, betting shops, eating houses, or grocery shops, catering for the needs as well as the comforts and weaknesses of their own community. Later these tradespeople could think of sending their children to university, by which time they would have moved out of the immigrant neighbourhood, even if much of their livelihood still derived from it.

Until well into the twentieth century, the absence of good educational facilities was an obstacle to upward mobility. Catholic education was very rudimentary, school buildings were of inferior standard, and the meagre resources at hand were barely able to provide the three Rs and religious instruction to a minority of Catholic children. In Glasgow, Catholic schools such as St. Aloysius and St. Mungo's, which would enjoy prestige in times to come as institutions turning out well-educated young adults, had been built by 1870 but it is a revealing comment on their limitations that the emerging middle-class in the immigrant community preferred to send their children elsewhere. John Maguire, the first archbishop of Glasgow to emerge from the local community was a pawnbroker's son who went to Stonyhurst, the Jesuit college in Lancashire.

In 1872 under the Scotch Education Act, new school boards took over the church schools, making attendance at school compulsory from five to thirteen years. Guarantees offered to the Presbyterian churches about religious education seemed sufficiently reassuring for them to transfer their schools to the new school boards. But the Catholic authorities chose to remain outside. Viewing the classroom as a vital forum, alongside the church and the home, for ensuring that children had a Catholic upbringing, the church wished to provide its own management. But Catholic school costs could not be charged on the local school rates and it was only when they had been built and equipped that some aid could be claimed on a direct grant basis from the Scotch education department.[36]

After prejudice and discrimination, educational backwardness must be counted as a prime reason why Catholics coming on to the labour market were unable to compete for jobs and opportunities on equal terms with other young Glaswegians until the 1970s at the very earliest. Sometimes rich Catholic benefactors aided Catholic schools but they were mainly dependent on the voluntary efforts of local congregations. 'Charity' sermons by well-known preachers and charity balls and concerts were typical methods of raising funds and, once each quarter, wage-earners were urged to donate a day's wages but the most lucrative method tended to be the holding of bazaars in town halls.[37] Such endeavours enabled the roll in Scottish Catholic schools to rise from 47,000 in 1883 to 85,000 in 1908.[38]

Catholic ratepayers were required to pay rates for the support of these schools, which was a longstanding source of grievance. The church decided to participate in triennial contests for local education boards through the

Catholic Union, which was its spokesman on political affairs. Senior priests as well as approved lay Catholics were regularly elected to school boards throughout industrial Scotland and often it was Catholic voters who turned out in the greatest numbers.

The school board is also significant due to it being the first elected body on which representatives of the Glasgow Irish were to be found. However, Catholic education languished while the national system expanded. In 1895 a Catholic teacher training college run by the Notre Dame sisters, was established at Dowanhill, Glasgow but this was not destined to be one of the supporting pillars for a future middle-class. It was a female college, many of whose graduates would remain single since marriage and attendant child rearing would have taken them out of teaching. They earned far less than state teachers and a revealing statistic shows that, before 1918, the minority of male Catholic teachers (one-fifth of the total), earned in a week, half of what a steelworker could expect to earn in a day.[39] So 'teaching was not a prestigious calling in the Catholic community and within the denominational system, teachers were a compliant group. Overall, after prejudice and discrimination, educational backwardness must be counted as a prime reason why Catholics coming on to the labour market were unable to compete for jobs and opportunities on equal terms with other young Glaswegians until the 1950s and 1960s at the very earliest.

Strong political feelings first became evident in the west of Scotland immigrant communities at the start of the 1870s. Here, as in other British centres of Irish settlement, Irishmen were chiefly concerned with events back home, a preoccupation that, in many cases was passed on to sons and grandsons who were destined never to set foot in Ireland. In November 1871, a Glasgow branch of the Irish national movement, then known as the Home Government Association, was formed. In the next forty years, this association would go through several name changes but the Home Government branch would always be one of the strongest in Britain. After 1880, the Home Rule movement was known as the Irish National League and between 1883 and 1890 the number of British branches rose from fifty-two to 630 and the registered membership from 4,000 to over 40,000.[40]

Archbishop Eyre opted for a policy of coexistence with the league which left school board elections to the Catholic Union and focused on local and parliamentary contests.108 In the West of Scotland, the most senior Home Ruler could not be described as a typical member of the exile community. John Ferguson was born in 1837 and came to Glasgow in 1860. His interest in nationalist politics was only kindled after he left Ireland. Entering the publishing business, he rose to become a partner in the firm Ferguson and Cameron, and a fairly wealthy man by the standards of the day.[41] Ferguson chaired nearly every Irish meeting of importance in the west of Scotland from 1873 up to his death in 1906.[42] His solid financial background meant that he was able to devote more time to politics than almost anybody else in the Irish community and he represented stability at the top of a movement which had a highly mobile rank-and-file.[43]

A close ally was John Torley (1851-1897) who, in 1990, became the first Catholic country councillor in the West of Scotland, representing Duntocher. He had been Scottish leader of the Irish Republican Brotherhood (IRB), more commonly known as the Fenians. He campaigned on behalf of evicted Irish tenants beyond Scotland, visiting the United States to fundraise for the IRB. Upon his death the Irish in Clydebank lined the funeral route and local industrialists contributed to a memorial over his grave.[44]

Ferguson brought Irish leaders to speak in support of the struggle in the Highlands against evictions. These links produced greater understanding between the Irish and that large part of the city's working-class that was of Highland descent.[45]

He was a conciliator who tried to settle internal feuding between the two largest branches of the city's Home Rule movement which delayed the election of the first Home Ruler on the city council until 1893. The Home Government branch and the William O'Brien branch were locked in fierce rivalry over many years, which events like the divorce scandal leading to the downfall of the Irish leader Charles Stewart Parnell in 1890 only helped intensify. A new organisation, the United Irish League (UIL) continued to mobilise the Irish vote until after the First World War. These voters were usually placed at the disposal of the Liberal Party which introduced Home Rule bills into parliament in 1886, 1892, and 1912. But this alliance was a marriage of convenience rather than a genuine partnership. League policy demanded that the Irish vote should not be committed to any British party, Tory, Liberal, or Labour, but directed where the interests of Ireland demanded such action'.[46] Sometimes the Liberals calculated that it was tactically shrewder to put up a candidate who was lukewarm or even hostile to Irish self-determination. When this happened, the league would direct its vote to the Tory or Labour camp. An extreme case occurred in 1900 when the local branch of the UIL in the Blackfriars division of Glasgow fell out with the defending Liberal and placarded the constituency with emerald green posters in favour of Andrew Bonar Law, the Tory, who won and later was to loom large in the demonology of Irish nationalism.[47]

After 1905, with the foundation of Sinn Fein, a movement wanting to take Ireland right outside the British orbit, nationalists dissatisfied with the league had an alternative movement with which to identify. In 1908, a branch of Sinn Fein was formed in Glasgow, the year in which its leader Arthur Griffith visited the city. [48]But Sinn Fein posed little threat although its visitors might be revered in years to come, they got a far less warm reception than Joseph Devlin, the leading home ruler in Belfast, who was a very popular figure in the Glasgow Irish community from the turn of the century onwards.[49]

Without the Irish Question it is unlikely that so many unskilled workers would have acquired a degree of political awareness that in time spilled over into British political involvements. James Connolly (1868-1916), arguably the best-known revolutionary socialist in these islands, entered politics through this route.[50] Less well-known has been John Wheatley (1869-1930), perhaps unfairly so, since more than any other individual, he was responsible for pushing the descendants of Irish immigrants in a leftward direction and for making Glasgow, by 1922, a strong Labour city.[51]

Irish-born, he was reared in the mining village of Baillieston, near Glasgow, and was one of a number of young intelligent members of the Irish community to come under the influence of Dutchman Peter Terken, who was the local priest. He placed a high value on education and had the strength of personality to enforce his belief in temperance. He doubled as the teacher and six of his pupils became shopkeepers in Glasgow, which is a striking incidence of upward mobility for such a small community.[52] At the age of twelve, he was already working as a miner underground in the pits but, after attending evening classes in Glasgow, he was able to find alternative employment in local shops and licensed premises, although he himself would be a lifelong abstainer from alcohol. Along with his younger brother Patrick, he set up his own small grocery business when in his mid-twenties and he was active in Irish Home Rule politics, first joining the Baillieston branch of the league, then led by the tailor, Denis Brogan, head of a talented family which would make its mark in different walks of life.[53]

Wheatley was one of the radical Home Rulers unhappy with the lack of democracy inside the movement and drawn increasingly to Labour politics. Early in 1906, he derived great encouragement from the success of the Labour Party in capturing Blackfriars, its first Glasgow seat whose large Irish electorate generally heeded the advice of the Home Government branch to vote for the winner George Barnes. Later that year, Wheatley publicly declared himself to be a socialist and formed the Catholic Socialist Society along with his brother Patrick, his lifelong collaborator.

The aim of the CSS was to win Catholic workers over to the Labour Party by demonstrating that belief in socialism and adherence to Catholicism were not incompatible. Wheatley was to remain a committed Catholic, one who had turned leftwards from the belief that 'capitalism and what it did to people was a destroyer of faith', and it was from the standpoint of radical Christianity and not Marxism that he was to justify his socialism.[54] But he had deep suspicions to confront.

When, in 1879, a young trade unionist called Keir Hardie innocently compared Alexander McDonald, the miner's leader, with Martin Luther, he was immediately heckled by the Catholic miners in his Lanarkshire audience. Events like the execution of the archbishop of Paris by the communards in 1870, and the great battles between church and state in Italy, Germany, and France made many pious Catholics willing to listen to the warnings of their priests about sacrilegious ideas drifting across from the continent. Many of the priests who had come to the Scottish mission from Ireland hailed from comfortably-off parishes in the southern grassland counties of Limerick and Cork, some came from garrison towns and were the sons of tailors and boot-makers,[55] so they were inherently conservative in their social outlook and were ready to denounce radicalism in whatever guise it might appear. Wheatley was soon embroiled in controversy with local clergy who automatically viewed socialism as anti-Christian. The *Glasgow Observer* was the stage for the debate between John Wheatley and his religious detractors that went on intermittently right up until 1910. Charles Diamond had discarded many of his suspicions of socialism which he had colourfully assailed in 1891:

> 'It means a nation of paramours, bastards, and profligates. It is
> Manichaeism, Montanism, Waldensianism, Mormonism, and
> Divorce Court Protestantism rolled into one'.[56]

Wheatley was also fortunate in that Archbishop Maguire, Eyre's successor, was a socially conscious prelate who, in a number of speeches, had displayed enthusiasm for the cause of organised labour.[57] He never endorsed Wheatley in public, but he refused to accede to the wishes of those priests who wanted him to be denounced. condemned for contravening the Papal encyclical *Rerum Novarum*.

Wheatley emerged unscathed from his jousts with hostile clerics where a lesser figure, in a more hostile climate, might well have been crushed by the weight of church hostility. Possibly the trickiest moment for him came in 1912 when Andrew O'Brien, the outspoken parish priest in his own parish of St. Mark's Carntyne, denounced him from the pulpit. That evening, a threatening mob gathered outside his home and burned his effigy, but Wheatley outfaced the mob by standing at his front door, and calmly puffed his pipe with a cool courage that was long remembered.[58] Wheatley's achievement has been expertly summed up in the following way:

> 'As far as can be seen, this is the only instance in Europe of a formal
> Catholic socialist movement emerging from within Catholic ranks
> and not being condemned but, in fact, tacitly accepted by the
> ecclesiastical authorities.'[59]

Before 1914, the CSS held speaking tours and debates in order to convince Catholic voters that socialism could be embraced from a clear-cut ethical standpoint. One of the most dramatic encounters took place one Sunday afternoon in November 1909 when 2,000 men and women assembled in Glasgow's Pavilion Theatre to hear Wheatley debate the question, 'Should Catholics Support Socialism' with the writer Hilaire Belloc, a favourite on the Catholic lecture circuit.[60] Belloc was unexpectedly worsted in this encounter by the local speaker who was acquiring impressive dialectical skills which would be demonstrated even more effectively once he entered parliament. He was elected to municipal office in 1909 and he soon became financially secure – a small publishing business, Hoxton and Walsh, which he and his brother had launched in 1906 was prospering, and by 1921 would have an annual turnover of £21,000.[61]

Wheatley was on his way to becoming a socialist entrepreneur before 1914 as he was creating a strong local power-base as a member of the Independent Labour Party (ILP); it was affiliated to the British body and, to all intents and purposes, *was* the Labour Party in Scotland since it was only after 1918 that it began to set up branches of its own. Within the ILP, anti-clericalism was largely absent and during the 1913 transport dispute in Ireland known as the 'Great Dublin Lock-Out', *Forward,* the Glasgow ILP paper was able to raise over £3,000 for the families of the victimised workers.[62]

In Glasgow, radicals who wished to break down strictly communal allegiances and replace them with a more universal kind had more space in which to operate than in Liverpool or Belfast, both badly scarred by sectarianism.[63] As early as the two elections in 1885 and 1886, it is reckoned that 'the language of working-class solidarity was. . . dominating political discourse in Govan and Kinning park', two inner city areas of Glasgow whose equivalents in these cities were often prone to strife. [64]Labour historians have claimed that 'For those coming into the area, especially those with experience of the bitter Ulster conflicts in the 1880s, local employment and residence brought them into contact with an entirely different social universe'.[65]

Across the river, in Springburn, Patrick O'Hare, on the council from

1897 to 1906, built bridges between the two communities. Earlier, as a member of the parochial board, he had gained the appelation of 'Watchdog of the Poor' because of the interest he showed in the system of granting poor relief. In a a district with a strong Orange presence, he was twice re-elected without opposition.[66] His descendants continued his tradition of service; two grandsons, Eugene and Patrick Connolly won the affection of several generations of residents in the Gorbals and Govanhill areas of Glasgow, where they had a medical practice for forty years up to the 1980s.

From 1913, Patrick Dollan drawn from an archetypal immigrant background, was a councilor for Govan. A year earlier, he had married Agnes Moir whose father was a leading Orangeman. The early socialist movement had brought them together and for others it created a new environment where ancient prejudices and misunderstandings could be breached. In Glasgow, at least, the left had a forum where a feeling of common humanity posed a strong challenge to sectarian identities. So, by 1914, with Ulster seemingly about to plunge into a sectarian civil war and Liverpool divided against itself, Glasgow and the west of Scotland generally presented a more hopeful picture, although once the guns on the western front fell silent, it would become speedily apparent that the city's sectarian ghosts were far from being exorcised.

NOTES

1 See James Walsh, 'Archbishop Manning's visitation of the western district of Scotland in 1867', *Innes Review*, 18, 1, 1967, p. 15.

2 Lord Bute to Lord Rosebery, 3 November 1881. Rosebery Papers, National Library of Scotland, quoted in 16 H. J. Hanham, *Scottish Nationalism*, Harvard University Press, Cambridge, Mass., 1969, p.85.

3 McClelland, 'A hierarchy for Scotland', p. 490

4 McClelland, p. 490.

5 James Darragh, 'The hierarchy of Scotland' *Catholic Directory for Scotland*, 1982, Burns, Glasgow, 1982, p. 39.

6 Cooney, p. 74.

7 Cooney, p.47.

8 *Scottish Catholic Observer*, 5 March 1965.

9 Drummond and Bulloch, *The Church in Victorian Scotland*, p. 74.

10 Handley, p. 223.

11 M.A.G. O'Tuathaigh, 'The Irish in nineteenth century Britain, problems of integration', in *Transactionsof the Royal Historical Society*, 5th series,m 31, 1981, p. 166.

12 Lobban, 'The Irish community in Greenock', p. 279.

13 Compton Mackenzie, *Catholicism and Scotland*, Routledge, London 1936.

14 Interview with Dr. Patrick Connolly, 29 April 1984.

15 O'Tuathaigh, 'The Irish in nineteenth century Britain', p. 166.

16 Sheridan Gilley, 'Catholics and socialists in Glasgow, 1906-12', in *Hosts, Immigrants and Minorities in British Society*, (ed.), C. Lunn, Dawson, Folkestone, 1980, p. 165.

17 John Lynch, 'Catholic lay societies, 1878-1956', *Glasgow Observer and Scottish Catholic Herald*, Scottish Survey, p. xxi.

18 Interview with John McLaughlin, 21 August 1984.

19 William Walker, 'Irish immigrants in Scotland: their priests, politics, and parochial life', *Historical Journal*, xv, 4, 1972, p. 658.

20 Canning, *Irish-born Secular Priests*, p. 135.

21 Bill Murray, *The Old Firm, Sectarianism, Sport, and Society in Scotland*, John Donald, Edinburgh, 1984,p. 19.

22 Brian McGuirk, *Celtic FC, The Ireland Connection*, Edinburgh: Black and White, 2009, p.20.

23 Murray, p.p. 17-8.

24 McGuirk, *Celtic FC*, p. 24.

25 Murray, p. 68. C.

26 G. Brown, Religion and the Development of an Urban Society: Glasgow, 1780-1914, Ph.D. thesis, University of Glasgow, 1981, p. p. 323-4.

27 Brown, thesis, p. 166.

28 John Denvir, *The Irish in Britain, from the Earliest Times to the Fall and Death of Parnell*, Kegan Paul, London 1892, p. 451.

29 Canning, *Irish-born Secular Priests*, p.107.

30 Norman Stone, *Europe Transformed, 1878-1919*, Fontana, Glasgow, 1983, p. 92.

31 Hugh G. McEwan, *Bishop Grey Graham, 1874-1959, an Essay on his Life and Times*, Burns, Glasgow, 1973, p. 93.

32 Drummond and Bulloch, *The Church in Victorian Scotland*, p.p. 100-1.

33 Sheridan Gilley, 'The Roman Catholic Church and the 19th Century Irish Diaspora', *Journal of Ecclesiastical History*, Vol.35, no 2, 1984, pp. 204-5.

34 David McRoberts, 'The archdiocese of Glasgow'. *Glasgow Observer and Scottish Catholic Herald*, Scottish Survey.

35 *Glasgow Observer*, 19 March 1904.

36 Ian Wood, 'Irish immigrants and Scottish radicalism, 1880-1906', *Essays in Scottish Labour History*, (ed.), Ian McDougall, John Donald, Edinburgh, 1979, p. 74.

37 Handley, *The Irish in Modern Scotland*, p. 237.

38 Handley, p. 236.

39 Colm Brogan, 'Catholics in changing social conditions', *Glasgow Observer and Scottish Catholic Herald*, Scottish Survey, p. iv.

40 Handley, p. 280.

41 E. P. M. Wollaston, The Irish Nationalist Movement in Great Britain, 1886-1908, M.A. thesis, King's College, London, 1968, p.p. 21-2.

42 Handley, p. 270.

43 Hutchinson, thesis, p. 488.

44 Florence Boyle, 'The forgotten rebel', *Open House*, February 2013.

46 A. G. Hepburn, 'Political and industrial relationships', *Glasgow Observer and Scottish Catholic Herald*, Scottish Survey, 18 78 1955, p. xv.

47 Wood, p. 81.

48 Handley, p. 291.

49 Handley, p.287.

50 James Connolly's early life in Scotland is dealt with to varying degrees in the following works: Ruth Dudley Edwards, *James Connolly*, Gill & Macmillan, Dublin, 1982; Owen Dudley Edwards, *James Connolly, the Mind of an Activist*, Gill & Macmillan, Dublin, 1971; and Donal Nevin, *James Connolly: A Full Life*, Dublin: Gill and Macmillan, 2004.

51 The best account of his life is by Ian S. Wood. See *John Wheatley*, Manchester: Manchester University Press, 1990.

52 Sir Patrick Dollan, 'Memories of fifty years', Mercat Cross, October 1953, p. 110.

53 Dollan, Mercat Cross, July 1953, p. 8.

54 Wood, *John Wheatley*, p. 73.

55 Interview with Bishop Joseph Devine, Glasgow, 26 August 1981.

56 *Glasgow Observer*, 17 January1891.

57 Gilley, 'Catholics and socialists', pp.164-6, 184-5.

58 Ian Wood, 'John Wheatley', *Scottish Labour Leaders, 1918-39, a biographical Dictionary*, (ed.), William Knox, Mainstream, Edinburgh, 1984, p. 277.

59 McCaffrey, 'Roman Catholicism in Scotland', p. 293.

60 Gunnin, thesis, p. 1.

61 Wood, 'John Wheatley', *Scottish Labour Leaders*, p. 275.

62 Joan Smith, 'Labour tradition in Glasgow and Liverpool', *History Workshop*, No 17, Spring 1984, p. 43.

63 Quoted in P. J. Waller, *Democracy and Sectarianism, a Political and Social History of Liverpool, 1868-1939*, Liverpool University Press, Liverpool, 1981, P. 249.

64 John Foster, Muir Houston and Chris Madigan, 'Sectarianism, Segregation and Politics in Clydeside in the later Nineteenth Century, in Martin J. Mitchell (ed), *New Perspectives on the Irish in Scotland*, John Donald, Edinburgh 2008, p. 94.193. .

65 Ibid.

66 *The Bailie*, 4 January 1905.

CHAPTER 3

Community in transition: Ireland, the rise of labour and the church resurgent

At the outbreak of World War I, there was a favourable response to the recruiting drive from the Irish in Scotland. Their religious leaders, such as the archbishops of Glasgow and Edinburgh, blessed and approved the war against Germany in unequivocal terms.[1] So did Charles Diamond, fiery editor of the *Glasgow Observer*, at least in the earlier stages. The influence he wielded in a community whose manpower was valued by the British authorities, saved him from prosecution after he made a pointed reference to the royal family's German ancestry. [2]

The death-columns on the back page of the *Observer* were well filled with the names of first and second generation immigrant Irish volunteers killed on the western front and elsewhere.[3] By the end of the war, six soldiers hailing from the Catholic community in Glasgow had been decorated with the Victoria Cross.[4] Shared war comradeship held out the promise that religious barriers would be far less relevant for those whose horizons had been expanded by participation in gruesome trench warfare.

But in the midst of war, the Irish crisis was revived when news trickled across from Ireland of a separatist uprising that had broken out in Dublin on Easter Monday 1916. The Easter Rising was condemned by nationalist opinion in Ireland and in immigrant circles in Britain. It was widely viewed as an insane enterprise that had placed in jeopardy the peaceful realisation of Irish Home Rule after the war. Charles Diamond was particularly damning in his condemnation:

> 'The Irish people . . . will not manifest the slightest sympathy or approval with the madly criminal action of the pro-German plotters who resorted to insurrection in Dublin. . . Their action . . . was needless, foolish, wicked, and unjustifiable. Irish nationalists will . . . condemn it as unpatriotic folly: rash, blind, headlong, stupid and wrong.'[5]

He almost seemed to justify the court-martial sentences which were shortly to be passed upon the rising's leaders: 'their doom is just. They got, or will get, no more than they gave. They shed blood and took life recklessly.'[6]

But the mood in Ireland and its satellite communities across the world changed rapidly when the British took out and shot the 1916 leaders. Rebels and fanatics were transformed into heroes and martyrs, a metamorphosis that was fully reflected in the columns of the *Glasgow Observer* and its numerous local editions. Charles Diamond bestowed the status of martyr on a few isolated separatists, and he went on to lend his backing to Sinn Fein, the separatist party which, by the general election of 1918 had displaced the Home Rule Party as the main spokesman for nationalist Ireland.

As the political crisis in Ireland spilled over into outright warfare between the British forces and Sinn Fein's military arm, the Irish Republican Army, ties between the left and the immigrant population were strengthened. John Wheatley found it easier to preach socialism to them now that it was widely known that the Edinburgh-born James Connolly, one of the leaders of the 1916 rebellion, had been a lifelong socialist.[7] In 1919, Wheatley spoke at the May Day demonstration in Glasgow, along with Countess Markiewicz of Sinn Fein, an occasion in which the Irish tricolour was carried in the crowd of 100,000 and the Irish national anthem, 'The Soldier's Song' was sung along with The Red Flag.[8] At the Scottish conference of the Independent Labour Party (the ILP: which *was* the Labour Party in Scotland till the early 1930s) in 1920, the Irish Republic was recognised, but the vote was surprisingly narrow (268 to 207), indicating that many had deep reservations about complete Irish separation.

Many of the Irish on Clydeside found themselves caught up in the Irish war of independence and made a substantial contribution to the achievement of self-government in 1922. Things got moving in 1919 when Sean O'Sheehan was sent from Dublin to build up a solidarity movement in Scotland. Within a year, the number of Sinn Fein clubs rose from twenty to eighty, 'income increased forty times and membership eightyfold'.[9] A military wing of the IRA sprung up and by September 1920, the Procurator Fiscal estimated that the size of the IRA in the Glasgow area had risen to 3,000 men: 'they have no rifles but the police have now obtained information. . . that they are in possession of numerous revolvers which have been picked up here and elsewhere'.[10]

The chief constable of Paisley reported how the mood of the Irish in his locality had greatly changed in recent years: 'at the outbreak of war, the young men of the Catholic religion in Paisley enlisted in greater proportion than the rest of Paisley's inhabitants; they were apparently loyal but their attitude has changed since the Dublin rebellion.' [11]

The role allocated to the Irish in Scotland was to provide money and military supplies to keep the war effort going back home and safe houses for IRA men on the run from British or Irish gaols.[12] By 1921, almost every Scottish town with a sizeable Irish presence had its own IRA company that was required to send a regular quota of revolvers, ammunition, and rifles to headquarters in Glasgow; from quarries, coal pits, and shale mines powder and gelignite was obtained; eight successful raids were carried out on Clyde shipyards engaged in munition works; a gunboat being overhauled at Finnieston dockyard was raided, the skeleton crew surprised, and small arms taken.[13] Many ex-servicemen belonged to the IRA while women supporters, such as Julia Foy, the owner of a second-hand-clothes shop in Glasgow acted as couriers or provided safe houses; men were trained for service in Ireland and, on two occasions, high-ranking IRA officers crossed to Scotland to 'review the troops' on remote moorlands.[14]

Local police forces mounted a close watch on Sinn Fein, but their most sensitive operations eluded their gaze and they were unable to penetrate the organisation, a great obstacle being the fact that so few policemen came from the immigrant communities. In December 1920, the Chief Constable of Lanarkshire recommended that Sinn Fein be suppressed, but the Scottish Office commented that 'there seems nothing here on which we can take action'.[15] Months previously, the Procurator Fiscal's Office had commented realistically that 'so far there has been no outbreak of disorders on the part of Sinn Feiners and, so far as I can judge, this state of matters is likely to continue as long as they are not interfered with '.[16]

Afterwards, the Irish leader de Valera emphasised just how important a role nationally minded immigrants in Scotland had played in Ireland's bid for freedom, 'The financial contribution to the Irish struggle from among the Scottish communities was in excess of funds from any other country, including Ireland.[17] But the events of the Anglo-Irish war remain a forgotten chapter in the story of the Irish in Scotland largely due to what happened after the 1921 ceasefire with Britain. A peace treaty was agreed which fell short of an outright Irish Republic but gave Ireland far more autonomy than it would have enjoyed under home rule. Even though the treaty contained the signature of Michael Collins, the legendary head of the Republican movement's military wing, the IRA, it produced dissension in Dublin and soon cries of sell-out were heard. Soon, Sinn Fein split into Republicans and Free Staters (i.e. those who endorsed the treaty from which emerged the Irish Free State), and full-scale civil war broke out in June 1922.

Among the Irish in Scotland, as indeed in the rest of Britain, news that the movement had split over the new state's constitutional relationship with Britain was greeted with sadness and dismay. In and around Glasgow, there was far more anxiety about the plight of Ulster Roman Catholics in the newly formed state of Northern Ireland, which remained linked to Britain while enjoying internal self-government. Controlled by the local Unionist Party, and comprising six of the nine counties of the province of Ulster (so that Protestants were left in a permanent two-thirds majority), the partition of Ireland (even though deemed a temporary expedient until the cooling of passions allowed nationalists and unionists on the island to be reconciled) was a far more emotive issue on Clydeside. Ulster was close by, the bulk of the Irish hailed from there, and many still had deep family links through which they learned about the rough treatment meted out to Roman Catholics who attempted to challenge the new *status quo*. Nevertheless, it was not long before the divisions in Ireland were duplicated inside the solidarity movement in Britain. A majority of active Sinn Feiners in Scotland aligned with the Republicans and Glasgow seems to have been the headquarters of the IRA's propaganda machine after the rebels were forced out of Dublin early in the civil war. [18]

Even before the dramatic events of 1922-23, much evidence points to the Irish in Britain showing a willingness to throw aside their absorption in enclave politics connected with the situation in Ireland. There is no doubt that the Irish civil war greatly hastened this process of disengagement. The spectacle of Irishman killing Irishman greatly weakened Irish political and cultural movements in many British cities. 1922 may be a appropriate point at which to discard the word 'immigrant' as a term of identification for the Glasgow Irish. Those Irish political movements that continued to exist, did so largely in the shadows.

With the dropping of Ireland from the British political agenda, there was now one less issue to engender misunderstanding between workers with different religious and national allegiances in Scotland. A sign of the times was the election of two Roman Catholic miners to parliament as Labour MPs in 1922. Joseph Sullivan (1866-1935) North Lanark and Hugh Murnin (1861-1932) Stirling and Falkirk, representing mining seats where the workforce had in the past been too bitterly divided to use their numerical strength to return one of their own leaders to parliament. But it has to be said that the Labour Party was extremely fortunate that Ulster had remained aloof from the warfare which had engulfed much of the rest of the island. Hundreds died in Belfast street-fighting during 1921-22, but if these sectarian pogroms had been supplemented by direct confrontation between the unionist north and the nationalist south, then it is quite likely that Protestant sympathisers on Clydeside would have been able to organise a movement of solidarity with even more teeth than that which emerged from the Catholic community. A split Republican movement may therefore have prevented a bloody showdown, not just in Ulster but possibly also in Scotland and Liverpool, while enabling the Unionist state to consolidate itself.

But as Labour made inroads elsewhere, working-class wards near the Glasgow shipyards, where there was regular contact with Belfast, remained staunchly Tory. In 1920, Labour was heavily defeated in Patrick and Whiteinch which *Forward* described as 'a noted stronghold of Carsonism', where 'at election time the primitive passions of the people are easily roused into violent opposition to Labour'.[19] In 1923, Hugh Ferguson, the candidate of an ephemeral Orange and Protestant Party was actually returned to parliament for Motherwell. This party was formed in protest

61

at the fact that the Tories had associated themselves with the 1921 Irish peace treaty, but Ferguson took the Tory whip in parliament. An ex-soldier, scrap metal dealer, and member of the Plymouth Brethren sect, he called in parliament for another Cromwell to get to work in Ireland,' but he was only there a year before being rejected by the electors of Motherwell in favour of Rev. James Barr for the Labour Party.[20]

In some parts of Scotland, sectarianism intruded into politics even without the stimulus of the Irish question. This was clearly seen in 1918 when Colonel A.C. Stirling lost the seat of West Perthshire which he had won for the Coalition Unionists at a 1917 by-election. Despite coming from a landed family with an illustrious military record, he was the only member of the government party to lose his seat in Scotland where it recorded sweeping gains, an outcome which the *Glasgow Observer* did not hesitate to ascribe to his Catholic religion.[21]

In at least one major respect, Scotland generated a form of communal friction that was peculiar to itself and could not be said to be an importation from Ulster. This was the fierce rivalry between the respective followers of Glasgow's principal soccer teams Rangers and Celtic. Supporters drew upon their respective Protestant and Catholic allegiances to give a sharper edge to their rivalry than almost anywhere else in the footballing world. The two teams had become locked in competition as the era of mass spectator sport dawned around 1900. It was becoming a well-established pattern for many British industrial cities to provide two rival teams before which other local sides paled and the competition was friendly enough until after World War I. Rangers, although drawing its support from the overwhelmingly Protestant craft workers who lived and worked not far from its ground at Ibrox in the west of the city, signed players from other denominations as Celtic has always done. But, after World War I, the team's players came to be drawn from one religion in a city where almost one-third of the inhabitants were Roman Catholic.

Rivalry took an increasingly ugly turn in the shadow of the escalating crisis in Ireland between 1912 and 1922. The arrival from Belfast of Protestant shipyard workers in 1912 to build a new yard near Ibrox at a time when feelings in their community was running dangerously high over

Irish Home Rule, possibly aggravated matters.[22] The war, and the depression which threw members of the aristocracy of labour onto the dole as some better-educated Catholics began to compete for more skilled jobs in the labour market, cannot have helped. Through its shareholders and directors, Rangers had close ties with the Freemasons and, in a time of uncertainty and shrinking economic horizons, it is not to be wondered at that such a powerful social institution, by its signing policy, emulated the Protestant-only recruitment policy long associated with the Freemasons in skilled industry. The Masonic lodge drew craft workers, foremen, and white-collar staff under its protective umbrella. Catholics were banned from joining on pain of excommunication by their church. Some viewed it as a devilish cult, but it encouraged religious observance among skilled workers, thus reinforcing the Protestant identity of skilled workers on Clydeside. One historian has estimated that one in ten adult male Scots had been enrolled into the Freemasons by the 1920s.[23] By drawing masters and men together, it impeded the rise of class consciousness, although it should not be forgotten that the severe industrial unrest on Clydeside between 1915 and 1919 mainly involved skilled workers anxious to protect their differentials.

The Labour cause appealed to a wide spectrum of Scottish Catholics because of the hope that social justice would not retreat if it progressed in politics. ILP branches were not divided on religious grounds because of the absence of complete residential segregation in Glasgow, so immigrants who got involved were able to put behind them the enclave mentality associated with home rule politics. Activists from a Glasgow Irish background were rewarded for their enthusiasm and commitment and, indeed, the Labour movement was practically the first 'secular' body where they made their mark. Many immigrants must have drawn encouragement from the rise of John Wheatley, returned to parliament in 1922 and a member of the cabinet two years later, and from the emergence of his protégé Patrick Dollan, who masterminded the 1922 electoral campaign which saw ten of Glasgow's fourteen parliamentary seats fall to Labour.

The immigrant districts still had ethnic bosses, many of whom belonged to the licensing trade. But the power of these Irish community leaders has been overstressed, not least in Iain McLean's *The Legend of*

Red Clydeside. Politically, it is an oversimplification to say that the Catholics were 'bound together by the bar, the pulpit, and an "ethnic" press'.[24] If more attention had been paid to the Catholic Socialist Society (and to the backing for radical politics from Irish community leaders in the Home Government branch of the UIL before 1914), the author might have found significant divergences from the Tammany Hall stereotype in the behaviour of Irish voters and activists. Of especial importance is the fact that many immigrants only came on to the electoral rolls thanks to the 1918 Representation of the People Act, by which time the home rulers were in retreat. By now, they were just as likely to be receiving their first instructions in politics from the Labour Party as from any old-fashioned ethnic source.

The Labour Party could count itself lucky that the burning question of Catholic education and who should pay for it, had largely been settled by the time it began to court working-class Catholic votes. The 1918 Education (Scotland) Act removed nearly all of the burden for maintaining and financing Catholic education from the religious authorities. It was one of the last important acts of the Liberal Party in Scotland, its architect being Robert Munro, Secretary of State for Scotland, who later became Lord Alness (1868-1955). Negotiations with the Catholic authorities were protracted since many important issues were at stake. The passages dealing with Catholic education were contained in Section 18 of the act which has been hailed as the Magna Carta of twentieth century Scottish Catholicism. The relevant Catholic authorities agreed that its schools could be transferred to the local authorities in return for certain safeguards about their religious character: only teachers acceptable 'in regard to religious faith and character' to the church authorities could be appointed; religious instruction was to be kept up at the same level as before; and priests were given full access to the schools where, on an unpaid basis, they could oversee religious instruction and worship.[25] Catholic schools thus became part of the state system and were known as *denominational schools*.

As will be seen, the 1918 settlement produced a storm of protest from Protestant spokesmen who complained about 'Rome on the Rates' and lobbied vociferously for the offending Section 18 of the act to be rescinded. The schools question breathed life into the No Popery movement to an alarming degree in the two subsequent decades and was responsible for giving it a legitimacy in Scotland which it had never previously enjoyed in modern times. It may now become clearer why the Labour Party was extremely fortunate that the tricky matter of bringing Catholic education into the state system, under terms favourable to the church trustees, was not left for it to accomplish. If it had been, the balancing act of satisfying Catholic voters and keeping in line Protestant workers unsympathetic to the new arrangement, might have proved extremely difficult to bring off. Church pressure on the party could have split specific constituency parties and given an extended lease of life to ethnic politics, enabling the Tories to acquire working-class voters by a straight appeal to religion, and allowing Catholic ward politicians to do likewise in their own bailiwicks.

The Labour Party's backing for the 1918 educational settlement, despite the presence of secularists who would have preferred to see all children educated under the one roof, raised the party's standing in the eyes of the Catholic press. Triennial elections for the education boards of Scotland's local authorities fell due in 1919 and provided another opportunity for co-operation between church interests and the forces of the left. Fought under proportional representation, they demonstrated the political influence clerics had over Catholic voters, at least where education was concerned. The Catholic Union, composed of active laymen in each parish, made sure that a maximum number of Catholics were enrolled on the electoral register and it campaigned for the return of senior clergy as well as respectable laymen, each of whom was nominated by the archbishop. Invariably, there was a much higher turnout of Catholics than non-Catholics and the discipline of the Catholic vote gave the Catholic Union the appearance of an embryo political party.

Until World War II, the main Catholic voice on social, political, and moral questions was the Catholic Union whose object was 'the protection and advancement of Catholic interests in the public sphere'.[26] The Catholic Union operated in most parishes under the patronage of the archbishop. In 1919 it was to enjoy its best-ever results in any educational election. Catholics headed the poll in each of the seven Glasgow districts, except Partick and Hillhead, four of the victors being clergy, while in Dundee, Catholics came top in all three districts. The *Observer* gave its readers minute instructions about which order of preference candidates should be backed in and it urged that second preferences should go to Labour. [27]

The quixotic relationship between Diamond's papers and the mass working-class party of the British left continued to flourish up to and beyond the 1922 general election when the Labour Party made an impressive breakthrough in nearly all the industrial areas which had working-class communities of Irish descent. In a special article which appeared in *The Times* after the dramatic advance of the left in Glasgow, the swing to Labour by the Scoto-Irish was singled out as one of the keys that explained the scale of the victory.[28]

The exact role of the *Observer* in this major political realignment is hard to judge since it is never easy to measure the impact of the press on political attitudes and voting behaviour. Iain McLean suspects that locally, the Catholic press was more influential than *Forward,* the socialist weekly, because of its much higher circulation.[29] Thus its political line is worthy of examination.

At the 1922 general election, Diamond's papers began to criticise 'pro-Bolshevik' elements within the Labour Party but, strangely enough, he was relatively slow to direct his fire at the Communist Party of Great Britain (CPGB) itself. Gradually it dawned on the church that the atheistic CPGB was capable of drawing recruits from Catholic workers, especially in mining areas in Fife and, to a lesser degree in Lanarkshire. Of the 407 men listed as killed fighting with the British International Brigade for the Republican side in the Spanish civil war of the 1930s, no less than ninety-one were from Scotland, many with names such as Burke, Casey, Connolly, Duffy etc. [30]

John Campbell, secretary of the Catholic Union in Glasgow later claimed with a little hyperbole in 1951 that the Communist Party was dominated by renegade Catholics and that fact had to be faced up to.[31] The activities of militants like Lawrence Daly and Mick McGahey of Lanarkshire, showed that the Catholic community was yielding talented recruits for the party even after 1945. From 1923 onwards, Catholics were instructed at every opportunity by clergy, the religious press, and the Catholic Union to have no truck with the CPGB or any communist front and it was only non-communist candidates whose views were canvassed on matters deemed relevant to Catholics. Such hostility contributed to the failure of the party ever to win a single parliamentary or even municipal seat in Glasgow. In single-industry towns and villages, where the church's resources were weaker and where the class struggle made the economics of survival drown out the appeal of religious salvation, the battle between the pulpit and the party was less of a foregone conclusion as was shown by Willie Gallacher's tenure as MP for West Fife from 1935 to 1950.[32]

Time would ultimately show that the extreme-left only had a distant appeal for small sections of the Catholic community at specific moments. Even in the midst of industrial turmoil, the power of the church could be vividly demonstrated as in the small Lanarkshire mining community of Carfin in the early 1920s. During a prolonged stoppage, striking miners erected a small grotto at the request of the local priest, Thomas Nimmo Taylor (1873-1963). Soon this bleak and ugly mining village became a place of pilgrimage for thousands of Scottish Catholics.[33] Its appeal grew as the waters of the shrine, dedicated to Our Lady of the Rosary in 1922 were claimed to have miraculous properties. Over one-quarter of a million pilgrims visited Carfin in the summer of 1923.[34] The shrine's appeal was undiminished even when the authorities prohibited an open-air procession due to be held on Corpus Christi Sunday, 22nd June 1924. At the behest of Hugh Ferguson, Orange MP for Motherwell, the police had activated legislation dating from 1850 which had rarely ever been used. His move prompted Francis Blundell, the Tory MP for Ormskirk, and the member of an old Lancashire Catholic family, to propose a private members bill designed to sweep away archaic laws prohibiting Catholic religious processions and public ceremonies.[35]

The Roman Catholic Relief Act passed into law in 1926 at a time when the image of the church in Scotland increasingly was becoming a devotional one. In Glasgow, Archbishop Donald Mackintosh was concerned not to provoke the traditional opponents of the church and religious events were usually held at discreet locations away from the city centre. The popular fury which erupted in Edinburgh, the venue of a Eucharistic Congress in June 1935, showed Mackintosh's caution to have been far from misplaced.[36]

The hierarchical structure of the church inhibited lay initiatives with a practical purpose and episcopal approval was not always a foregone conclusion. Backing withheld for a Young Catholic Workers Movement influenced by Dorothy Day in the USA and the Belgian priest, Canon, later Cardinal Cardjin. Caution was preferred over innovation which meant that much of the potential of the engaged laity (which as a proportion of the entire Catholic community was high compared to the rest of Britain), went to waste.

Archbishop Mackintosh was a rigid but increasingly ineffective autocrat. His style appealed to senior priests who wished to manage a church suspicious of change that might even be in its own interest. This may help to explain why some priests reacted with barely concealed hostility to new Catholic state secondary schools like Holyrood in Glasgow, opened in 1936. The reason? It was staffed by lay teachers, the tiny Catholic secondary sector having hitherto been dominated by the religious orders.[37]

Before long, Archbishop Mackintosh fell victim to heart disease and turned into an invalid for long periods so that, in the words of a successor, 'he grew rather out of touch with the problems of the archdiocese'.[38] In the view of a well-informed Catholic layman, a number of clerical 'godfathers' were able to wield considerable power in Glasgow down to the 1970s. They could make or break a bishop's plans by their willingness or unwillingness to raise money for him. A large number were Irish priests who headed 'great clans of priest relatives' – one priest having as many as twenty relatives (cousins and nephews) as priests in the diocese. It has been claimed that many Irish priests were slow in encouraging vocations to the priesthood among Scots-born boys in their parishes. Such boys sometimes never had their applications answered, but bishops accepted the situation because it meant that they could get Irish-trained priests 'free' at no cost to diocesan funds. The source for this information linked the post-1975 acute shortage of vocations with the traditional lack of encouragement in many parishes for boys to try their vocations. Many of those Scots who did enter the priesthood preferred to join the religious orders. So pronounced was this trend that, by the 1950s, the British province of the Franciscans was estimated to be almost two-thirds Scots-bom, mainly from Glasgow or Dundee.[39]

It was members of the religious orders like the Jesuits or the Dominicans who very often provided the initial spur for movements of the laity whose objective were more social than devotional. In Edinburgh, where Roman Catholics made up less than 10% of the population, a bid was made to relate Catholic principles to modern society in the 1930s and 1940s. It coincided with the two decades as archbishop of Andrew Joseph McDonald (1871-1950), former head abbot of the Benedictine monastery at Fort Augustus. Both laymen and priests were given more autonomy to organise a Catholic social movement than elsewhere in Scotland. He sent some of the most promising younger clergy to universities in England and abroad. There they studied sociology and other liberal arts subjects that might equip them for new responsibilities the church needed to face up to in a rapidly changing age.[40]

In 1919 only 8.5% of the Catholic school population benefitted from some form of post-elementary education, a figure that had risen to only 13.9% by 1939.[41] The prospects of Catholics at university began to rise following the decision in 1924 that all Catholic male teachers had to be graduates.[42] The 1918 Act greatly expanded that part of the Catholic middle-class based on teaching.

But attendance at university was often not a transformative experience for Catholic students Many found themselves in an environment which they suspected of being at best apathetic and at worst hostile both towards their religious faith and national origins.[43] It was not long before nearly all Catholic students at Glasgow found their way to the Catholic chaplaincy. It had been opened in 1925 and, by 1930, almost 500 Catholic students were studying at Glasgow. The first chaplain was William Eric Brown, a convert and former Glasgow history lecturer who influenced the views of a great number of Catholic students in the 1920s and 1930s.[44] Another significant experience for many was membership of the University Distributist Club founded in 1930 and which celebrated fifty years of existence in 1980.[45] Distributism is the theory that personal freedom can only be safeguarded if there is widespread personal ownership of property. The theory was popularised by Hilaire Belloc and G. K. Chesterton, the best-known Catholic intellectuals of the inter-war period. To combat the evils of industrialism, distributism urged the revival of small-scale family farming, small units of trade and industry, and the encouragement of the craftsman. It had a strong impact on Glasgow university Catholics for a number of reasons. It blended with the Papal encyclicals that addressed social questions and, in an industrial city stricken by the depression, it provided an attractive theoretical alternative to 'the rule of the machine' for students from a subordinate closed community unable to play a major role in the technological field, at least locally.

The Church authorities were ambivalent about lay Catholics getting actively involved in public affairs. The Catholic Union before 1945 appeared most concerned with what it perceived as the dangers of the modern age rather than major economic issues. It campaigned against artificial birth control and the sterilisation of mentally handicapped people. The boarding out of orphaned Catholic children to Protestant homes or state orphanages continued to be a very sensitive issue. Bitterly fought court cases where the church sought to have orphaned children, one of whose parents was a Roman Catholic, placed in the care of co-religionists, were not unknown.[46]

Surprisingly, the inter-war Scottish church seemed unperturbed by the rise of the mainstream left. Pressure for a Catholic political party to cater for Catholics dissatisfied with those already on offer was weak. Not only did the British electoral system make its success unlikely but there was not enough common ground among Catholics to make it a practical proposition. The church and its allies avoided situations which would have shown that Catholics did not have an identity of outlook on political issues and that the pull of class loyalties could in certain recurring situations be stronger than the wish to obey the priest.

The political content of speeches made by autocratic clergymen hostile to the claims of socialism were usually discreetly ignored by parishioners who instinctively felt differently. The concentration of Scotland's urban Catholics in the lower income groups which were faring worst of all in the post-1929 depression and experiencing the full rigours of unemployment, means test, workhouse, and general deprivation meant that the left was their natural home despite the outbursts of nervous clergy.

The Catholic Union backed the ILP in most electoral contests even when, estranged from the Labour Party in the 1930s, it advocated confronting the capitalist system. The atheism of its leader James Maxton was overlooked as was the early anarchist sympathies of John McGovern, Wheatley's successor as MP for Glasgow Shettleston. In 1935, not long after the MP had been collaborating with the Communist Party in organising the unemployed, John Campbell in a letter to another prominent Catholic wrote that 'I am very glad to see Maxton's result in Bridgeton and particularly the unexpected majority he had'.[47] Much earlier, in 1923, the *Glasgow Observer* wrote: 'His favours to Catholic interests and his special knowledge of school questions and of the natural need for absolute equality in education legislation will render him a particularly useful friend to Catholic school interests if these should be attacked by bigots hereafter.'[48]

Maxton always cultivated the Catholic community in his Glasgow Bridgeton seat. From it he derived proportionately more votes than from non-Catholics which is confirmed by the attitude of the two main juvenile gangs in his constituency: the Protestant 'Billy Boys' were staunch supporters of the Unionist cause at election time while the Catholic 'Norman Conks' 'are in the main devoted followers of Maxton'.[49]

Towards John Wheatley, the Catholic establishment was less indulgent and his untimely death in 1930 was a hammer-blow to the left. In 1931, the defection of Labour leader Ramsay MacDonald enabled the Conservatives to dominate the politics of the 1930s. Maxton proved to be mistaken in his belief that the economic crisis had created something approaching a revolutionary situation that would enable the ILP to supplant Labour as the party of the working-class. Among much of the unemployed the depression bred grim resignation rather than a defiant espousal of socialism. The erratic Maxton was sidelined by the more effective Patrick Dollan. He moved from being an anti-war foe of the economic bosses to being a machine politician with an increasingly cautious agenda for change. As early as the mid-1920s, he was working hard to stitch up an alliance with fellow moderates from the trade unions and the Co-operative Society so as to keep Glasgow safe for reformist socialism.[50] He managed to keep the bulk of the Scottish ILP loyal to the Labour Party after 1932 but the crusading educational work and general propaganda of the ILP soon lapsed.

In 1933 the first Labour administration was formed in Glasgow and

Dollan became city treasurer. He became Lord Provost in 1938 and his gift for public relations won round many of those in important walks of life apprehensive that an ex-agitator with an Irish name had become Glasgow's first citizen. He accepted a knighthood in 1941 after having declared in 1937 that 'we socialists are bound to admit that our movement has made more progress under the monarchy than the pioneers thought possible . . . there is no evidence that the monarchy in this country has, at any time, tried to interfere with working-class aspirations'.[51]

A reconciliation with the Catholic church occurred in the early 1940s and his wife became a Catholic convert. In an epoch when the church was obsessed with 'leakage' from the faith, his status as a lapsed Catholic during his years at the political helm would have troubled church leaders. Trade union officials and members of the Co-operative societies seem to have been far more reliable allies than the Catholic Union in Dollan's drive to push the Labour Party in Glasgow rightwards. A mere six out of 116 Glasgow councillors in 1933 were Roman Catholics, a figure that only began to appreciably rise in the 1950s.

Knowledge of the balance of forces on the left in the West of Scotland in the 1930s tends to dent the view that influential 'co-religionists' of Dollan, organised into 'a Catholic machine', played a crucial role in helping him to tame the left. Only the Spanish civil war and the persecution of clergy and nuns there produced a collision between the Catholic Union and the ILP. Stormy public meetings pitted John McGovern against religious detractors.[52] But his backing for the Spanish Republic cooled after he narrowly escaped death at the hands of Spanish communists on a visit to Spain. Like George Orwell he had been dismayed by the way the Republican government had allowed local communists under instructions from Moscow to crush the libertarian left in the Barcelona fighting of May 1937.[53] In later years he became one of the most inveterate anti-communists in the Parliamentary Labour Party which he joined after Maxton's death in 1946. General Franco's British allies were unsavoury ones for devout working-class Catholics. The Earl of Glasgow, Ayrshire landowner and backer of various far-right causes between the wars, was a patron of the Friends of Nationalist Spain. But Catholics would have drawn little comfort from the fact that he had earlier founded a Union of Scottish

Loyalists, a name that would have conjured up unfavourable images for many of them.[54]

The inter-war years were ones of searing hardship for many Catholics but also ones of brightening prospects in other respects. The 1918 Education Act helped emancipate growing numbers of Catholics from permanent immersion in the unskilled working-class. It was an advance jealously defended by the church which managed to obtain near unanimous endorsement from its members for the Catholic schools system. But the new education settlement underscored the separateness of the Catholic community while giving its clerical and lay leaders more time to focus their energy on other areas of community life. The emergence or revival of a wide range of Catholic bodies with charitable, political, social, or devotional aims sharpened the identity of Catholics as a distinct grouping, but the restraints placed on 'Catholic Action' by the church, allied to its own hierarchical character, prevented most of these groups fulfilling their promise; as did the absence of a cultural infrastructure encompassing a Catholic daily paper, a political party, or a Catholic university, all of which the community was too poor to provide.

If Catholics had sought to create a parallel society, it could have produced an even more hostile response from those Protestant Scots still unwilling to accept Catholics as fellow citizens even with the Irish question in cold storage. As it was, Scotland was fortunate that the delicate web of community relations was not rent asunder in the inter-war years. World war, the relegation of the Irish question, and the rise of the Labour and Communist parties subtly altered the character and broadened the horizons of the immigrant community. They also made the majority much more aware of its presence than before. This did not necessarily lead to greater mutual respect. But opportunities for cooperation did arise even in the depression-ridden 1920s. Sections of both communities were able to co-operate in struggling against the hardships and injustices of an economic system whose harsh effects were not respecters of religious difference.

NOTES

1Cooney, *Scotland and the Papacy*, p. 17.

2 Michael Maguire, 'Charles Diamond reappraised', *Irish Post*, 7 May 1983.

3 Ian Wood, 'John Wheatley, the Irish, and the labour movement in Scotland', *Innes Review*, 31, 2, 1980, p. 80.

4 *Scottish Catholic Observer*, 19 April 1985.

5 *Glasgow Observer*, 29 April 1916.

6 *Glasgow Observer*, 16 May 1916.

7 Nan Milton, *John Maclean*, Pluto Press, London 1973, p. 129.

8 Wood, *Innes Review*, p. 248.

9 Handley, *The Irish in Modern Scotland*, p. 298.

10 Scottish Record Office (SRO), HH/31/ 34, Procurator Fiscal's Report, Glasgow, with reference to Scottish Office file No. 25478/Q/ 92: 'Hostile Propaganda – "Proposed Irish Massacre" ', September 1920.

11 SRO, HH/55/68, William Duncan, chief constable of Paisley, to Secretary of State for Scotland, 10

12 *Scottish Catholic Observer*, 24 October 1969.

13 Handley, p. 299.

14 Handley, p. 299.

15 SRO, HH/65/62, Part 30033/8, Chief Constable of Lanarkshire to the Scottish Office, 9 December 1920.

16 SRO, HH/31/34, 'Police Reports of Political Meetings 1918-', Part 25478A/ 79, Report by Procurator Fiscal, Glasgow, 3 September 1920.

17 Kevin O'Connor, *The Irish in Britain*, Torc, Dublin, 1970, pp.141-2.

18 Ernest O'Malley Papers, P17a/ 182, University College, Dublin: they contain vital information about the operations of the Republican movement in Glasgow during the civil war.

19 *Forward*, 29 October 1921. 'Carsonism' referred to Sir Edward Carson, leader of the Ulster Unionist resistance to Irish Home Rule.

20 *Motherwell Times*, 14 December 1923, for Ferguson's biographical details; Hansard, 15 April 1924.

21 *Glasgow Observer*,4 January 1919.

22 Murray, *The Old Firm*, pp.84-5.

23 Christopher Harvie, *No Gods and Precious Few Heroes*, Scotland 1914-80, Edward Arnold, London, 1981, p. 100.

24 Iain McLean, *The Legend of Red Clydeside*, John Donald, Edinburgh, 1983, p. 185.

25 John McKee, 'Catholics and education', *Scottish Catholic Observer*, 10 March 1978. For the 1918 Act see also James Treble, 'The development of Roman Catholic education in Scotland, 1878-1978', in McRoberts (ed.), *Modern Scottish Catholicism*, pp. 111-39.

26 *Glasgow Observer*, 18 September 1937.

27 *Glasgow Observer*,12 April 1919.

28 'Socialism on the Clyde', *Times*, 28 December 1922.

29 McLean, *Legend of Red Clydeside*, pp. 185-6.

30 James Darragh, 'The Catholic population of Scotland, 1878-1977', in McRoberts (ed.), *Modern Scottish Catholicism*, p. 246, n. 36.

31 *Irish Weekly* (Glasgow edition), 31 March 1951.

32 For the communist presence in Scottish industrial communities with a significant Catholic presence,see Stewart McIntyre, *Little Moscows, Communism and Working Class Militancy in Inter-warBritain*, Croom Helm, London,1980, p. 161.

33 See Susan McGhee, *Monsignor Taylor of Carfin*, John Burns, Glasgow, 1972.

34 The Carfin phenomenon elicited mixed views from Scottish commentators. For a sceptical account tinged with sarcasm see George Malcolm Thomson, *The Rediscovery of Scotland*, Routledge, London, 1928, pp. 53-61. The writer and critic Edwin Muir was more favourably impressed in his *Scottish Journey*, Mainstream, Edinburgh, 1979 (first published 1935), pp. 176-7.

35 Susan McGhee, 'Carlin and the Roman Catholic Relief Act of 1926', in *Innes Review*, n 16, 1, 1965, pp. 56-78.

36 See chapter 4.

37 Information from retired teacher who has taught in both state sectors

38 Information from a private source.

39 Information from the late James Darragh.

40 Interview with Fr. Anthony Ross, O.P., December 1981. For McDonald's work as archbishop, see also his obituary in CDS, 1951, and W. P. Crampton, 'The archdiocese of St. Andrews and Edinburgh', Scottish Survey, *Scottish Catholic Herald and Glasgow Observer*, 1878-1956.

41 McCaffrey, 'Roman -Catholicism in Scotland', p. 298.

42 McCaffrey, 'Roman -Catholicism in Scotland', p.p. 297-8.

43 Ian 0. Bayne, 'A university institution with its own proud record',*Scottish Catholic Observer*, 9 May1980.

44 See Alice Ivy Hay, *Valiant for Truth, Malcolm Hay of Seaton*, Neville Spearman, London, 1971, p. 95.

45 The story of the Glasgow University Distributist Club is related by Ian 0. Bayne (see note 43).

46 The correspondence relating to specific court cases can be found in the Catholic Union files, Glasgow Archdiocesan Archives (GAA).

47 John Campbell to John Cruden, 16 November 1935, Catholic Union files, GAA.

48 *Glasgow Observer*, 1 December 1923.

49 Gilbert McAllister, *James Maxton: Portrait of a Rebel*, John Murray, London, 1935, p. 95.

50 See Helen Corr and Bill Knox, 'Patrick Dollan', in W. Knox (ed.), *Scottish Labour Leaders 1918-39*, Mainstream, Edinburgh, 1984,

51 *Forward*, 8 May 1937.

52 *Forward*, 21 January 1937.

53 See Ian Wood, 'Scotland and the Spanish civil war', *Cencrastus*, autumn 1984, p. 14.

54 *Forward*, 18 June 1932.

CHAPTER 4

'The Scottish lion and the Irish bull will not lie down together'

HOSTILITY to the Catholic or Irish presence (and the two terms were interchangeable in describing a population that was now mainly Scottish-born) mounted as Scotland entered the post-World War I era in a depressed and troubled state. The low morale of Scottish public opinion and of the various institutions and pressure groups which defined it, was due to a variety of factors. Among Scottish troops (who had flocked to the colours in greater numbers than people anywhere else in the United Kingdom), there had been a disproportionately high casualty rate in World War I. [1] There was a crisis in Scottish heavy industry upon which rested the local economy, that was triggered off by the post-war fall in demand for ships, engineering products and coal, but was made worse in Scotland by the failure of conservatively-minded industrialists to diversify into other areas. And there was a conversion of much of the working-class to parliamentary and even extra-parliamentary forms of socialism which, in their different ways, were seen to pose a threat to the security and cohesion of Scottish and British society.

As Scotland moved from being almost a co-partner in the British Empire to being an internally divided and increasingly peripheral part of the United Kingdom which had recently shed the troublesome sister isle of Ireland, the mood of sections of the middle-class darkened. This spelt trouble for a marginal and unassimilated minority like the Irish in Scotland whose presence 'is regarded with little favour even by enlightened Scottish opinion', the words of a jaundiced nationalist spokesman as late as 1950. [2] Throughout the interwar period, even neutral commentators described a community that had been predominantly Scottish-born by the 1890s as 'the Irish' in Scotland, a telling indication that they were regarded almost as strangers in their midst.

Vocal elements not without influence in the political parties, the Protestant churches and, to a lesser extent in the professions and the business world, viewed them as interlopers who had transformed some of the most densely populated areas of industrial Scotland into alien enclaves and who, by withholding loyalty to their adopted country and scorning its educational and popular institutions, had contributed in no small measure to its malaise.

In the brighter atmosphere before the war, the Irish community was generally ignored by institutions and individuals who later spoke out about its presence, even though it afforded far more examples of being a separate enclave. Scots then looked outwards to the empire and to London where they were influential in politics, journalism and many of the other professions. Statements and developments emanating from the Catholic Irish community which, in the past, would have been overlooked by a confident bourgeoisie, elicited a forthright response in a new and unhappier age.

The new highly-charged atmosphere helps explain the violent reaction to a speech made at the end of 1921 by John Phillimore, the Catholic convert and professor of Greek at Glasgow University when he delivered a prize-giving address at St. Aloysius Academy. He told the audience, made up of Catholic pupils, some of whom were bound for higher education, that the universities were open to capture and that education could be used as a means of converting Scotland to Roman Catholicism. . .'[3]

Protestant opinion viewed the speech as an 'insidious plan to infiltrate the universities and turn them into Catholic institutions'.[4] With elections for the Glasgow Education Authority due in April 1922 the Protestant church mobilised its members as it had never done before. The turnout leaped from 27% to almost 60% of the electorate and Catholics lost nearly half their seats on the authority. The *Glasgow Herald* was to the fore in sounding the alarm, the paper claiming that so effective had been its appeal to Protestant creed and heritage that even 'the bulk of Labour voters did not transfer to Catholic candidates but to Protestant "Anti-Socialist" ones'.[5] But by the next round of education elections in 1925, the hubub had died down and all twelve Catholic candidates were returned in Glasgow on a more reduced overall turnout.

Strongly worded attacks on the Catholic Irish presence in Scotland became a feature of the General Assembly, the annual gathering of the Church of Scotland, starting in 1923. In that year, the Assembly's influential Church and Nation committee formally approved a report entitled *The Menace of The Irish Race to Our Scottish Nationality*. It had carried out an investigation into the Irish presence after strong representations on the matter from the Presbytery of Glasgow, so it was no isolated outburst but resulted from a groundswell of concern from presumably ordinary Kirk members. Published in pamphlet form to ensure wider circulation, the report speculated about whether Scotland might not be on the verge of committing 'race suicide' and demanded that means be devised to 'preserve Scotland and the Scottish race' and 'to secure to future generations the traditions, ideals, and faith of a great people unspoiled and inviolate'.[6]

The report carried the signatures of the Rev. William Munro and of a High Court judge. It produced a fierce response from the *Glasgow Observer* which showed how little common ground existed then between the two main branches of Christianity in Scotland:

> 'What is an Irishman? What is an immigrant? (For instance, is Bonar Law one?) . . . When does an Irishman become a Scotsman. (Is it when recruits are wanted to prevent a Hun invasion?)
>
> 'There is a complaint that the ancient glory of Scotland must depart if Roman Catholics or Irish are allowed to increase and multiply. When was Scotland glorious? Was it not in its Catholic days? Did it not owe its proud position among the nations of the world above all to immigrants like Columba and St. Margaret . . .
>
> 'It is time Parliament curtailed the power of such people? The simplest way would be to abolish the stipends of the parish ministers. The rest would follow naturally.' [7]

With falling church rolls causing much worry, economic prosperity apparently a thing of the past and emigration removing many of the most energetic Scots, the Kirk seemed inward-looking and dispirited if a perusal of the topics featuring prominently in the resolutions of church synods and debated at the annual General Assembly in the 1920s and 1930s is any guide. By contrast, the Catholic population of Scotland was increasing, new parishes were being built, influential people were going over to Rome, and the Catholic church was not so reticent as before in displaying its strength in public processions and rituals.

It was rare for those who were vocal on the question of the Irish presence to distinguish between first generation Irish and those whose parents or more distant ancestors hailed from Ireland. All too frequently commentators wishing to prove the urgency of their case, mixed together the Scoto-Irish with the Irish-born to arrive at a figure of anything up to three quarters of a million 'foreign Irish' in the country.

One factor that ensured that this state of affairs would continue into future generations was Section 18 of the 1918 Education (Scotland) Act which preserved and upgraded Catholic schools by bringing them within the state system. It was this issue, more than any other, which was a rallying-point for Scots unable to come to terms with the fact that theirs was a multicultural society possessing an active minority whose religion Scots had historically come to fear and distrust. The issue was put in a nutshell by Rev. F.E. Watson, parish minister in Belshill West in Lanarkshire, a depressed mining area where Catholics and Protestants lived in uneasy proximity. He was already the main church opponent of the 1918 Act, and in 1935, he wrote:

> 'The indignant opposition to the provision of Section 18 of the Education (Scotland) Act, 1918, is that public money is being expanded in educating an increasing section of the population, in the main Free Staters or their offspring, in a faith and a loyalty hostile to the tradition and religion accepted by the vast majority of the Scottish nation.
>
> 'Why should we feed, clothe, and educate these people who everywhere plot and plan for the downfall of Great Britain?'[8]

Many Protestants felt it a travesty of justice that a suspect minority faith had been able to receive more generous educational terms from the state than the Church of Scotland had in 1872. Priests had free access to Catholic schools which ministers did not have in state ones. There was an angry reaction to the fact that many teachers in Roman Catholic schools were members of religious orders who would not keep their salary but

80

rather pass it on to the church. Thus it was alleged that the state was directly subsidising its general operations. Perhaps fortuitously, opponents of state-financed Catholic schools were deprived of a powerful forum in 1929 when the government abolished directly elected education authorities and replaced them with ones whose members were nominated by local councils and the various church groups involved. If they had remained as forums for contentious debate into the 1930s, when militant religious parties were picking up council seats in Glasgow and Edinburgh, it might even have further aggravated an already troubled situation.

Denunciation of Popery was a feature of General Assembly debate well into the 1930s and in one particular year, an Edinburgh daily paper was moved to remark that 'from yesterday's speeches in the General Assembly, one could gather the impression that the most formidable enemy is the Church of Rome'.[9] Some churchmen may have half-believed the talented journalist, George Malcolm Thomson when he wrote in his book *The Re-Discovery of Scotland*:

> 'Well the truth is that Calvinism is going. As a creed it is as dead as
> the doornail already; as a system of Church government, it has still
> as vigorous a life as is possible to any institution whose soul is
> departed.'[10]

But it would be wrong to give the impression that all, or perhaps even most, Church of Scotland ministers felt that they were in deadly combat with a resurgent Catholic faith for the hearts and minds of the Scottish people. The protagonists were a small but vocal minority of ministers who had a larger element of the faithful behind them. Most ministers were probably careful to keep out of the firing line and preferred not to get involved while a smaller number, little more than a handful, spoke out when they felt feeling was running dangerously high, against hotheads inside or outside their own church.

For instance, in 1930 the Rev. John Kennedy of St. Paul's North Church, Glasgow, repudiated a co-religionist for voicing concern that 12.3% of Scotland's population was comprised of Catholics:

'he makes no comment on the fact that 36% (i.e. three times the number of Catholics) belong to no church at all. He unabashedly admits that this pagan million 'are predominantly Presbyterian in their training and outlook'. It may further be added that they are the products of secular education to which we have betrayed our children as Catholic Churchmen refuse to do . . .'[11]

In 1935, after militant Protestants had made successful forays into local politics, the Rev. J.M. Dickie was moved to ask in a debate at the General Assembly on the 1918 Education Act: 'was it possible when nationalism was rampant and sheer paganism existed not only beyond the frontiers of the Rhine but in their own midst, that they should engage in a campaign against a Church which, however they deplored its errors, did stand for spiritual things and on the side of Christ'.[12]

Within weeks of this sobering intervention, Edinburgh, the site of the General Assembly, was convulsed by angry religious rioting which greeted a three-day Roman Catholic Eucharistic Congress, even though it was an indoor occasion mainly held on Catholic premises. Exultant hardline Protestants felt that Scotland's capital had been reclaimed for John Knox and Catholics seeking to flaunt their religion taught a well-deserved lesson, but the scale of mob violence alarmed many in the Church of Scotland. Even a convinced opponent of the 1918 Act like the Rev. D. M. McGregor felt obliged to write to the *Scotsman* to warn that 'if Protestantism can only be vindicated in such crude ways, its day is nearly done'.[13]

A few bold spirits in the Church of Scotland went beyond conciliatory words and took practical steps to build bridges in their community often at no small risk to themselves. In the Gorbals district of Glasgow, J. Cameron Peddie, an Aberdonian, and minister of Hutcheston parish church in the Gorbals for twenty-seven years up to the 1950s found that, contrary to popular belief, rival gangs could be composed of both Protestants and Catholics. He won the respect of many of the young in Glasgow's South-side, irrespective of religion, by treating them seriously and giving them premises where they could meet instead of on the streets. He felt that poverty and unemployment were the main causes of Glasgow's gangsterism and he was not the only observer to find that the Gorbals was 'not as black as it was painted'. His congregation 'were quiet decent folk' while the people he met 'in the closes and the streets were friendly, kindly, appreciative'.[14]

Another minister who broke down barriers of mistrust was Henry C. Whitley during years spent in Port Glasgow in the late 1930s. During his first week there, he sought out the local parish priest, Simon Keane (1888-1951), a redoubtable individual, and their combined efforts managed to extinguish the weekend sectarian brawling which disfigured the town.[15]

Rev. Whitley served on the local council in Port Glasgow while in Glasgow, the Episcopal Canon John McBain was a much respected Labour councillor for Mile-End in the 1920s and 1930s. But perhaps it was the United Free Church minister, James Barr (1861-1949) who made the greatest contribution of any churchman to community harmony by his political interventions. He was based in Govan after 1905 where he won the respect of a Protestant congregation in an area with strong Ulster ties that also included many Catholics who admired his work on the Glasgow School Board.[16] In 1924 Barr defeated a hardline Orangeman to be elected Labour MP for Motherwell and in 1935 he came out of retirement to stand as MP for Coatbridge and Airdrie, another of Glasgow's satellites where religious rivalry had blighted local politics, which he represented until 1945.

These individual efforts deserve not to be overlooked because they show that even in the most perilous years of community relations in lowland Scotland, there were outspoken figures giving a lead in the direction of sanity and mutual toleration for respective creeds.

The Catholic church passed up chances of more bridge-building. Talks between Catholic students at Glasgow university and members of the Student Christian Movement presided over by their respective chaplains appeared imminent in the late 1930s. A proposal for discussions actually came from the SCM which William Brown, the Catholic chaplain at Glasgow was willing to accept. However, on the eve of the first meeting they were unexpectedly overruled by Archbishop Mackintosh, one Catholic student still being able to recall how Fr. Brown broke down and wept on receiving the prelate's veto.[17] By deliberately isolating itself in this way, the Catholic church invited suspicion and reinforced the ignorance of what ordinary Catholics were like.

The eruption of discord on religious and racial grounds was, from time to time, reflected in the statements and actions of the Tory Party which between 1911 and 1964 was known in Scotland as the Unionist Party. In the aftermath of the Anglo-Irish war, a number of its MPs and parliamentary candidates pointedly referred to the unwelcome presence of the Irish in their midst. The intention behind such statements was often to use ethnic solidarity in a bid to get workers to resist a class appeal. By the collapse of Lloyd George's coalition in 1922, the Tories were able to lay claim to the bulk of the anti-Socialist vote in the main Scottish towns and cities. It was a straight fight between them and Labour now that the Liberal Party's power had been largely broken. But, in these straight contests, unorthodox tactics were sometimes used.

One of the worst examples arose at the 1924 general election in the seat of Glasgow Shettleston. John Wheatley, the sitting Labour MP and minister of housing and health in the outgoing Labour administration returned to campaign in his constituency with the reputation of having been the most effective member of the outgoing government. But his Tory challenger, Major Reid Miller, a one-armed war veteran, waged a vitriolic campaign against him that dwelt on his Irish birth and religious attachments and he was returned with only a seventy-four vote majority.[18] After the election Reid Miller waged a vendetta against Wheatley which was too much for the Tories who dropped him as the Shettleston candidate.

Until the 1930s officers of the Orange Order sat on the Scottish council of the Tory Party.[19] The local Orange hall was often utilised as an election headquarters for the Tories, the practice being maintained in Ayrshire, according to David Lambie MP up to the 1960s.[20] By using the premises of a body that was non-Catholic by its statute and decidedly anti-Catholic in its behaviour and outlook, the Scottish Unionists were effectively snubbing the Catholic minority. Even Liverpool had Roman Catholics sitting in parliament as Tories by the 1930s but this development did not arise in urban Scotland till the 1970s.[21]

In order to cultivate the Protestant grassroots, members of the Tory aristocracy sometimes consented to being given titular appointments in the Orange Order. This meant reviewing Orange parades and turning up to sit on the platform at annual general meetings. Sir John Gilmour,

Secretary of State for Scotland from 1924 to 1929 was an honorary deputy grand master and, before leaving office, he announced his 'intention of seeking an amendment of the law in virtue of which an Irishman landing on these hospitable shores was immediately entitled to the benefit of the Poor Law without the least risk of being returned to his parish and country of origin'.[22] This gesture did no harm among working-class Tories and, in 1931, the year of Labour's electoral crash, a few new MPs even more in tune with their feelings were returned. One such was William Templeton, an advocate of the compulsory inspection of convents[23] who was Tory MP for the divided but solidly working-class seat of Coatbridge and Airdrie from 1931 to 1935. This was also the parliament in which the most forceful cries for a regulation of Irish immigration to Scotland were heard but Scottish members were unable to convince English fellow Tories of the urgency of the problem.

Reliable evidence gathered by the *Glasgow Herald* (see p. 94) and found in government statistics showed that Irish immigration to Scotland in the 1920s and 1930s was miniscule compared with previous decades. However, popular perceptions were at variance with cold statistics and even liberal Tories like Robert Boothby and John Buchan, felt obliged to table questions or make representations about the 'Hibernianisation of Scotland'. In a parliamentary debate, on 24 November 1932, Buchan linked the Scottish malaise with the Irish presence, albeit in a low-key manner:

> 'something must be done, and done soon if Scotland is not to lose its
> historic individuality. All is not well with our country. Our
> population is declining; we are losing some of the best of our race
> stock by migration and their place is being taken by those who,
> whatever their merits, are not Scottish. I understand that every fifth
> child born in Scotland is an Irish Roman Catholic'.[24]

Electoral successes had already occurred for the Scottish Protestant League led by Alexander Ratcliffe, a full-time anti-Catholic preacher. His election to Glasgow corporation in 1931 at the head of an unknown party, after having lived in the city for less than a year, demonstrated how susceptible part of the electorate was to a religious appeal couched in political terms. In 1934, keen to prevent the Labour Party consolidating its newly won majority on Glasgow corporation, the Moderates actually struck up an electoral pact with the anti-Catholic SPL. It was given a free run in seven working-class seats while the Moderates were unopposed in more affluent districts where the SPL had taken seats from them last time. No terms were published but, in his election address, the SPL leader declared that 'the Moderate Party have entirely changed their view on . . . my appeal for a revision of the 1918 Education (Scotland) Act as they recently in the Council unanimously supported my motion for action'.[25]

Orange support for the Tories was concentrated in working-class strongholds stretching from Renfrewshire through Lanarkshire across to West Lothian, where Labour only stood a chance of being toppled in an specially disastrous year like 1931. Sometimes, Orangemen would protest that they were being taken too much for granted and that their elected representatives were dragging their feet over issues dear to their hearts. In 1923, an Orange and Protestant Party had actually been formed when the Scottish Unionist leadership was seen to back the Anglo-Irish peace settlement. However, it had the half-hearted support of Orangemen and quickly disappeared once it was apparent that the 1921 treaty was far from being a sell-out of the Ulster Unionist cause.

If it had been the Unionists and not the religious fringe which had used extremist rhetoric to try to weaken the Left, then Orangeism's political visibility would probably have been greater. But there was no Scottish Sir Oswald Mosley prepared to appeal to the atavistic feelings of a section of Protestant workers and middle-class elements. In some ways, this is surprising. The Orange card had helped to dethrone the Scottish Liberals in 1886 and there is a lot of circumstantial evidence to show that religious disgruntlement was just as strong in the 1920s and 1930s among parts of the working-class and the church-going lower middle-class.

While Glasgow acquired political stability in 1933 with Labour winning contol of the council and keeping it for many years, it was in Edinburgh that religious extremism shattered civic calm. Here, although Catholics comprised less than 10 per cent of the population, Protestant extremists enjoyed greater political success than in Glasgow and their campaign was laced with violence. Catholic functions were attacked, priests were assaulted in the streets and threatened in chapel houses, and many ordinary Catholics were victimised at work. The eruption of strife on such a scale was difficult to explain because the Orange presence was weak in Edinburgh, street violence fuelled by religious misunderstanding was previously virtually unknown, and the Ulster question had not divided the city as had happened in Glasgow.

The rise of Protestant Action owed more to the angry eloquence of its leader, John Cormack than to the prevailing political situation or previous sectarian unrest. For a brief period he showed that, even in the absence of deep divisions, a city or a community can almost be torn apart by the sudden emergence of a charismatic individual who can move people to deeds which they would never normally contemplate.

Born in 1894, the son of Highland parents, he was brought up in a devout Baptist household and, at the age of fifteen, he joined the Argyll and Sutherland Highlanders as a boy soldier. Serving in the trenches in World War I he later saw action in Ireland during the 1919-21 War of Independence. Collusion between Catholic priests and Sinn Fein separatists made him strongly anti-Catholic.[26] By the end of the 1920s, he was speaking on Sundays at the Mound, the venue for open-air speakers in Edinburgh. Initially, this was a gesture of solidarity with his father, a lay preacher who was being maltreated by young Catholics in the crowd when he spoke.[27]

Cormack gathered around him a growing band of supporters who clashed with young Catholics who lived in the crowded tenements of Edinburgh Old Town. These clashes sharpened his anti-Catholicism, he found that he could attract a following on account of his physical boldness and speaking abilities, and his thoughts soon turned to politics; in 1933 he formed the Protestant Action Society and one year later he decided to stand for the ward of North Leith in the Edinburgh municipal elections. He was elected, defeating the sitting Moderate, even though Leith, Edinburgh's port was not his home area, nor did it harbour a 'No Popery' tradition at least on the scale of that found in similar small towns in the west of Scotland. But in the 1920s, Leith was reeling from the depression. The export of coal and ancillary trades upon which the viability of the docks depended, ground to a halt. Severe hardship ensued but the Labour Party, which had received its worst Scottish results in the black year of 1931 in and around Edinburgh, was unable to make much headway.

Cormack owed his first and many subsequent victories in Leith to an unusually high poll. In 1934 the average Edinburgh turnout had been 40% but in North Leith it was 58.4%, the highest in the whole city. Rowdiness characterised the contest in 1934 and in 1935 when he fielded more candidates, much to the dismay of the local press.[28]

Protestant Action's manifesto was bound to attract controversy. Cormack was on record as advocating the disenfranchisement of Roman Catholics in Britain and their expulsion from Scotland. No less absurdly, he promised to remove local Catholics from all public employment, ban them from having the use of corporation halls, or going ahead with public processions if his party ever won a controlling majority in Edinburgh.[29]

In 1935 he took advantage of his mandate to embarrass and intimidate the Catholic authorities in Edinburgh. He gave a warning of the lengths he was prepared to go to shortly before the city council was due to give a civic reception to the Catholic Young Men's Society:

> 'On the 27th day of April, the peaceful, cultured, enlightened city of Edinburgh, that has never known in my lifetime at least what a real smash-up means, is going to know it that day, if this civic reception comes off.'[30]

Councillors Cormack and Marr (the latter newly returned for Central Leith at a by-election) duly turned up outside the City Chambers with over ten thousand people, many of whom barracked the arriving council guests. Fearing trouble a detachment of Gordon Highlanders stationed in Edinburgh Castle was placed in readiness.[31] When the Archbishop of Edinburgh arrived, his car was almost surrounded by a hostile mob before the police brought him to safety. Later, on 10th June 1935, Cormack interrupted the ceremony in which Joseph Lyons, the Australian Prime Minister and a Roman Catholic, was being given the freedom of Edinburgh along with John Buchan.[32] Still more unruly scenes occurred later when a Catholic Eucharistic Congress was held in Edinburgh. Since the first one in Lille during 1882, Eucharistic Congresses had been held to propagate the uniquely Catholic doctrine of the real presence of Christ in the Eucharist. This doctrine of transubstantiation was anathema to Cormack and on the evening of 24th June, there was much disorder in Waverley Market where a woman's eucharistic meeting was being held and four priests were set upon by a hostile mob.[33]

However, the worst scenes of all occurred at the climax of the Congress on 25th June at an open-air procession of the Blessed Sacrament. This avoided the city-centre and was held in the grounds of St. Andrew's Priory, Canaan Lane, in the Morningside district. The next day, the *Scotsman* related how 'as the hour of the gathering approached, tramcar after tramcar brought Protestant extremists and others to the scene . . . By 7 p.m., there must have been at least 10,000 people in Morningside Road. Gangs of youths and women shouted "No Popery" . . .' It went on to report that special coaches containing women and young people were stoned, fighting broke out in the crowd, the police were attacked and baton charges were made.[34]

Nearly eighty years later, four academics arguing in their book that sectarianism was fast vanishing and that it had never been as ugly or widespread as analysts of the phenomenon had claimed, went to some pains to show that it was not rioting that Edinburgh witnessed in 1935 but 'large and boisterous' demonstrations.[35] When Archbishop McDonald wrote to Prime Minister Stanley Baldwin that 'priests were savagely assailed, elderly women attacked and kicked, bus-loads of children mercilessly stoned and inoffensive citizens abused and assailed in a manner that is almost unbelievable in any civilised country today', the response of Steve Bruce and his co-authors was in effect that he would say that, wouldn't he?[36] They offered no evidence as to why he might be dramatising a troubling episode.

Examining the public profile of the Catholic hierarchy since its 1878 restoration, Archbishop McDonald's decision to go public was unprecedented even though there had been no shortage of sectarian disorders in Scotland in previous times. Church leaders were prepared to put up with attacks, even violent ones, as long as core church interests, such as Catholic schools were not under threat. McDonald's successor, Gordon Gray gently rebuked me in 1985 for setting out to unpack the Edinburgh troubles of the mid-1930s in a book.[37] If it had been high spirits among crowds of people that had occasionally got out-of-hand, he would surely have been more relaxed about the affair being chronicled.

The future Cardinal and members of his family had actually been caught up in the 24th June 1935 disturbances at Waverley Market as his brother George Gray related to the historian Michael Turnbull:

'I drove my mother up there. My father and Gordon came with me. . .

'When the meeting was finished and the women came out to get into buses and coaches, a terrible noise started. . . there was hammering on windows, the sound of breaking glass, and my father, who was standing between Gordon and myself, on the other side of the road, said in his quiet way – "I've travelled all over the world. I've lived among natives and savages, but I've never seen people behave like this!" As he said that the crowd turned on him. Gordon got him round one side, I got the other, and managed to get him down a side street with the help of the police.'[38]

The next day Fr. Gordon Gray was actually the priest carrying the cross at the head of the open-air procession in Canaan Lane. His brother recalls a baton charge, buses stoned and overturned and 'a great deal of fighting. . . especially on Bruntsfield Links.'[39] In his letter to me exactly fifty years later, the then retired church leader could have been forgiven for still being traumatised by these events.

The atmosphere was ugly and the intimidation of Catholics continued on and off for the rest of the summer. Catholic activists stood on all-night vigils guarding their churches and a Catholic Vigilance Association was formed when it was feared that this might have to be a long-term precaution.[40] Worshippers were jeered and taunted as they entered St. Mary's Cathedral and retired accountant, John McLaughlin, can still recall how, at midnight mass on a Christmas Eve in the mid-1930s a few of Cormack's supporters entered St. Mary Star of the Sea Church in Leith 'when it was packed to the doors' and 'went to communion simply for the sake of coming out and waving the host saying this is what they believe and it is not true'.[41]

Other Edinburgh Catholics still recall how attempts were made to pressurise Catholics in their workplace. Archbishop McDonald spoke out at the time about the intimidation of Catholics in factory employment.[42] Some Catholics in the retail trade were laid off on account of their religion;[43] in other concerns, such as the printing trade, they kept their jobs but none were taken on in future. Some large shopkeepers had already operated a Protestant only staffing policy over many years so that Cormack's views were not particularly new. It was rather the extreme methods he used to enforce them that were striking. Even Catholics working for the Co-operative Society in Edinburgh were not immune from pressure and they were harassed or intimidated by fellow workers or managerial staff, according to the testimony of at least one Catholic who worked for St. Cuthberts Co-operative Society.[44] From his own memories of the 1930s, Hugh Brown, Labour MP for Glasgow Provan recalled in 1984 that there was a distinct lack of sympathy for Roman Catholics in the co-operative society.[45] No Catholic ever became a director of the largest Scottish society, the SCWS at least before 1945 and, earlier in the century, a separate Catholic Co-operative society nearly got off the ground in Lanarkshire because of perceived anti-Catholic bias.[46]

In 1930, the Kirk's general assembly approved a call for a boycott of 'Irish' labour in Scotland, 'Irish' and 'Catholic' at that time being seen as interchangeable terms. Professor Bruce and his co-authors, who disparage claims about long-term economic discrimination mention the successful motion in their book, adding that 'the new strategy quickly flopped' without any supporting evidence being offered which would suggest that Edinburgh Catholics had once again been over-reacting, this time about being squeezed out of parts of the labour market.[47]

The Co-operative movement had strong Masonic affiliations and Freemasons were also strongly entrenched in many local Scottish police forces up to and beyond the 1930s. The police is the other well-known institution which Hugh Brown MP identified as not being particularly sympathetic to Catholics at this time. It was not just in the Edinburgh force that Catholic officers were conspicuous by their absence. Between the Masonic order and the Roman Catholic church there was little love lost and it would not have been surprising if this was reflected in relations between the police and ordinary Catholics; they were, by and large, low wage earners who dwelt in the overcrowded tenements of the Old Town in Cowgate, the Grassmarket, and the Canongate. These were areas where the police frequently had to investigate crimes, albeit of a petty kind linked with drunkenness and petty thieving and, although most of the Old Town's inhabitants somehow managed to remain law-abiding in the fight for economic survival and the maintenance of self-respect, it did not incline the police to view them always in a sympathetic light.

Cormack singled the police out for praise at the time of the most serious public disturbances in 1935.[48] So did Professor Bruce and the co-authors of the 2004 study: 'the police handled the militants with skill, as the absence of any serious or sustained violence demonstrates'.[49] But Scottish Office records, released a full decade before their book's appearance, showed real frustration with the approach of the Edinburgh police. In early 1936, continuing unrest was discussed between the Lord Advocate, Thomas Cooper and his civil servants and a memo written by the civil servant indicated the matter was to be brought to the attention of the chief constable.[50] For several years, the police insisted that there was insufficient evidence to support a prosecution, (presumably one that an Edinburgh jury would return a conviction on.) This remained the case even in 1940 when Cormack was asserting at regular public meetings in central Edinburgh that Scottish Catholics were more suitable targets than Nazi troops. A police intelligence report claimed that he had urged: 'That when Protestants went "over the top" with Roman Catholics, the Protestants should shoot them'.But the Lord Advocate continued to be stonewalled by the police that there was no 'feasible case' against him.[51]

Cormack was adamant that Roman Catholics were beyond redemption even if they displayed a willingness to abandon Romish doctrines and embrace the Reformed tradition. He disavowed any connections with fascism. But slogans like 'Toleration Overdone is an Evil' or 'Better a Competent Dictatorship than an Incompetent Democracy' were used by Cormack in public and private and show his authoritarian political outlook.[52] At its peak, Protestant Action boasted a membership of 8,000 people in Edinburgh which showed the lack of inhibitions about his chilling attitude towards a highly visible minority.

At the 1935 local elections Protestant Action (PA) gained nearly one-quarter of the city's votes and Cormack kept the temperature high into 1936 by holding outdoor and indoor meetings on every day of the week, three on Sunday, and occasional rallies in the Usher Hall which held over 3,000 people and which he regularly filled. His arrest, following disturbances at a Catholic Truth Society meeting in February 1936 addressed by Monsignor Ronald Knox, brought more publicity especially when he elected to conduct his own defence at the subsequent trial. Women queued all night to be guaranteed seats in the public gallery and hundreds of his supporters escorted him to court.[53] When he was briefly imprisoned for non-payment of his fine, his hero status was confirmed.

Women would comprise a far higher proportion of Cormack's municipal candidates than was customary for any party in the 1930s. There were few other openings for them in Protestant life with membership of the Freemasons and any kind of influence in the Orange Order denied to them. One commentator reckons that an important element of his success was the ability he possessed to pour 'excitement into lives that were a vacuum of inactivity . . . and frustration'.[54] Certainly, the feminine dimension visible in PA dents the widely-held assumption that involvement in sectarian actions has primarily been a male phenomenon.

In 1936 PA was able to capture 30.84% of Edinburgh's municipal vote. Labour was driven into third place and Cormack realised his aim of driving all Catholics from the council. He claimed to have received telegrams of congratulations from businessmen in all parts of the city after his 1936 electoral triumph. But thereafter Protestant Action grew too unwieldy. Opposition to the church of Rome was not enough to keep its elected members united when most of council business concerned non-religious matters.[55] Various councillors defected and in the 1937 local elections, Cormack found himself suddenly out of the council when he stood for two wards, neither of which returned him; presumably, voters were indignant that he would not be giving them his undivided attention. However, his movement was strong enough for him to be returned for South Leith in 1938, a ward he represented without interruption until his retirement in 1962.

As protest movements the SPL and Protestant Action did well because they echoed the prejudices of certain groups of voters at a time when the major parties were exhausted or else divided. But the stable structure of British politics prevented them exploiting persistently low-levels of sectarian tension. They were hampered by local constraints. The community that was their chief antagonist acted in a low-key manner even when the provocation reached a striking level as undoubtedly happened in Edinburgh. Protestant bodies like the Orange Order have usually distrusted populists. Cormack later became a folk hero in east of Scotland Orange circles, and his portrait adorned several Orange banners. But he quit the order in 1939 after its refusal to sponsor a full-scale Protestant party, only rejoining several decades later.

Media hostility also held back the religious parties. Back in 1929 in response to both public interest and mounting agitation on the question, The *Glasgow Herald* undertook a detailed investigation of the facts concerning the immigration of the Irish into Scotland. After publishing its findings in five lengthy articles, the conclusion of the journalist investigating the question was as follows:

> 'I am satisfied that the current Irish immigration is not large, that compared with the stream of the past it is the veriest trickle, and that it is practically negligible in bearing upon the development of the Irish community in Scotland. That development proceeded almost entirely from the multiplication of the Scoto-Irish – natives of this country but of Irish extraction.'[56]

The occasional journalist was to be found who reflected popular unease about the Scoto-Irish and who used his pen to magnify the ill-effects of their presence. In the late 1920s the Leith-born George Malcolm Thomson (1899-1996) did this in a number of remarkable books where, with much eloquence, he sought to convince his complacent fellow countrymen how their very national identity was in peril.[57]

The Irish in Scotland are not the only symbols of decline examined in his books but some of his most angry prose is reserved for them. The Scots, 'a nation waiting for a boat', are 'a dying people . . . being replaced in their own country by a people alien in race, temperament, and religion'.[58]

Thomson regarded the 'miracle-working' Grotto of Carfin as 'a landmark of the religious and racial revolution. . . changing the spiritual face of Scotland'. Its location was no accident, 'situated in. . . the very heart of industrial Scotland and within easy reach of the main industrial towns'.[59] He recalled how 'the sight of three Irish Catholic priests walking in Princes Street came upon me with the shock of a portent. I waited for some demonstration of wrath from heaven. I looked around appealing to some solid outward symbol of Knox's presence in his own land to fall down and crush the Papistical intruders.' [60]

A close collaborator in those days was Andrew Dewar Gibb, an early figure of influence in the Scottish National Party (SNP) who became Regius Professor of Scots Law at Glasgow University. In his *Scotland in Eclipse* published in 1930 he made his views plain about the Irish in Scotland:

> 'In the heart of a dwindling though virile and intelligent race there is
> growing up another people, immeasurably inferior in every way, but
> cohesive and solid, refusing obstinately, at the behest of obscurantist
> magic-men, to mingle with the people whose land they are
> usurping; unaware of, or if aware, disloyal to all the finest ideals and
> ambitions of the Scottish race: distinguished by a veritable will to
> squalour which is mainly responsible for Scottish slumdom;
> squatting and breeding in such numbers as to threaten in another
> hundred years to gain actual predominance in the country. . .'[61]

> 'No amount of anti-immigration legislation', he argued 'can
> prevent Irish labourers from having families of twelve nor Irish
> priests from telling them that to attend a birth-control clinic is a
> deadly sin.'[62]

Unlike George Thomson (who later regretted his anti-Irish outbursts),[63] Dewar Gibb never repudiated this outlook.

John McCormick, the leading figure in the SNP in the 1930s and early 1940s, tried to preserve a balance between nationalists favourably disposed towards the Irish because they had broken away from British rule, and hardliners like Gibb. Most of the time he 'wanted no part in an appeal to anti-Irish populism'.[64] But in 1934, he drafted a conference motion demanding a overhaul of the 1918 Education Act.[65]

Overall, McCormick was a benign influence, steering early Scottish nationalism away from scapegoating the Scoto-Irish. He was in favour of assimilating them rather than expulsion and he placed the blame for their 'un-Scottish social habits and standards' not on their priests or on any racial inadequacy, but on the failure of Scots to develop a healthy national life to which the newcomers could relate.[66]

But even if the Nationalists had, without exception, been sympathetic to the Scoto-Irish or had sung the praises of Irish independence, it probably would not have made much difference to their electoral fortunes in the west of Scotland. In the 1930s and beyond the Scoto-Irish were more concerned with material advancement or simple survival than with sorting out their relationship with the Scottish nation and the Labour Party was the obvious vehicle for them.

NOTES

1 Harvie, *No Gods*, p.p. 10-11.

2 Andrew Dewar Gibb, *Scotland Resurgent*, Observer Press, Stirling, 1950, p. 180.

3 *Glasgow Herald*, 21 December 1921.

4 Cohn Brogan, 'Catholics in changing social conditions', *Glasgow Observer and Scottish Catholic Herald*, Scottish Survey, p. 4.

5 *Glasgow Observer*, 1 April 1922.

6 *The Menace of the Irish Race to our Scottish Nationality*, William Bishop, Edinburgh, 1923.

7 *Glasgow Observer*, 19 May 1923.

8 *Glasgow Herald*, 8 May 1935.

9 *Edinburgh Evening News*, 2 June 1932.

10 George Malcolm Thomson, *The Rediscovery of Scotland*, Kegan Paul, London, 1928, p. 35.

11 *Glasgow Observer*, 6 November 1930.

12 *Scotsman*, 31 May 1935.

13 Quoted in Mackenzie, *Catholicism and Scotland*, p. 169.

14 Rev. J. Cameron Peddie, The man who really broke the Glasgow gangs', *Evening Citizen*, 19 January 1955.

15 Henry C. Whitley, *Laughter in Heaven*, Hutchinson, London, 1962, pp. 47-8.

16 See Albert Bogle, 'James Barr, B.D., M.P.', *Records of the Scottish Church History Society*, 21, 1983, pp. 189-207.

17 Recollection of James Durkan.

18 Ian S. Wood, *John Wheatley*.

19 Harvie, *No Gods*, p. 100.

20 Interview with David Lambie, MP, London, 26 April 1984.

21 James Reynolds, Liverpool Exchange, 1929-32; John Shute for the same seat from 1933 to 1945.

22 Dewar Gibb, *Scotland in Eclipse*, p. 59.

23 *Glasgow Observer*, 5 July 1930.

24 *Hansard*, 261, 24 November 1932, p. 262.

25 Ratcliffe's election address is quoted in a memorial of the Archbishop of Glasgow, 1935, in the Catholic Union files, box 11, Glasgow Archdiocesan Archives.

26 See John Cormack, 'My hectic life', *Protestant Telegraph* (Belfast), 11 January 1969.

27 The personal details about John Cormack's early life were provided by his sister, Mrs Dora Wight, in an interview on 18 July 1983. Additional information about how he came to form Protestant Action was given by McDonald Morris in a series of interviews carried out in December 1984.

28 *Edinburgh and Leith Observer*, 25 October 1935.

29 John Cormack, 'If I were dictator of Edinburgh', *Daily Record*, 6 October 1937.

30 *Daily Record*, 18 April 1935.

31 *Protestant Times*, 4 May 1935.

32 *Glasgow Observer*, 15 June 1935.

33 *Scotsman*, 25 June 1935; *Scottish Daily Express*, 25 June 1935.

34 *Scotsman*, 26 June 1935, *Daily Record*, 26 June 1935, *Scottish Daily Express*, 26 June 1935.

35 Steve Bruce, Tony Glendinning, Iain Paterson and Michael Rosie, *Sectarianism in Scotland*, Edinburgh: Edinburgh University Press, 2004, p.53.

36 Bruce et al, *Sectarianism in Scotland*, p. 54.

37 Letter from Cardinal Gordon Gray to the author, 9 January 1985. Tom Gallagher, *Edinburgh Divided*, Edinburgh Polygon, 1987.

38 Michael Turnbull, *Cardinal Gordon Joseph Gray*, St. Andrews Press, Edinburgh 1994, p. 17.

39 Turnbull, *Cardinal Gordon Joseph Gray*, p. 18.

40 *Glasgow Observer*,10 August 1935.

41 Interview with John McLaughlin, Edinburgh, 21 August 1984.

42 Archbishop McDonald's statement about the Edinburgh riots was issued in

July 1935 and is reproduced in full in Compton Mackenzie's *Catholicism and Scotland*, pp. 178-9.

43 Mrs Molly Regan, interviewed in Edinburgh on 18 June 1985, was able to cite a number of examples from her own experience.

44 Mrs Molly Regan.

45 Interview with Hugh Brown MP

46 I am grateful to Professor John Butt for this information.

47 Bruce et al, *Sectarianism in Scotland*, p. 44.

48 *Protestant Times*, 18 May 1935.

49 Bruce et al, *Sectarianism in Scotland*, p.55.

50 'Police lenient with anti-Catholic extremists', *Scotsman*, 25 August 1994 (based on memo of 24 July 1940 from a senior Crown Office civil servant.

51 Ibid.

52 'Toleration overdone' was displayed in Cormack's newspaper in a prominent position; 'Better a competent dictatorship . . .' was a favourite saying of Cormack's, according to James Russell. Interview with James Russell, former vice-president of Protestant Action, Glasgow, 10 June 1985.

53 *Edinburgh Evening News*, 8, 14 April 1936.

54 Colm Brogan, 'Catholics in changing social conditions'.

55 Interview with Lionel Daiches, Edinburgh, 22 August 1984; conversation with David Daiches, Edinburgh, March 1984.

56 *Glasgow Herald*, 25 March 1929.

57 See George Malcolm Thomson, *The Rediscovery of Scotland*, p. 86; *Caledonia, or the Future of the Scots*, Kegan Paul, London, 1927, p. 10.

58 Thomson, *The Rediscovery*, p. 86; *Caledonia*, p. 10.

59 Thomson, *The Rediscovery*, p.p. 53,54.

60 Thomson, *The Rediscovery*, p. 34.

61 Andrew Dewar Gibb, *Scotland in Eclipse*, Toulmin, London, 1930, pp. 56-7.

62 Dewar Gibb, *Scotland in Eclipse*, p. 57.

63 Interview with George Malcolm Thomson, London, 26 March 1982.

64 Wood, *John Wheatley*, p. 83.

65 Dewar Gibb collection, National Library of Scotland, letter from George Malcolm Thomson dated 8 March 1934. The Scottish novelist Neil Gunn (1891-1974) is referred to in this quote.

66 John McCormick, *The Flag in the Wind*, Gollancz, 1955, p. 53.

CHAPTER 5
Sectarianism and Social Democracy Co-Exist, 1945-70

ON SHOWING the Duke of Kent around early wartime Glasgow Sir Patrick Dollan managed to put a brave face on it when the royal visitor remarked that he must have a difficult time because of the large number of Irish in Govan and elsewhere:

> 'I told him that I had represented Govan for thirty years during which I had never had trouble with any of the citizens and that he was on his way to inspect the Govan Civil Defence Force. At the end of the inspection, he had a tremendous reception from the Govan boys and when we went out into the street I said, "You have just now been cheered by the Irish and the Scots of Govan. Could you tell me which was Irish and which was Scots?" ' [1]

Shared wartime experiences made such a sectarian remark, from the younger brother of the then king, unfashionable. The case of the Glasgow doctor Patrick Connolly, grandson of an Irish Nationalist MP, is eloquent in this respect. Although indemnified by his Irish nationality from being called up, he saw the Nazi threat and volunteered for war service with the Royal Air Force. His obituary relates that:

> 'Eventually he was captured and incarcerated in various Japanese prisoner of war camps, where he was a medical officer with little or no medical supplies and where starvation, malnutrition and disease were rife. When faced with men returning to camp in extremis from gross malnutrition and dehydration, caused by enforced labour in brutally high temperatures, he took bold decisions. He persuaded the better nourished kitchen staff to donate blood which he transfused into the dying men. In dire circumstances he would run the blood directly from donor to recipient to save their lives. All whom he treated in this way survived.

'On liberation, and while on board the MV Cilicia taking them
home, 82 survivors wrote a letter to Flight Lieutenant Connolly
expressing their thanks: "In the new era which we are about to begin
the kindness and devotion to duty and the deliverance of thé
extortionate demands we made upon you, your example should
prove an ideal for every one of us throughout the years".'[2]

In 1945, as troops were demobilised, Scottish Catholics had grounds
for displaying some guarded optimism. Those of military age who had
enlisted in the armed services generally found that domestic rivalries were
put aside: they were not systematically discriminated against on a religious
or ethnic basis, promotion was often open to those who displayed aptitude
or courage, and more than a few were decorated for action on the
battlefield. This disarmed some of their critics who had previously viewed
them from afar as an un-assimilable sub-group immersed in ghetto life
and unlikely to acquit themselves well in the patriotic struggle against
Hitler because of past anti-British associations.

The wartime emergency and attendant labour shortages had created
some openings in skilled occupations which for generations had been the
reserve of the Protestant labour aristocracy, but the ending of the war
showed that the extent of change in recruitment practices, especially in
private industrial concerns, had only been limited. However, the expect-
ations of working-class Catholics were raised just at a time when the state
was proving more responsive to the needs of underprivileged sectors of
the population as a whole. A comprehensive set of educational and social
reforms were approved by parliament even before the termination of the
war. The desire for a fairer distribution of wealth and resources was
confirmed when the Labour Party was swept into office with its first ever
overall majority. For the first time, the party which the Catholic minority
had broadly identified with since the settlement of the Irish question, was
now in a position to act decisively to remedy some of the outstanding
grievances which the community shared with others in the lower-income
bracket.

These plans included the introduction of a free health care service for
all citizens and the provision of state assistance for the unemployed or
those unable to earn a regular income. The welfare state was the corner-

stone of Labour's reforming programme and, along with the expansion of state education, it greatly contributed to reducing tensions and rivalries within the working-class as indeed did the gradual onset of full employment.

Rev. David McRoberts, the most authoritative Scottish Catholic historian of the post-war years, has described a church that was emerging into 'a rather strange new world of problems and ideas where the nineteenth century tradition was no longer adequate'.[3]

Only a relatively small number of priests and laymen were actively involved in checking communism. In the post-war decades, the church was fully stretched trying to cope with the enormous population shifts brought about by the need to rehouse families outside the densely overcrowded inner city of Glasgow.

The 1951 census had shown a population of 119,000 in Clydeside living three to a room, the average in England being one person per room except for a very few areas. Glasgow corporation had 80-90,000 families on its housing waiting list in the early 1950s. It responded by building large housing estates around the perimeters of the city, allowing for density a great deal higher than had previously been thought appropriate in such developments. They were put up with such haste that there was minimal provision of facilities and amenities.[4] Ten per cent of Glasgow's population was decanted on to these estates, others moved into high rise flats in the 1960s (the decade when multistorey housing was seen as the exciting answer to remaining housing needs), while new towns were built at East Kilbride and Cumbernauld to which upwardly mobile working-class Catholics were able to gravitate. Between 1961 and 1975, when the human exodus from the city was at its height, Glasgow's population fell from 1,055,000 to 825,000;[5] between 1951 and 1977 the population of the eight inner city Catholic parishes slumped from 69,000 to 13,000.[6]

Glasgow in 1948 was left with an estimated Catholic population of almost 300,000 people whose spiritual care was in the hands of 298 priests in fifty-eight parishes.[7] The creation of two new dioceses was an admission that the old archdiocese had outgrown the administrative capabilities of the church. The Catholic population had risen from 309,700 in 1900 to

522,900 in 1951 (that represented an increase of six per cent in the west of Scotland which stood at 24% of the region's total in 1951).[8] Inevitably, there were critics with eyebrows being raised about including new Glasgow housing estates like Easterhouse and Garthamlock in the Motherwell diocese in order to ensure a sensible spread of population. The viability of the Motherwell diocese itself had been questioned because it has no recognised urban regional centre and comprises an area facing a difficult economic future as coal and steel, the mainstays of the local economy, were relentlessly scaled down.

But generally, people grew accustomed to new adminstrative ecclesiastical arrangements which were far easier to come to terms with than the wholesale change in the fabric of Glasgow life wrought by the planners in the post-war years. Large dreary housing schemes situated miles from traditional centres of activity and lacking amenities such as cinemas, libraries, social clubs or public houses were the unimaginative outcome of what had been one of the most ambitious slum clearance schemes in Europe. They were a kind of parody of Glasgow's traditional tenement life, quite incapable of generating the same kind of community spirit.[9] One of the few voices raised against these 'concrete jungles' had been Cornelius O'Leary, parish priest of St. John's in the Gorbals.[10] This was appropriate since the area that had been the hub of Glasgow Catholic life up to the 1950s was to suffer more completely at the hands of the planners than possibly any other working-class community in Glasgow.

The area certainly had its share of social problems thanks to over-crowding and the 1930s slump. Gangs existed, but they were a threat to one another rather than the general public. The Gorbals was Scotland's most cosmopolitan district, (having absorbed a succession of immigrant groups – Irish, Highlanders, Jews, Lithuanians) through which people could walk in safety in the 1930s.[11]

Glasgow was not alone in witnessing such cataclysmic changes. In Edinburgh a Tory council ensured that most of the working-class was banished to rather desolate housing schemes on the outskirts of the city so as to sweep social problems from view and cash in on tourist receipts by enhancing the city's picture-postcard image. The population of the five oldest city parishes declined from 22,000 to 9,000 as Catholics from the old town began to trek to windswept estates. But, in the east, the pace of change for Catholics was altogether less drastic than in the west.

Gordon Gray was appointed Archbishop of St. Andrews and Edinburgh on the death of Andrew Joseph McDonald in 1950. Although then, at forty years of age, the youngest bishop in the world, he was essentially a traditional figure. One outspoken priest remembers a favourite motto of his having been 'you must not disturb our good ordinary Christian people'.[12]

Having his roots in Banff, Gray wished to uphold the Scottish identity of the church and remained shaken by the eruption of Protestant Action in the 1930s. In the 1950s, he even banned the sale of *The Irish Weekly* at the back of churches in his archdiocese. Edited by Edinburgh Catholic Michael Fallon, it provided news for Irish immigrants in Scotland and enjoyed a circulation of 16,000 in the late 1940s.[13] The ban was not always enforced by priests in outlying West Lothian parishes with mining communities of Irish descent and it gradually fell into disuse. But one well-known Glasgow Catholic, a resident of Edinburgh for over fifty years has been able to detect a difference of attitude among Catholics towards their Irish ancestry in these two principal centres:

'Those in Edinburgh tend to conceal their Irish connections more often than in Glasgow. Under the influence of traditional Scottish Catholics from the north, they can be disparaging of the Irish in a way that is not often heard in Glasgow'.[14]

This underlying feeling was referred to with unusual frankness in a Catholic press article marking the retirement of Gordon Gray in 1985:

'He opened a seminary at Drygrange to allow the future priests to be trained within their own diocese and their own traditions. He championed the training of teachers at Craiglockart in Edinburgh in the sound belief that teachers needed to be seen by parents and pupils alike as products of their own region and not imports from Ireland or Glasgow'.[15]

The east-west tension between the upholders of the native Catholic tradition and those representing the immigrant stream was not exacerbated by Gray who placed a strong emphasis on tact and diplomacy in most of his relationships. His predecessor had dreamt of a national seminary at St. Andrews with the west, inevitably, being the only reliable source of finance. The idea was promoted in Glasgow by Archbishop Campbell but it was opposed by his chapter (senior clergy). Campbell prudently decided not to force the issue since he would merely have alienated his leading priests for the foreseeable future.

This incident graphically illustrates the limits of a bishop's power. The tensions producing it stemmed in part from the fact that the Scottish Catholic church had no recognised head or Primate. St. Andrews and Edinburgh is the senior diocese but the incumbent does not have the formal authority over his fellow bishops that the Archbishop of Westminster has in England. Inevitably, a situation of overlapping powers, and no clearly defined responsibility, has hampered long-term decision-making, encouraged a degree of inertia, given bishops with strong personalities an advantage, and led to a degree of duplication of resources best seen in the creation of separate seminaries in the east and the west when the numbers of vocations warranted one establishment.

In the immediate post-war years the strength of west of Scotland Catholicism was celebrated by public events such as the mass at Celtic Park in 1949 said by Archbishop Campbell in the presence of the Papal representative in Britain, on the centenary of the formation of the CYMS. Docility was a virtue stressed from seminary days onwards; it was dangerous to ask too many questions.[16] Firmly orthodox priests could even be suspicious of the work of the Newman Association, an organisation of Catholic graduates formed in 1945 which stimulated a wide range of study through lectures and conferences. In Glasgow, when it began to make use of the facilities for study offered by the university, this was not universally welcomed. 'Aquinas,' growled Canon Joseph Daniel when he heard that the teaching of Aquinas was to be the subject of a course one winter, 'Give them Aquinas and you'll turn them into Marxists.' [17]

Such attitudes did not encourage a tradition of Catholic intellectualism to take root among the new middle classes. And clerical domineering in general is bound to have repelled orthodox but independent-minded Catholics, exactly the kind needed to confront the 1967 Abortion Act perhaps even through civil disobedience. Though the Society for the Protection of the Unborn Child (SPUC) came into being, a sinister piece of legislation met surprisingly little opposition from the church-directed lay Catholic bodies.

Monsignor David McRoberts, who taught church history and scripture at the Glasgow diocesan seminary from 1948 to 1963, often had occasion to rail against the short-sighted and anti-intellectual character of the bishops, and much of the clergy. From 1951 until his death in 1978 he edited *The Innes Review,* the journal of the Scottish Catholic Historical Association which was launched in 1949. In 1960, on the 400th anniversary of the Reformation in Scotland, when *The Innes Review* produced a special issue on how and why it occurred, the journal was accused of spreading 'Protestant scandal' after a contributor mentioned that the sixteenth century Cardinal Beaton had fostered illegitimate children. The matter went before a meeting of bishops but was dropped when Bishop Scanlan of Motherwell quietly declared that the claim indeed had validity and that Beaton had tried to legitimise his offspring.

The peak years for seminary students and ordinations were 1959 and 1960 (both at 184 students). A fairly steady decline set in thereafter which 'thus pre-dates the second Vatican Council.[18] The community which used to yield up a plentiful supply of vocations was slipping into history. Scottish Catholics were `no longer so concentrated geographically, or so unified in outlook and social experience as . . . in the inter-war period'.[19] The levelling of old communities, the drift to the suburbs, housing estates and new towns, the growth of a professional class, the rise of the consumer society, the arrival of the mass media with its jarring values, and the alteration of the status of women could not fail to affect Catholics, often profoundly. An estimated 120,000 Catholics lost contact with the Church in Scotland between 1951 and 1976 compared with some 52,000 between 1931 and 1951.[20]

Upon Archbishop Campbell's death in 1963, while on a pilgrimage to Lourdes, he was succeeded by Bishop Scanlan of Motherwell. He was a law graduate from Glasgow University and only the second native of the city to be appointed its archbishop. As a conservative extrovert, he relished his time in Rome during the pathbreaking Vatican Council while being determined to keep unorthodox ideas at bay in Glasgow.[21] His elevation symbolised the appearance of a less insular community. The expansion of secondary and tertiary level education and the growth of local employment as a result in the upsurge in the world economy and greater investment in the public sector, were creating opportunities for upward mobility which had proved elusive for even the brightest members of past generations of immigrant Catholics.

By the 1940s the time had long gone when the only professions open to Roman Catholics who wished to break out of the working-class were bookmaking or pub ownership.[22] The burgeoning responsibilities of the state in the post-war world meant that Catholics could now aim to enter the local or national civil service in the hope that their religious or school background would not be a hindrance.

The lower-income groups were among the principal beneficiaries of post-war expansion and Catholics benefited disproportionately because they were massively over-represented in these categories. The raising of the school leaving age to fifteen in 1947 placed an extra 60,000 Scottish pupils on school roles and a disproportionate number were Catholics.[23] Whereas in 1921 Catholic secondary pupils in Scotland had only been 3.3per cent of the Catholic school population, by 1972 the proportion had risen to 31.2per cent; [24] even more significantly Catholics made up no less than 39per cent of secondary school pupils in Glasgow by 1972.[25]

After 1945 a grant was automatically available from the Scottish Education Department for university applicants who fulfilled the conditions of entry while grants were also available for ex-servicemen as well as for trainee teachers.[26] The number of Catholic students at Glasgow University trebled from 700 in 1956 to an estimated 2,000 in 1972.[27] In a given year many more were to be found at Scotland's other seven universities as well as at technical colleges and, by the 1980s, it was estimated that the Catholic student community in Glasgow was the largest such in Britain .[28]

If they did not emigrate from Scotland altogether, a very high proportion of graduates still headed for a career in teaching by the 1960s. Family and peer group influence combined to make this seem the natural thing to do. Any with business flair were quite likely to be in the ranks of those who moved away from Scotland. An estimated 900,000 people left Scotland between 1945 and 1975, effectively wiping out the nation's natural population increase. James Darragh reckons that Catholics 'were at least proportionately represented in this great movement and . . . because of their circumstances in Scotland, may have been proportionately over-represented'.[29] He himself rose to a senior level in the Board of Trade before being appointed in 1972 to oversee the rescue of shipbuilding on the Clyde, an ironic responsibility given the past lack of success of Catholics in securing employment there. James McGuiness, once a leading member of Walter Glancy's Association of Catholic Trade Unionists, became a senior civil servant in the Scottish Office charged with responsibility for drawing up the legislation for the Scottish Assembly of the mid-1970s.

One aspirational Catholic Tom Carberry went on to become professor of business studies at Strathclyde University, having entered the ministry of labour in the 1950s. By the end of that decade it was found that west of Scotland Catholics were heavily represented at clerical officer level in this ministry. Questions were discreetly asked and it was discovered that with religious discrimination still being quietly practised in areas like banking and accountancy, they were naturally gravitating to areas in which it was thought to be absent.

Slowly the legal profession drew recruits from Catholics of an immigrant background. This was especially true of the solicitors' branch of the legal profession. Although not as prestigious as the bar, the financial rewards were easier to come by than those at the bar while the social status of a solicitor was at least as high as that of a family doctor; a very high proportion of Glasgow Catholic lawyers had previously trained for the priesthood.

The trek out of the immigrant Catholic enclave to a socially and religiously mixed neighbourhood was a decisive event for those who undertook it. Professor Tom Carberry recalls moving from a room and kitchen in Cumberland Street, the Gorbals, to a three apartment corporation house in Govanhill when aged nine in the 1930s. Although the anti-Catholic Scottish Protestant League had enjoyed some success there earlier in the decade, he does not remember the family encountering positive hostility:

'One sensed various things though . . . Firstly . . . that we were the first Catholics living up that close and that our arrival was viewed with some apprehension by the neighbours; mind you they were very discreet in giving voice to that apprehension. . .

'The first day that we were there after the removal my mother was told in a very nice and polite way what was expected of her. I think that would have been told to any incoming neighbour but, looking back on it, I think it was done with a certain emphasis to make sure we did not step out of line . . . Occasionally there was a little flurry . . . around things like silver jubilees and coronations. The expectation was that everyone should put out flags. We didn't put out Union Jacks
. . . and there was maybe the odd comment made. However, that being said, I think we were pretty readily assimilated.' [30]

It is surprising that the wholesale relocation of tens of thousands of people gave rise to surprisingly little sectarian friction between uncongenial neigbours, at least of the kind that reached the courts and was reported in the press. Gang warfare was a feature of life on some of the new Glasgow housing estates, especially in the late 1960s, but the evidence suggests that these gangs were formed on a territorial rather than a religious basis;[31] no evidence has emerged that, in allocating tenancies for new corporation housing, factors paid especial heed to the possibility of religious friction emerging and took steps to offset it. Officials in corporation housing departments wielded immense power and, if they reflected the disparaging view of working-class Catholics held by other power-holders, it may help to explain why, starting in the 1930s, they were sent in large numbers to a poorly constructed estate like Blackhill. It was allocated for those among the working-class who could not be designated 'clean and respectable' and it rapidly developed 'a reputation for illness and violence that surpassed that of the old slums themselves'.[32]

Scope for misunderstanding existed in at least one middle-class community, Eastwood, in the southern suburbs of Glasgow but located in Renfrewshire. By 1966 there was a demand for a denominational school and a suitable site was available. However, the locally dominant Conservative Party dragged its feet over allowing planning permission. It reflected the views of many residents, who were soon aware that the proposed school would also cater for children from nearby Glasgow council estates. But Catholic parents had no wish to continue sending their children to over-crowded schools in Glasgow and, according to one observer, were keen to see their desire for full equality met by sending their children to a good school in the area where they lived.[33] This dispute split a suburban community. In the mid-1970s Thomas Winning, the new Archbishop of Glasgow, is reported to have told the Tory Party leader, Margaret Thatcher, in no uncertain terms while she was visiting Glasgow, of the importance the Catholic hierarchy attached to the building of the school.[34] In the hierarchy's eyes it would ease the worrying temptation for middle-class Catholics to send their children to a more convenient non-Catholic school.[35] Whether or not this apocryphal story is strictly accurate, solidarity for Eastwood Tories from Conservatives outside the area quickly dried up and the school was eventually built.

This episode may have shown aspirational Catholics that advancement was an uphill business. It is likely that very few Orangemen were to be found in Eastwood. But the Masonic Order remained a potent social force in middle-class Glasgow as a glance at the still copious Masonic notes in the daily press in the 1950s and 1960s would soon make clear.

It was middle-class businessmen with Masonic loyalties who (as directors and senior shareholders) ensured that Rangers football club still retained an all-Protestant image by declining to sign Catholic players in the forty years after World War II. An unguarded statement in 1967 by Matt Taylor, the club's vice-chairman, showed how outdated religious ties blended in with strong financial considerations to account for this anachronistic policy: 'it is part of our tradition. We were founded in 1873 as a Presbyterian Boys' Club. To change now would lose us considerable support.'[36]

Only in the late 1960s, when recurrent crowd trouble from a section of Rangers' following began to mar the image of Scottish soccer, did the local press begin to campaign in earnest against its religious exclusivity. Alex Cameron of the *Daily Record* demanded 'a vigorous clean-out of inbred bigotry which coincidence no longer begins to explain or excuse'.[37] Earlier, in the mid-1960s, various Glasgow elites had begun to be outspoken perhaps aware that a correlation existed between football disorder and

Glasgow's accelerating industrial decline. Magistrates were instructed to hand down stiff penalties to soccer hooligans; Sheriff Daiches QC spoke in 1965 of 'this disgraceful behaviour which is making this city a byword in Europe'. The chairman of the Scottish TUC wrote to the city's magistrates arguing that Old Firm violence was having a damaging effect on Scotland's image among industrialists while the Lord Provost made a plea to both clubs to sever their sectarian identities.[38]

But the inertia of Scottish society allowed the waves of criticism to lap harmlessly around Rangers; earlier, Celtic had been under greater pressure from the administrators of Scottish football. In 1952, it was almost expelled from the Scottish Football Association for refusing to cease the practice of flying the Irish tricolour at its ground. Its antagonists were George Graham, secretary of the SFA since 1928, a powerbroker who had risen to be grand master of the Scottish Freemasons and Harry Swan, who in 1931 had become the first non-Catholic to hold shares in Hibernian FC and, three years later, became the club's chairman.[39]

He strove to dilute the Hibs connection with things Irish: the harp which had adorned the main entrance at Easter Road was removed; the right of priests to attend free of charge was ended. When it looked as if they had the backing of a majority in the SFA, Robert Kelly, the Celtic chairman, made what looked like an ethnic appeal to West of Scotland Catholics to shed their passivity. He was speaking to the Glasgow Province of the Knights of St. Columba, a charitable body founded in Glasgow in 1918 which eventually became the largest organisation of Catholic laymen in Britain.[40] An historian of Celtic Brian Wilson relates that 'its subject matter went far beyond the immediate problem faced by Celtic. . . It was about a more general threat to the standing of the Catholic community in the West of Scotland.'[41] Kelly declared:

> 'it is necessary that Catholics should become more and more organised because at present in the West of Scotland, they are not making their presence felt in sufficient proportion to their number. We are not wielding the same influence as our fathers and grandfathers did. In such societies as the Knights of St. Columba, it is one of our duties to make sure that Catholic laymen, in whatever profession they have been called, exert their influence to the fullest possible extent'.[42]

Such was the importance of the speech in the eyes of the *Glasgow Observer* then with a massive circulation exceeding that of Scotland's best-known daily papers today, that it took the highly unusual step of printing Kelly's speech on its front page. At the climax of the dispute, Celtic was supported by John Wilson, chairman of Rangers and a vote to defuse the crisis was carried by the narrowest of margins, sixteen to fifteen.[43] Rangers were aware, according to another Celtic historian, that a Scottish league without Celtic was scarcely worth winning.

This sense of mutual dependency was already at work in the 1920's according to the journalist Sir Michael Kelly. He revealed that when his grandfather, James Kelly was chairman of Celtic, there was an unexpected overture from Rangers. The club had a temporary cash flow problem and their board came out to his house in Blantyre to explain the problem and seek help. Celtic gave them an unconditional short-term loan, according to Kelly because it was the sporting thing to do and was also eminently practical.[44]

But after the 1953 crisis, for the next forty years at least, Celtic was disinclined to abandon its distinctive heritage and blend into the scenery of Scottish football by adopting an identity more in keeping with mainstream Scotland.

For much of their chequered histories, Rangers and Celtic were like Siamese twins dependent on each other for their economic well-being. One would not enjoy the same economic success and prestige without the closing of ranks induced by the other's presence. But there were occasional moments of solidarity as when Rangers chairman, John Lawrence travelled to Glasgow airport in 1967 to be among those welcoming back the Celtic team from their European Cup triumph in Lisbon; the Church of Scotland later passed a motion of congratulations at its General Assembly. However, many supporters blocked out such gestures and preferred to see Rangers (with its Protestant-only signing policy) as the chief symbol of their subordinate role in Scotland. It was still a very tangible one in the 1950s.

Richard Buchanan, then a Glasgow Catholic councillor with a surname that gave no clue to his religious identity, recalls what he found on being appointed to the board of the Royal Infirmary in Glasgow. Interviewing applicants for a senior nursing post, he was struck by the fact that the retiring matron ruled out the most promising candidate with the words, 'Oh but she's a Catholic'. However, her abilities impressed the other members of the interview panel and she got the job, but Buchanan still remains appalled at the open and obvious way that her religion was treated as a disqualification by an older member of the nursing profession who, by the candour of her remarks, did not feel she was expressing views that were in any way unusual.[45]

Professor Tom Carberry is just one of several interviewees in the 1980s who mentioned that in the post-war decades, a whole range of establishments (some, well-known names), would still not take on Catholics. Old recruitment patterns based on Protestant solidarity or disdain for a community that had hitherto been regarded as synonmous with the underclass, began to alter. Local family-based concerns were increasingly taken over by national or multinational firms whose personnel section had a more meritocratic set of criteria for recruitment. If local managers remained in charge, scope existed to continue with the old hiring practices, but 'if a *debacle* occurred, you had to justify your approach to someone coming up by train or plane from London or across the Atlantic.[46]

Leading trade-unionist, Alex Ferry, President of the Confederation of Shipbuilding and Engineering Unions in the early 1980s, was able to comment authoritatively about the changes he glimpsed on the shopfloor in the west of Scotland during this period. Born a Catholic in Glasgow in 1931, the son of an Irish father and a Scottish mother, on being widowed she remarried a Protestant who became a convert (though he did not practice the faith) and the children were brought up as Catholics. He entered the job market in the 1940s when he recalls the question of one's denomination still played a significant part in deciding what type of job a Glaswegian acquired:

> 'It was still much more difficult for a Roman Catholic to be employed
> in the craft trade than it was for others . . . I discovered that myself
> when I was trying to find an apprenticeship. The employer . . . would
> ask you what school you had gone to (that was the immediate give-
> away) and if you tried to cover it up, you were then asked about the

Boy Scouts and the Boys Brigades; this was supposed to see what kind of individual you were but really it was a hidden questionnaire about your background and religion.

'Notwithstanding that, I managed to get an apprenticeship in one of the less desirable engineering companies in Clydebank . . . When I moved into the Singer Sewing Machine Company in 1954. . . the effects of discrimination were even more glaring. The tool room where I was, employed around 300 people . . . You could have counted the Catholics on the digits of your two hands and, in the shop in which I worked, I was the only Catholic.' [47]

Alex Ferry relates that the situation changed between 1954 and1966 not through any affirmative action on the part of trade unions or employers but owing to the shortage of skilled men which made it difficult to adhere to the old recruitment policy. The better conditions of the 1950s reduced rivalry within the working-class but mutual suspicion could be rekindled in surprising ways. Alex Ferry recalls that in 1956 when the unions in the engineering industry negotiated an extra day's holiday and recommended to members that it be taken on Christmas Day, 'all hell broke loose' at Singers. December 25th was still not a recognised holiday in all walks of Scottish life and it was felt that Catholics would be the chief beneficiaries since for them it was a more significant occasion on which they were required to attend Mass. The matter had to be put to a ballot and it was carried only by a small majority despite the fact that more than half the workforce were women who might have been expected to be keen to be with their families on that day.[48]

Alex Ferry was already a union officer at Singers by 1956 and he recalls attempts by the Singer management to take advantage of religious differences to split up the workforce. A lever was to hand in the Freemasons who had many adherents among the rank-and-file who were keen to seek promotion up the ranks of this male-bonding organisation:

'You could actually see people changing . . . With those you had been on friendly terms with, a wall was erected once they joined . . . When they went to a meeting or a function of the Masonic Order and the managers were there, somehow this gave them the impression that they were important. And that was reflected in their attitude when industrial disputes arose.' [49]

113

Standing for his first elective office in 1964, Ferry found that his religion was so unpalatable for some engineers that they preferred to vote in the first ballot for his Communist rival despite their lack of sympathy for the Communist cause. This was particularly the case in the Dennistoun area of Glasgow which had been the power-base of Ratcliffe in the 1930s. In the second ballot, the branch swung into line after remonstrations from other Protestant engineers supporting Ferry who then went out of his way to win the trust of branch officials in that district. He reckons that he managed to 'prove to them his determination to serve the entire membership irrespective of what anybody's religion was'.

Near the end of his union career, Ferry glimpsed progress but he was still able to point to some employers who 'want to know what religion you are':

> 'Of course when you query that and say that it leaves room for discrimination, you are told that it is just in case somebody is taken ill and we know that we've got to send for a minister or a priest. But when you look at the proportion of Catholics employed by companies who operate in this way, you often find it is amazingly low and that they are usually in the worst types of jobs'.[50]

But, as late as the 1980s, anecdotal evidence pointed to a large number of working-class Scots still having a subliminal or active fear that public officials, whether they be policemen or social security officials, are liable to discriminate against them on religious grounds. This became obvious to one social security officer with militant Protestant affiliations, when he was placed in charge of one urban district for five years:

> 'If I went to a house and saw a nail on the wall, then I guessed that nail had contained a holy picture which had been removed when the householders discovered that I was coming to do an inspectoral visit – just in case they didn't get a grant which they were entitled to.
>   'It was a completely irrational fear.' [51]

The upheavals of war, the relocation of so much of the urban population in new communities, and the onset of moderate prosperity, certainly dealt a blow to old religious prejudices and rivalries, but their banishment to the darker corners of Scottish life was a slow process as the above illustrations have shown. The differing receptions Catholics received as they moved into new housing estates, middle-class suburbs, the factory shop floor, or the university showed how community relations remained in a state of flux well after 1945.

Old political moulds also remained obstinately in place on Clydeside after 1945. In the general election of that year there was only a 2.5per cent swing to the Labour Party in Glasgow compared with Edinburgh's 14.5 and the UK average of 12per cent.[52] Glasgow had the lowest turn-out of any one of Britain's fifteen largest cities which, at 6per cent was 7per cent down on the 1935 figure.

Donald MacDonald, a Church of Scotland minister, recalls that his Highland background had not prepared him for the rigours of Glasgow, which he came to in the 1950s. He arrived from North Uist, an island largely inhabited by Presbyterians; neighbouring Benbecula was comprised almost equally of Protestants and Catholics while South Uist was 90per cent Catholic, yet he recalls 'there was really no friction . . . no strong awareness of difference between us'. In Glasgow he 'came down to earth with a thud in his first summer' on taking a part-time job in a Bridgeton photographic factory 'where suddenly you discovered that there were some people who did not sit with one another at teabreak, people who did very different things over the weekend. . . it was really then that I discovered how badly divided the community actually was.'[53]

Living in the Partick district he 'discovered that there were Protestant and Catholic pubs . . . that some people . . . would cross the road rather than walk in front of the Catholic chapel; I remember the intense Catholicism there was on the other side of the coin – people passing the chapel who would take their hat off . . . These were the formative impressions.'

The local media had learned from experience not to probe too deeply into these tangled mix of loyalties. No lead was forthcoming from the BBC, which failed to beam a spotlight on Scotland's religious and social problems. From 1933 to 1957 BBC Scotland 'became a by-word for puritanical parochialism' under its Controller, the Rev. Melville

Dinwiddie.[54] That a Presbyterian minister could hold down such an influential post in the public domain and mould it to his own narrow tastes shows how invisible were the Roman Catholics (14.7% of Scotland's population in 1951, 25.6% of Glasgow's).[55]

The 2nd Vatican Council, inaugurated by the liberal Pope John XXIII in 1962, set in train changes which made the Catholic church far less dogmatic and introspective in its style and teachings and opened the way for meaningful dialogue with many of the Protestant churches. It thus signalled the end of the Cold War between Protestants and Catholics in all but a few parts of the world and 'ecumenism' became the new catchword for those on both sides of a previously gaping chasm wishing to build bridges and establish realistic inter-church contacts.

A landmark in ecumenical relations was the visit paid to the Pope in 1962 by the Moderator of the General Assembly, the Very Rev. A.C. Craig, the first holder of the office to make that journey.[56] In 1969 Fr. J.H. Dalrymple took up the invitation for a Catholic priest to attend the General Assembly. In 1971, a member of the Catholic Church hierarchy, Bishop James Monaghan was present and in 1975 Archbishop Thomas Winning addressed the Assembly in 'a speech that was very warmly received'.[57] The first official talks between the two churches since the Reformation had taken place in 1971 when the Catholic hierarchy accepted an invitation from the Assembly to establish a dialogue on the meaning of marriage.[58]

In the Church of Scotland the driving force behind ecumenism was the Iona Community led by the redoubtable Very Rev. Dr. George MacLeod, later Lord MacLeod of Fuinary. He raised issues such as the Catholic church's hostility to mixed marriages in the hope that a meaningful dialogue could ensue with beneficial results. In 1966 a warning note was sounded by him on this question in the *Scotsman* which showed how slow progress had been in places:

> 'It is surely improper for public monies, monies subscribed by members of other branches of the Christian Church in Scotland to be used in part to facilitate the teaching of young children that a Roman Catholic married, in say St. Giles Cathedral, to another member of Christ's Church is living in sin.' [59]

The attitude of many Catholic priests to a mixed marriage was conveyed in the official obituary of Canon William Mallon (1904-73), a Glasgow priest:

> 'Firmly and trenchantly he preached the old faith. Mixed marriages were not encouraged. "Trust Our Lady and she will get you a good Catholic husband" – this was the advice he gave many a girl considering a mixed marriage, and he was often proved right.' [60]

Canon Mallon operated in the era when Catholics had to seek clerical permission to attend Protestant weddings or funerals or to eat meat at weddings held on a Friday. If a Catholic was asked to be the best man at a Protestant wedding, again permission was required and it was not always forthcoming. These ground-rules applied in many Catholic parishes up to the 1960s. Parents who accepted the prevailing orthodoxy were often devastated if one of their children contracted a marriage with somebody not belonging to the church. But the church gradually modified its line on mixed marriages after 1970. A written undertaking from both priests that they would do everything in their power to ensure that their children would be brought up in the Catholic faith was replaced by a verbal promise to that effect from the Catholic partner.

The unguarded observations by Catholics that a reunited church would be predominantly Catholic in doctrine and ethos roused suspicion in some quarters that ecumenism was a 'takeover bid'. The Right Rev. Andrew Herron, a Church of Scotland administrator and former Moderator, remained wary about where the ecumenical movement might be leading and was critical of George MacLeod's stance on the issue.[61] Both men were on opposite sides of the debate over whether bishops should be appointed and placed in charge of kirk presbyteries which gripped the church in the mid-1950s.[62] Herron thought that diversity in the Christian tradition was enriching and was not prepared to discount the possibility of a split occurring in the Kirk – with himself among the seceders – if the ecumenical movement progresses so far as to cover the essential differences between the Reformed and Roman tradition in the Christian Church. [63]

The official obituaries of Scottish priests who died in the 1970s and 1980s show far more examples of priests who had misgivings over the major religious changes taking place in the 1960s than of any who had positively welcomed change and sought to implement it in their parish work.[64] If instructed by a higher authority, some priests reluctantly went along with ecumenical initiatives while inwardly desiring to tell non-Roman Catholics the errors of their ways; 'they believed themselves to be in possession of everything that was good and true,' recalls Fr. John Fitzsimmons, an ecumenically-minded priest. Donald MacDonald, in his Partick parish, found that the scope of dialogue depended on the individual response to churchmen on the ground rather than the policy of their superiors, or the wishes of parishioners:

> 'One of the Presbyterian misconceptions is that everything is decided from Rome . . . but I discovered that if the priest up the road just wants to shut the door of the Presbytery and says none of these new ideas are coming in, they don't come in.' [65]

When a charming but conservative Irishman was replaced in Partick by Fr. Gaetano Rossi, 'you could practically feel the atmosphere changing overnight . . . anything he was asked to participate in he agreed to.' This accord bore practical fruit when the clergymen realised that the council had plans to demolish the whole of Partick. A local association was formed to save the district: 'it was the sort of thing that could not have been done by the minister or priest alone, but with the two of us, it was almost an unstoppable force in the area,' [66] What remains of tenement life in Partick today was saved by their timely co-operation.

Archbishop Scanlan of Glasgow was able to break down barriers at a higher level:

> 'He and his attire were to become very familiar in George Square and other public places in the city. It was a side of life of which the clergy knew very little. Where he got the key I do not know, but in a short time he had opened all doors to the civic and social life of the city.' [67]

The climax of his open diplomacy came on 5th January 1971 in the aftermath of the Ibrox disaster in which sixty-six Rangers supporters were crushed to death at the end of an Old Firm match. The archbishop arranged a Requiem Mass to which he invited the leaders of the city along with the

Rangers and Celtic football clubs. His obituary records that 'when the manager of Rangers FC appeared on television to announce that Rangers as a club would attend Requiem Mass in St. Andrew's Cathedral, it was the greatest piece of religious news ever heard in Glasgow in my time.' [68]

Gestures which received far less publicity also had a vital bearing on community relations: in Partick, Donald MacDonald records the atmosphere in 1967 when he invited a nun to preach at one of his services, an event unprecedented in Scotland:

> 'Quite a number in my congregation were suspicious. . . the usual question was raised: 'Are you likely to get asked back yourself?' There was a massive turnout . . . and we got picketed by Pastor Jack Glass . . . . His supporters infiltrated the congregation and. . . the moment Sister Catherine got up to start speaking, pandemonium broke out.'

> 'It was fascinating to see some of the congregation who I knew had Orange leanings, grabbing hold of Jack Glass's supporters and physically flinging them out of the door . . . He put people's backs up. It was. . . old-fashioned working-class courtesy– this was no way to treat a guest, no way to treat a woman in church.' [69]

A rebuke to bigotry which had even more resonance in wider society was the appointment of Jock Stein, a non-Catholic, as manager of Celtic in 1965. Stein's family associations (centred around the Lanarkshire coalfield) were emphatically Protestant, but he fitted in easily with the team seen as the tribal champions of Catholic Glasgow.[70] In 1967 Celtic won the European Cup in Lisbon, a victory seen as a great Scottish success by many non-adherents since Celtic was the first team from Scotland to win this coveted trophy.

But, in elections, evidence of a strong correlation between religious denomination and voting choice was easy to find up to the 1960s. In relatively harmonious Dundee, a survey into voting behaviour carried out in 1968 found that 3per cent of workers from a Church of Scotland background voted Conservative compared to only 6% of workers from a Catholic background.[71] Until the 1964 general election Scotland had a greater proportion of working-class Conservatives than the north of England which had a not dissimilar class structure.[72] The capture by the Tories of the shipbuilding constituency of Glasgow Govan in 1950 and 1951 (a Labour seat continuously since 1918) had shown that working-class Conservatism still had plenty of life in it. Until the late 1960s the Tories still held on to a swathe of working-class wards like Kinning Park, Whiteinch, Partick, and Govanhill associated with traditional Clydeside industries, the composition of whose workforce had remained solidly Protestant.

Labour's most loyal support group in Scotland provided very few of its MPs in the 1945-70 period. Selection meetings may have been reluctant to nominate Catholics in certain constituencies for fear of alienating Protestant voters. A bitterly fought contest in 1959 may have shown that it was not a groundless fear. A showdown occurred in the normally safe Labour seat of Coatbridge and Airdrie when Labour nominated James Dempsey, a Roman Catholic, to fight against Mrs C.S. Morton a sister of the great Rangers football hero of the inter-war years, Alan Morton, who was standing for the Tories. She lost by only 795 votes, an extraordinary result that went flatly against the trend in the rest of Scotland where Labour made spectacular gains. Clearly large numbers of Protestant working-class voters allowed their religious folk loyalties to gain precedence over their normal class allegiances.

When the history of Scottish Labour politics after 1918 began to be chronicled in the 1970s, it was tempting to ascribe the gradual slide towards anonymity and conformity on the Scottish left in large measure to the strong Catholic presence, especially at municipal level, and to the fact that the party drew much of its support from a community with strongly conservative social instincts. However, other Labour local authorities in England and Wales experienced the same regression without the presence of a Labour-voting Catholic community. Besides, it was only in the 1960s that the number of Glasgow Labour councillors from a Catholic background began to match the degree of electoral support which the community traditionally gave the party. By 1968 around one-quarter of Glasgow Labour councillors were Catholics. Their visibility coincided with a rash of corruption cases and rumours circulated about the existence of a separate Catholic caucus. MPs Hugh Brown and David Lambie who were familiar with the Glasgow Labour scene in the 1960s likewise failed to come across evidence of a religious caucus at work.[73]

The late 1960s saw the first real breakthrough for the Scottish National Party (SNP), initially among parts of the lower middle-class in small town Scotland, and among working-class 'floating' voters. Catholic fidelity to Labour irritated at least one future SNP MP, Iain McCormick:

> 'Politically many of these Scots fail to appreciate that they are now as Scottish as anyone else, and fail to see that Scotland's future is their future.
>
> 'It is more the pity that so many working-class Catholics regard it as an article of faith to vote Labour come-what-may. Such a vote is meaningless and only matched in futility by the ritual Conservative vote of working-class Orangemen.
>
> 'Catholics could make a great contribution to the Scotland of the future were they to cast aside the 'ghetto' approach to Scottish politics now.' [74]

The SNP's brief breakthrough in Glasgow municipal politics stemmed in part from internal Labour Party divisions over schools. In 1970 the Glasgow City Labour Party passed the resolution that 'segregation of schools on religious grounds be terminated but that provision for religious instruction be continued in accordance with individual belief'.[75] Senior Labour figures were aghast at the decision. Daniel Docherty, the Labour spokesman on education said:

> 'A decision like this is political suicide . . . If those people want to lose the next election; this is a sure way of doing it. There will be a riot in the country if this sort of thing is forced through.' [76]

Eventually, peace broke out on this issue. The Labour Party chose to support denominational schools as long as they were seen to have the backing of Catholic parents, although motions hostile to the segregated system continued to be submitted to the party's Scottish conference well into the 1970s.

The cracks in the consensus over education followed hard on the heels of disagreements within Scottish Catholic ranks over the extent to which the reforms emanating from Rome should be implemented. For news from Scotland the Vatican relied on the apostolic nuncio in London whose concerns were mainly with the English church. Scotland's remoteness was only partly assuaged in 1969 when Archbishop Gray was elevated to the rank of cardinal. Overall, the Catholic church in Great Britain had been ill-prepared for change and the result was considerable confusion about belief and practice, a sudden and widespread weakening of Catholic identity, a polarisation of opinion, and a weakening of acceptance of the authority of the Church.

This at any rate is how an official church agency described the reaction of the English church to 'Vatican II' and it would not altogether misrepresent the Scottish response either. Elderly priests and laity found it difficult to come to terms with the replacement of the Latin Mass with English, the repositioning of altars so that priests no longer celebrated with their backs to the congregation, and the phasing out of so much ritual and ceremony. The introduction of a new ritual, whereby worshippers wish each other the sign of peace by shaking hands was another unwelcome innovation for those priests reared in a more austere tradition.[77] Even Monsignor David McRoberts, who 'as a young man . . . had favoured change', felt little sympathy with many aspects of the post-Vatican II world. His obituarist recalls that:

> 'although he was no theologian, he had no difficulty in identifying the 'new insights' as simply old heresies writ fresh. The liturgical changes depressed him – maimed rites, as he somewhere describes them, with little of that liturgical orderliness, and nothing whatso-ever of the consoling beauty of the Church's traditional music . . .'[78]

Tensions between the generations was perhaps most strenuously reflected within the priesthood itself during the 1960s. Men still took charge of parishes after their prime and many tended to see the parish as their property. In the 1960s younger priests began to question their subordinate role to these autocrats. Since Scottish priests did not have a national council, as in England, they lacked the institutional forum in which to ventilate their concerns. Many who underwent a 'crisis of identity' and began to 'query the relevance of their reclusive seminary training to the realities of life' abandoned the priesthood and went to university as mature students to gain professional qualifications in law, social work or in education; some fell in love with women whom they later married, others returned to the ministry more qualified for the tasks ahead but the church could ill afford to forfeit the energy and commitment of those who cut adrift in the 1960s.[79]

The issue that undoubtedly produced the greatest degree of anxiety and unrest within the clergy and between the church authorities and the laity in the 1960s and indeed beyond was artificial birth control. Planning a family by the use of artificial contraception was an accepted convention in Scotland. In 1968 a commission set up by Pope Paul VI to review the church's prohibition on artificial birth control found itself split, but with a clear majority stating that the church's teaching could change without losing theological respectability. In the encyclical *Humanae Vitae* Paul VI chose to accept the minority report to the initial dismay even of Gray in Edinburgh and several other Scottish bishops. Henceforth, people began to 'shop around' and look for priests who appreciated the personal and family difficulties involved in arriving at a decision over birth control and who were prepared to underline the role of individual conscience in making a choice about regulating one's family. Rennie McOwan, a leading Catholic journalist, detected the growth of 'compartmentalised Catholicism' in the late 1960s whereby 'people said in effect that the encyclical was not an infallible document, that the hierarchy had got it wrong, and they carried on making decisions in conscience according to their circumstances.' [80]

In 1968 two Scottish-based priests actually debated *Humanae Vitae* from differing standpoints in the main Scottish Catholic weekly[81] although Gerard Hughes, the Catholic chaplain at Glasgow University was the only one in Scotland to publicly express his misgivings about the line taken by the encyclical. A small but highly articulate section of the laity then entered the fray with the Glasgow solicitor James Armstrong forming the Scottish Catholic Renewal Movement (SCRM) in 1969. He sought to 'encourage intelligent debate on the problems facing Christians', turning Glasgow a lively centre of theological and ecumenical discussion by inviting to the city some of the most progressive of contemporary Catholic theologians. A statement issued by the SCRM in 1969 complained that the laity 'who contribute all the financial resources of the Church, have little or no say in how these are deployed' and that 'the true status of women is not reflected in the Church'.[82] Fr. John Fitzsimmons who had attended the Vatican Council supported lay empowerment: 'I belong to a generation of clergy who did not see it as their task to tell people how to live, but rather to give them the Gospel so that they could make up their own minds how to live.'[83]

At Glasgow University, the Rev. Professor William Barclay, a well known biblical scholar and a Kirk minister, became the Catholic Society's honorary president in 1970 after having addressed it on scripture.[84] But in 1971 Fr. Hughes faced dismissal as university chaplain by the Archbishop who had objected to him giving Holy Communion at interdenominational services to non-Catholics. The case received prominent coverage in the local press and a petition carrying 3,000 signatures gathered by the students was presented to Scanlan who retreated.[85] But as the 1970s wore on those Scottish Catholics who wished the clergy and the laity to cooperate in efforts to renew the faith found an unresponsive church leadership. At the 1965 session of the Vatican Council it had been agreed that the laity 'share in the priestly, prophetic and royal office of Christ, and therefore have their role to play in the mission of the whole People of God in the Church and in the world'. In Scotland the concessions to the 'lay apostolate' that had been made in England were not forthcoming. Many radical Catholics drifted away once it became clear, with the installation of John Paul II as Pope, that order was going to be restored to the heart of the institutional church. Older priests had, in the 1960s, seen traditions they had long accepted being swept aside and now it was the turn of younger priests to find that hopes for a radical new ministry were going to be dashed. The destruction of long-established working-class communities as part of an ambitious and flawed process of urban development, had weakened the hitherto strong group identity of Catholics and now it was the turn of the church itself to confront crisis as a result of sudden and poorly implemented change.

NOTES

1 Patrick Dollan, unpublished memoirs, vol. 2, Glasgow Room, Glasgow, Mitchell Library, pp. 134-5.

2 Obituary, Dr. Patrick Connolly (1913-2011), the *Herald*, 27 December 2011.

3 McRoberts, 'Scottish Survey'.

4 Talk with Willie Hamilton MP, 3 April 1984

5 Checkland, *The Upas Tree*, Glasgow 1875-1975, p.67.

6 Darragh, 'The Catholic population in Scotland, 1878-1977', in David McRoberts, *Modern Scottish Catholicism*, p. 223.

7 McRoberts, 'Scottish Survey'.

8 Darragh, *Catholic population*, p. 230.

9 Checkland, *The Upas Tree*, p. 68.

10 Obituary of Cornelius O'Leary, CDS, 1975.

11 John Burrow, *Benny Lynch*, Mainstream, Edinburgh, 1983, p. 2

12 Private communication.

13 Interview with Michael Fallon, Edinburgh journalist, 1982.

14 Interview with Lord Wheatley, Edinburgh 1982.

15 James Coffey, 'Scotland's cardinal', SCO, 10 May 1985.

16 Interview with the Rev. Anthony Ross OP, 21 December 1981.

17 Anthony Ross OP, 'The development of the Scottish Catholic community, 1878-1978', in McRoberts, *Modern Scottish Catholicism*, p. 51. Fr. Ross later identified Canon Daniel to me as the author of this remark.

18 Darragh, 'Catholic population', p. 221.

19 Thomas J. Fitzpatrick, *Catholic Secondary Education in South-west Scotland before 1979*, Aberdeen University Press, Aberdeen, 1986, p. 115.

20 Cooney, *Scotland and the Papacy*, p. 95.

21 Obituary of Archbishop Scanlan, CDS, 1977.

22 View of David Lambie MP, interview, 26 April 1984.

23 Fitzpatrick, *Catholic*, p. 152.

24 Fitzpatrick, *Catholic*, p. 152.

25 Darragh, *Catholic population*, p. 234.

26 Interview with Professor Tom Carberry.

27 McRoberts, Scottish Survey; interview with Bishop Joseph Devine, 21 August 1981.

28 Fitzpatrick, *Catholic*, p. 152.

29 Darragh, *Catholic population*, p.224.

30 Interview with Professor Tom Carberry.

31 Interview with Hugh Brown MP, 26 April 1984; see James Patrick, *A Glasgow Gang Observed*, Eyre Methuen, London, 1972. This was the pseudonym used by the name of the son of a senior member of the Catholic teaching profession in order to penetrate the gangs.

32 Smout, *A Century of the Scottish People*, pp. 55-6.

33 W.J. McKechin, *A School in Eastwood Park*, Paisley College of Technology, Working Paper, No. 9, 1979, p. 49.

34 McKechin, p. 23.

35 McKechin, p.39.

36 Quoted in Murray, *The Old Firm*, p. 222.

37 Murray, p. 223.

38 Quoted in H. F. Moorhouse, 'Professional football and working-class culture: English thought and Scottish evidence', *Sociological Review*, 32, 2, 1984, p. 302.

39 See Tom Campbell, *Celtic's paranoia. . .all in the mind*, Ayr: Fort Publishing, 2004, p. 71; and Brian Wilson, *Celtic: A Century With Honour*, London: Willow Books Collins, 1988, p. 95.

40 *Glasgow Observer*, 26 September 1969

41 Wilson, *Celtic: A Century*, p. 97.

42 Ibid.

43 Campbell, *Celtic's paranoia* , p. 64.

44 Michael Kelly, 'Helping Rangers would be sporting thing to do', *Scotsman*, 15 March 2012.

45 Interview with former MP Richard Buchanan, 16 June 1986.

46 Interview with Tom Carberry.

47 Interview with Alex Ferry, 23 November 1984.

48 Alex Ferry.

49 Alex Ferry.

50 Alex Ferry.

51 Private information.

52 R. B. McCallum and Alison Readman, *The British General Election of 1945*, Frank Cass, London, 1964.

53 Interview with the Rev. Donald MacDonald, 16 April 1984.

54 Harvie, *No Gods*, p. 128.

55 Darragh, *Catholic population*, p.230.

56 Obituary of the Very Rev. A. C. Craig, *Times*, 28 August 1985.

57 James Quinn SJ, 'Ecumenism and Scottish Catholics', in McRoberts (ed.), *Modern Scottish Catholicism*, p. 208.

58 Quinn, 'Ecumenism', p. 208.

59 *Scotsman*, 23 April 1966.

60 Obituary of Canon William Mallon, CDS, 1974, p. 324.

61 Interview with the Rev. Andrew Herron.

62 Andrew Herron.

63 Andrew Herron.

64 These obituaries are carried in the *Catholic Directory for Scotland*.

65 Rev. Donald MacDonald.

66 Rev. Donald MacDonald.

67 Obituary of the Most Rev. Donald Scanlan, Archbishop of Glasgow, *CDS*, 1977, .p. 373-4.

68 Obituary, *CDS*, 1977, p.p.373-4.

69 Rev. Donald MacDonald.

70 Hugh McIlvanney, *Observer*, 15 September 1985.

71 J. G. Kellas and P. Fotheringham, The political behaviour of the working-class', in A. Allan MacLaren (ed.), *Social Class in Scotland Past and Present*, John Donald, Edinburgh, n.d., p. 159.

72 Kellas and Fotheringham, p. 150.

73 Interviews with Hugh Brown MP and David Lambie MP.

74 Iain McCormick, *Scottish Catholic Observer*, 19 May 1967.

75 *Glasgow Herald*, 10 March 1970.

76 *Glasgow Herald*, 18 March 1970.

77 See Pat Bolan, obituary of Canon Joseph Daniel, *SCO*, 6 February 1981.

78 Obituary of Right Rev. DavidMcRoberts, *CDS*, 1980, p. 387.

79 Cooney, *Scotland and the Papacy*, p. 78.

80 Rennie McOwan, 'Catholics and contraception in the real world', *GH*, 10 April 1985.

81 *Scottish Catholic Observer*, 16 August 1968.

82 Cooney, *Scotland and the Papacy*, p.101.

83 Private memoir.

84 Cooney, p.111.

85 Cooney, p. 104.

CHAPTER 6
Ulster's war fails to ignite Scotland, 1970-1990

SCOTLAND was taken as much by surprise as the rest of the United Kingdom by the eruption of bitter internal conflict in Northern Ireland starting in October 1968. The deceptive quiet of the previous forty-five years had caused most Britons from the political class to think that the Anglo-Irish conflict had been permanently settled by the device of partitioning the island and allowing the Unionists in six of Ulster's nine counties to have home rule within the UK. A navel-gazing Westminster was shown how wrong it was in 1968 when the downtrodden Catholic minority, comprising one-third of the population of Northern Ireland, began to campaign for civil rights and an end to blatant favouritism shown towards the Protestant majority in the allocation of jobs, housing and regional development.

Although the campaign was for the adoption of British democratic standards in Northern Ireland rather than Irish unity, the Unionists over-reacted; peaceful protests led by middle-class Catholics then gave way to furious rioting in the Catholic nationalist ghettoes. British troops were deployed in 1969 to prevent law and order collapsing altogether; Britain soon got even more deeply embroiled as extreme nationalists took advantage of the power vacuum to revive the IRA. Its bombing campaign of 1971-72 helped topple the Unionist government and Britain stepped into the Ulster cauldron by closing the Stormont parliament and introducing direct rule from Westminster but, not until the mid-1990s, was it able to end the violence or devise an acceptable political solution.

The west of Scotland was the part of mainland Britain closest to Northern Ireland not just geographically but emotionally and also in terms of the ethnic composition of its inhabitants and their religious ties. Journalists looking for a fresh angle on the conflict wondered whether it was not a matter of time before Glasgow, which had always enjoyed a turbulent image when Belfast was deceptively calm, erupted into fratricidal violence. It was noted that the behaviour of Orange and republican flute bands that travelled over to Northern Ireland rallies from Scotland was often more provocative than that of their local counterparts; and that it was soldiers in Scottish regiments who had been involved in the first clashes with Belfast youths in March 1970, disturbances that marked the end of the Catholic community's 'honeymoon' with the British Army. Not a few Glaswegians watched uneasily as fresh sectarian graffiti began to appear on bus shelters and on the walls of housing schemes. Insulting or complimentary references to the Queen or the Pope and dates marking earlier stages of the conflict, such as 1690 or 1916, gave way to slogans about 'Bloody Sunday', 'PIRA', and the UDA and UVF, two paramilitary responses to the Provisional IRA from the loyalist or Protestant side.

While trying to get on with their own lives Glaswegians cast an anxious glance over their shoulders and worried about the amount of local political fall-out from the Ulster explosion. Looking back in the mid-1980s Church of Scotland ministers Andrew Herron and Donald MacDonald still remained surprised that battle had not been drawn by some of the local factions that took their lead from the partisans of orange and green in Ulster.'[1]

But as the Northern Ireland conflict dragged on leaving Scotland relatively untouched, predictions of imminent disaster receded. Scotland's communal differences were homegrown ones, shaped around contested territory, sport, education and, to an ever lessening degree, religion, Those who wished, like nationalists in Ulster, the country to embrace a post-British future, were not contestants in the sectarian quarrel. Unlike in Ulster, state institutions were not citadels of discrimination; it was in the private sector that this hung on. Antagonism centred around Old Firm matches which helped divert intense rivalry into the recreational sphere and away from politics and religion. 'Perhaps', in the words of a Glasgow chief constable, 'the ritual of these events has been instrumental in providing an outlet for the differences between the two communities', however uncomfortable it has been for those neutral citizens inconvenienced by the anti-social behaviour of Old Firm supporters.[2]

The Orange Order, rather than Rangers, constantly renewed Protestant bonds with Ulster. This may have been vital in preventing the conflict taking root in Britain; lodges paid fraternal visits back and forth across the Irish Sea to commemorate the symbolic events of the Protestant calendar. identification with Irish republicanism has only been expressed in a sporadic or disorganised way. There is plenty of evidence to suggest that the post-1968 troubles helped revive the order at a time when nominal membership was increasing, especially among younger generations of Orange families where sons expected to don the Orange sash, preferred instead to follow, in their spare time, sport or other leisure pursuits. In Partick only a dozen old men could be found to assemble behind the Orange banner in the mid-1960s recalls Donald MacDonald, then a local minister, but once Protestant Ulster was seen to be under threat from enemies within or without, Orange events suddenly seemed less hackneyed and once more hundreds were to be found marching behind the banner in this working-class Glasgow district.[3]

Bulldozers had levelled areas like Kinning Park, and parts of Partick, Whiteinch and Govan where Orangeism had been especially strong thanks to their shipbuilding associations. The demolition of areas in the east end like Dalmarnock, Bridgeton, and Parkhead, associated with weaving or heavy engineering, came later but would be just as devastating. The decline of shipbuilding on the Clyde and the winding down of the Ayrshire and Lanarkshire coalfields in the 1950s removed industries around which the lodges had grown up. Emigration from the Orange heartlands of Ulster was also a casualty of the economic downturn. Some of the most dedicated Scottish officials had strong Ulster family connections and the damming up of this source of renewal stood to alter the character of the movement in subtle ways. But the institution clung to a mass membership despite such challenges and the growth in religiously mixed marriages and the further spread of secularism within the working class.

It is easy for journalists increasingly fenced off from social realities to overlooked the social role of the Orange Lodge. It manages to fill a void in the lives of men and women in dozens of anonymous towns and villages across Scotland with bleak economic prospects. There is keen competition to ascend the lodge hierarchy and pursue the degrees which denote a brother's seniority. The spread of licensed Orange social clubs shows how the Order has come to terms with the pub-orientated life of post-industrial Scotland in a way that its much larger Ulster counterpart refused to do. However divisive some of its features are, Orangeism remained an expression of communitarian values at a time when working-class lifestyles are becoming increasingly privatised and centred around the home with its consumer goods and television.[4]

Anyone aware of the degree of solidarity with the Irish republican cause emanating from Glasgow after 1918 might have been surprised at the lack of response shown in the 1970s. By now, most of Ireland was independent and emigration from Ireland to Clydeside had dried up several decades previously. Archbishop Thomas Winning was pleased that the vast majority of Glaswegian Catholics had no time for the IRA. But, In 1973, his church was briefly embarrassed when the police discovered a cache of weapons in the chapel house of St. Teresa's, Possilpark. Fr. Bartholomew Burns successfully evaded the police before returning to his native Ireland. Tensions existed at the top of the church over the handling of the affair. Traditionalists wished to minimse cooperation with the police due to a ghetto-like suspicion of most state institutions. Winning was appalled to find that his predecessor was almost talked into giving a reference to Burns after his flight from the law. [5]

Anyone with an extensive knowledge of West of Scotland might have expected high figures in the Orange Order and not the Catholic church to be naive or indulgent about terrorists. In the late 1950s Scottish Orangeism was briefly led by a firebrand Church of Scotland minister, the Rev. Alan Hasson who combined outright hostility to 'Popery' with a bid to re-dedicate the Order to firm Reformation principles. A nervous breakdown in 1960 forced him to stand down.

Level-headed figures dominated Grand Lodge, the order's ruling body at the start of the conflict. Still, the killing of three Scottish soldiers in March 1970 caused outrage.[6] But it was nothing like the shock in Scottish Orange ranks following a blatant sectarian attack on Tullyvallen Orange hall near the Irish border in south Armagh in which five Orangemen were killed. For a while, in 1975-76, a change of attitude could be discerned. Hitherto, Grand Lodge had kept its distance from paramilitary bodies like the Ulster

Defence Association (UDA) or to extremist politicians like Ian Paisley and his Democratic Unionist Party. The south Armagh massacre brought home the sense of common identity between fellow Orangemen as nothing previously had done. Meeting soon afterwards Grand Lodge suspended normal business and for hours talked only of Tullyvallen, security in Ulster, and what could be done to help. There was talk of organising a mass evacuation of Armagh Protestants to loyalist homes all over Scotland. One district lodge, acting hastily, bankrupted itself by buying dozens of camp beds, blankets and other emergency supplies. But of much greater significance was Grand Lodge's decision to send a delegation to Belfast where it secretly met a joint committee of paramilitary groups.[7]

One well-informed journalist reckoned that the Order planned to widen the scope of its charity work to include the welfare sections of these paramilitary groups as well as the Orange distress fund in order to help prisoners and their families.[8] David Bryce, the Grand Secretary who had handled public relations since 1975, stressed that the Order would not be giving money for the buying of arms.[9] But the prospect of a split loomed after Roddy MacDonald, an Orangeman and a foreman in the Edinburgh building trade declared on a 1976 BBC Scotland programme that there was a possibility of guns being shipped from Scotland to Ulster. The leadership was alarmed that it had been indirectly linked with unlawful activities and it sought to expel MacDonald at the end of 1976. However, the 300 delegates assembled at Grand Lodge refused to support the motion for his expulsion.[10] The ruling executive then threatened to resign *en masse* unless delegates at the Order's AGM endorsed a resolution which 'utterly rejected all support, be it active or tacit, of terrorist organisations whose actions contravene the law of the land'.[11] The motion was approved overwhelmingly. The leadership continued to be vigilant against any state move to sell out the Ulster Protestant cause but it never thereafter lost the initiative over grassroots militants.

In February 1977 *The Orange Torch*, the Order's monthly paper, promised to maintain continuous pressure on Westminster politicians to ensure that Ulster was never removed from the UK against the wishes of the majority and to provide 'massive humanitarian assistance' should the need arise, but flirtation with paramilitaries was firmly ruled out:

'Leaving aside . . . the question of the acceptability of members of a
Christian association such as ours involving themselves in unlawful
'military' activity,,how positive and effective has been the role of the
Scottish wing of the UDA?They have been blunderingly ineffective . .
. More serious still, they have endangered the credibility of the
Orange institution in Scotland. . . In plain language, who in Scotland
will want to listen to anything the Orange Order has to say about
Northern Ireland when misguided men claiming the name of
Orange are constantly in our newspapers on arms charges or
flaunting themselves on television boasting about shotguns and
flamethrowers.' [12]

In 1979, the Young Scottish Loyalists were founded by ten young
Glaswegians disenchanted by the Order's moderation.[13] By 1982 they were
claiming a paid-up membership of 1,500 and an ability to mobilise 5,000
supporters for street demonstrations.[14] Clashes took place with pro-
Republicans who belonged to the Troops Out Movement and during the
worst of these, at one rally in Glasgow on 14 February 1981, 152 people
were arrested. As early as 1972, one Scottish Labour MP, Hugh Brown the
member for Glasgow Provan,was already concerned about the strength of
feeling in his own constituency. He took soundings by approaching a
respected priest and the officers of a Masonic club in his constituency
which he had opened and asked to be put in touch with 'some wild men':
'so I had conversations with two groups separately . . . I was appalled by
the bigotry on both sides. Anybody who is complacent about the
underlying tensions is making a big mistake; they are there without a
shadow of a doubt.'[15] It may well have been that fall-out from the Ulster
conflict impeded initiative, such as that of the Church of Scotland's
Glasgow presbytery to try and shame Rangers into ending its bar on
Catholic players. In 1978 after *The Bush*, its monthly paper, issued a
scathing editorial, 'The Blue Barrier', some parishes cancelled their bulk
orders forthwith, and before long it folded.[16] At the 1980 General Assembly
of the Kirk a motion calling on Rangers to 'publicly disclaim a sectarian
bias in management and team structure' was passed by a majority of 200
but it was an ambiguous result since 400 commissioners abstained.

Perhaps some Protestant frustrations stemmed from the growing
success of Catholics in obtaining middle-class positions. Recruitment
procedure in council employment has become centralised. In Glasgow

District Council, a new director of personnel saw to it in 1975 that an applicant for a council job was no longer required to put down the name of his or her school in the application form which has always been the question asked by a west of Scotland employer anxious to identify a person's religion.[17]

Michael Kelly, a Catholic and a former lecturer, helped revive Glasgow's floundering image during his term as the city's Lord Provost from 1981 to 1984. He launched a public relations campaign entitled 'Glasgow's Miles Better', designed to banish the city's violent, unruly and run-down image by substituting a new one which stressed the warmth and wit of its inhabitants, the richness of its architectural heritage, and the open-air amenities and range of cultural events offered by the city. Some felt that at the height of a savage economic slump, Glasgow's image was beyond repair, others accused Kelly of self-promotion, but the campaign led to a sharp increase in tourism to the city as it painfully evolved from being a major industrial centre to being a city that relied on service industries that catered for the consumer and out-of-town visitor.

Fr. John Fitzsimmons, based for some years in what is arguably the most prosperous middle-class parish in Glasgow, St. Joseph's, Clarkston, considered that 'a Catholic mafia' had grown up in Glasgow based on white-collar professionals.[18] Archbishop Winning, by contrast, felt in 1986: 'there is no established Catholic middle-class in Glasgow yet' and he emphasises that those professionals who do exist 'are still only a generation removed from the working-class'.[19] Winning had still to meet a Scottish Catholic banker, banking being an area where others perceive some lingering discrimination. One respected administrator, stung by this fact, took the opportunity of sharing a train compartment with a senior director of a premier Scottish bank to ask: 'Isn't it time you ceased to ask an applicant's religion? After all, a person opening an account with your bank doesn't have to say what his religion is.'[20]

Thomas J. Winning, Glasgow's archbishop for nearly three decades, would, by the middle of his tenure, be viewed in the media as one of the most influential decision-makers in Scotland. Until his appointment in 1974, his predecessors had been self-effacing. They did not attract attention by making controversial statements, nor by contributing to the letter columns of the press and they expected the same introspection from priests. As a result, many found it difficult to follow the lead of their new archbishop who thought it necessary for the church to show concern about whether gospel values were being applied in the present time by governments that now had the means to decide the fate of mankind. Through his diocesan newspaper *Flourish*, Winning branded nuclear weapons as immoral as did his successors. The Catholic church's attitude was hailed in left-wing quarters as progressive while its stance on abortion was viewed as reactionary but the overriding consistency of the message which was that it was immoral to needlessly end human life, was overlooked.

Having grown up in a Lanarkshire mining community, the future archbishop studied for the priesthood in Rome and became a canon lawyer. Like most canon lawyers he was instinctively loyal to the Roman hierarchy of the church and most of his innovations have been in terms of organisation rather than ideas. Stints of parish work culminated in two years spent in Clydebank (1972-74) where he won the respect of the trade unions for his defence of endangered shipyard workers jobs at the time of the famous UCS 'work-in': its leader Jimmy Reid, was tipped as the first Communist MP to be elected since 1945 when he stood for parliament in 1974 but Winning did not hesitate to remind his parishioners that the church's view about the Communist Party had not altered despite the merits of the individual candidate and Reid lost.

Though not the most riveting of speakers Archbishop Winning's accessability and charm made him popular among ordinary Catholics who no longer felt they were in the presence of a remote potentate when he moved among them. Visits to the USA and Australia where Catholics 'often shout their faith from the rooftops' brought home to him the contrast with his own people who, weighed down by their past, 'are sometimes almost ashamed of being a Catholic':

> 'We form the working-class church in the country. . . We are very diffident about our faith. We are inclined to conceal it. We are afraid of making too much noise in case we disturb the tranquility of others'.[21]

He had his internal critics who argued that his energy has largely gone into shoring up the institution for its own sake rather than into forging a more democratic and visionary church which can fully respond to the material and spiritual crisis people are facing in urban post-industrial Scotland. Rennie McOwan, who had accepted his offer to form a Catholic media office in the 1970s, warned in a 1985 letter to the *Scottish Catholic Observer* (SCO) that:

> 'Church authorities cannot call on governments or local authorities or dictatorships . . . to be more open, honest, and more accountable unless its own life in this respect is a model for others to follow.'[22]

James Coffey, then the editor of the SCO, had warned around the same time that:

> 'Many young adults want a strong active Pope who will condemn injustice, shame governments into helping the Third World, outlaw nuclear weapons and put pressure on repressive regimes in South Africa and Latin America. For them, these are the real sins of the modern world. Not the private, personal matters the Pope so often deals with in his speeches.'[23]

Winning was an innovator, one keen not to be out-of-step with the Vatican (a perennial obsession for Scottish bishops). In a 1982 interview, he conceded that the Scottish Church may not have altogether understood the great implications of Vatican II:

> 'Vatican II was all about changing attitudes. It was not merely about changing vestments or externals. We've never really been told that till recently'.[24]

He was bound to have been concerned by the decline in people going to the priest for confession perhaps because of their defiance of *Humanae Vitae*. Perhaps he was also shaken by a survey which broke the alarming news that attendance at weekly Mass had plummeted from 50% to under 40% in less than a decade.' The figures suggested that attendance among Catholics was declining faster than among other Christian bodies in Scotland and Winning conceded that if avoiding action was not taken, 'by the end of the first quarter of the twenty first century, there will be very few committed Catholics in Scotland'!

He displayed uncommon diplomatic abilities in order to save the 1982 Papal visit to Britain. Years of planning had gone into it, but it was almost cancelled at the last moment due to the outbreak of war in the spring of 1982 between Britain and Argentina following the Argentinian invasion of the disputed Falkland islands, a British possession in the South Atlantic. As pressure from Latin America for Pope John Paul II to cancel the visit mounted, Archbishop Winning stepped in, realising that because of the cost involved, it would be difficult to rearrange the visit for a later date and that cancellation would be a great blow to the morale of the Scottish Church.[25] After sending a telegram to the Pope urging him not to call off the visit, he sent private messages to the Argentinian cardinals and on 17 May, with the Archbishop of Liverpool, he flew to Rome, where the Pope told him to do his best to save what would have been an unprecedented event in modern times.[26]

The prospect of a Pope being received in Scotland was bound to trouble foes of the Church of Rome. The Rev. Ian Paisley's had pressurised the organisers of the 1979 Papal visit to Ireland to scrap plans to bring him to Northern Ireland. For months in advance the press speculated that the thirty-six hours the Pope was scheduled to spend in Scotland would be the ones most likely to be marred by ugly protests. Opponents were not pacified by the hierarchy's insistence that the visit was a purely pastoral one designed to deepen the religious belief of Catholics. If that was the case, they demanded, why were all Edinburgh children being give a day off school when the Pope came among them, a council decision which the Secretary of State overruled.[27] The Orange Order sent a telegram to the Queen warning her that she would be in breach of her coronation oath if she met the Pope.[28] After lively internal discussions the Order opted for peaceful and orderly protests and the 10% to 15% of the Glasgow membership who allegedly felt inclined to assemble at the Glasgow open-air venue where he would say mass on 1 June, got no official backing.

Church of Scotland leaders had reacted negatively on being informed by those drawing up the Papal itinerary that the only time available for a meeting between the Pope and the Moderator would be in distant Canterbury where he would take his place in the queue with English Protestant church leaders. For a time it looked as if no meeting would take place which would have been a severe blow to Scottish ecumenism. Then the Pope's crowded schedule was rearranged to allow for a meeting with the Moderator, Professor John McIntyre in the courtyard of New College on the Mound leading directly to the steps of the General Assembly Hall in Edinburgh. In the courtyard stands a statue of John Knox and the two church leaders were to meet in its shadow which infuriated militant Protestants in Edinburgh. Eight hundred turned out to protest, the Pope blessing them as he passed by to meet the Moderator, their angry shouts remaining audible during the short meeting."

On 1 June 1982, an estimated 300,000 people packed Bellahouston Park in Glasgow to greet the Pope, the largest turnout of any of the British rallies. In his homily John Paul II referred to Ninian, Mungo, and Margaret, the chief saints of Scotland, though significantly not to Patrick.[29] His speech-writers were keen to stress that Roman Catholicism was an authentic part of the life and traditions of Scotland and that the church had ceased to be an immigrant one. The writer Allan Massie airily concluded that 'John Paul has completed the rehabilitation of Scottish Catholicism and its reintegration into the Scottish nation'. [30]

It is true that many Protestants packed into Bellahouston Park, one of them being the Rev. Donald MacDonald who felt that he must be among many co-religionists on noticing that in the enclosure in which he and his family was located, only 50% of people went to communion at the Mass being celebrated; it may also have been a sign that many Catholics there did not feel themselves to be in sufficient state of grace to partake the communion host or that to many it was as much a carnival as a religious event.

The Pope emphasised Scotland's nationhood and by kissing the soil of Scotland on his arrival at Edinburgh airport he allayed suspicions that the Vatican viewed the country as the northern extension of England.[31] It is ironic that the only local politician to make a controversial pronouncement in the run-up to the visit was William Wolfe, president of the pro-independence SNP. In the spring of 1982 he expressed concern about mainly Protestant Falkland islanders falling under the control of 'the cruel and ruthless fascist dictatorship of a Roman Catholic state' and he questioned the recent decision to raise the status of the Papal envoy in Britain to ambassadorial level.[32] Wolfe's was an isolated voice and Gordon Wilson, the party chairman was invited to attend the Bellahouston Mass by Cardinal Gray who, in his letter, reportedly assured the party leader that he was not at all worried by the Wolfe outburst and that Catholics in the SNP should carry on regardless. [33]

The SNP had just emerged from a period of electoral growth. In the October 1974 general election where it obtained 30% of Scotland's vote, ten of its seventy-one candidates had been Catholics, two of whom were elected. But most Catholics were numb to (or else apprehensive about) its sole policy which was to remove Scotland from the British state.

Upwardly mobile Catholics remained attached to the Labour Party, not surprising given that most upwardly mobile central Scotland Catholics were still disprorportionately located in public sector posts. In the February 1974 election it has been calculated that only 6-9% of Catholics voted SNP compared to 48.4% of voters who were linked to Protestant denomin-ations.[34] In the second election of 1974, held in October, evidence has been gathered to show that, of a distinct selection of groups, it was Catholics who showed the greatest resistance towards voting SNP.[35]

The Labour government elected in 1974 had been panicked into drawing up plans for a Scottish assembly in Edinburgh by the success of the SNP. The SNP was unable to convert Scots happy with the British link even to the moderate degree of home rule on offer. Hugh Brown MP, a firm devolutionist with many RC constituents (who, in 1978, addressed several Orange conferences about what devolution would mean), found more apprehension among Catholics than Protestants.[136] It was not completely far-fetched to believe that sectarian strife was more likely to occur in a Scotland which enjoyed much the same measure of home rule as Northern Ireland had done until the start of the 1970s than within a single British state. whose experiment with devolution failed disastrously earlier in the 1970s. Bishop Joseph Devine of Motherwell campaigned on the 'Yes' side and declared in a speech that:

'As a Catholic, I belong to an international church, but internationalism flourishes best when rooted in a keen sense of one's nation, culture and identity. After all, you cannot have internationalism without nations and Scotland is a nation'.[37]

In the referendum on 1 March 1979, Strathclyde region (in existence from 1974 to 1994 and covering most of the West of Scotland) returned a 54.0% 'Yes' vote in favour of a Scottish Assembly, the second highest in the country but on a low Scottish turnout of 63.8%. It is impossible to ascertain to what extent working-class Catholics with reservations about devolution turned out to vote 'No' or merely stayed at home. But devolution was lost, since Parliament required 40% of the Scottish electorate (voters and non-voters alike) to vote 'Yes' and the low turn-out ensured that only 32.9% actually did so.

Eighteen years of Conservative rule lay ahead and in each general election, the Labour Party consolidated its electoral hold in Scotland. Many Orangemen found themselves casualties of an industrial downturn which was put down to Prime Minister Margaret Thatcher's anti-manufacturing policies. Her willingness, in 1986, to give the Dublin government a consultative role in the affairs of Northern Ireland was another reason for Orange men and women to desert the Tories. A Scottish Unionist Party, sponsored by the Order, was formed in 1986 to exact revenge on the Tories. But most Tories drifted across to Labour. It was now a big tent party that accommodated not only an increasing swathe of middle-class voters but the bulk of a working-class that remained culturally fractured in parts of Scotland. The tensions that could arise were shown in the case of Sam Campbell, the Labour convenor of Midlothian District Council whose Scottish *Who's Who* entry listed 'supporting Glasgow Rangers' as one of his recreations. Having spent a lifetime in the mining industry, the then fifty-five-year-old councillor was returned unopposed for a Midlothian mining seat in 1985. But his political career collapsed overnight after a speech at an open-air rally in Leith on 28 June 1986 at the annual parade of the County Grand Orange Lodge of the East. Even Orangemen among the platform party were taken aback by the stridency of his remarks which received wide coverage in the press. The *Scotsman* reported it as follows:

'Campbell, a Church of Scotland elder . . . said ministers should be told to 'stop fraternising with the Church of Rome . . .' Lord MacLeod of Fuinary, founder of the Iona Community, had 'betrayed the church and lived 90 years too long.

'Priests who participated in radio counselling programmes had 'never been in a wedding bed, at least I think they haven't' but were advising on family life: 'let's get it stopped'. Protestants should withhold their TV licences until Roman Catholicism was 'cleared' off the screen. . .

'Campbell . . . said the best way to save money on education was to 'shut down the Papist schools' which were an insult and a memorial to Roman chains and darkness. . .

'After making more temperate points about resources for denominational education, he concluded: 'the moment that the Roman Catholic Church in this country loses its schools it is on the way down, so let's help it.' [38]

Tensions continued to bubble up in Scottish Labour ranks over Catholic schools. After five previous tries, a motion supporting integration was passed at the 1976 conference, prompting a nervous leadership to try and keep the issue under wraps. These motions came from working-class constituencies, from skilled trade unions likely to have relatively few Catholics or from middle-class branches which regarded separate schools as an offence to sensible secularist views. Polling surveys indicated that most Scots had *not* got used to denominational schools. A 1984 survey commissioned by *The Glasgow Herald* produced a result not very different from ones reached in the past:[39] 72% of the sample polled were opposed to state-funded Catholic schools, 20% in favour, and 8% didn't know; in addition, campaigns in favour of integration had recently been carried out by large circulation papers like the *Daily Record* and the *Sunday Mail* which may well have influenced popular attitudes on the subject.

Archbishop Winning was bound to be alarmed to hear Catholics prominent in Labour politics like Helen Liddell and Jean McFadden openly hope for the creation of an integrated system with provisions for religious education.[40] In a 1982 pastoral letter read out at all masses, Dr. Winning felt obliged to remind church-going parents that they were still required to send their children to Catholic schools despite recent legislation establishing a 'parent's charter' that gave them greater freedom of choice.[41] He would have been troubled by middle-class Edinburgh Catholics who increasingly chose to send their children to selective schools attended by other incipient members of the Edinburgh bourgeoisie. (Unwilling to go down this path Brian Gill, the future senior Scottish judge, sent his children through to Glasgow to attend his old school of St. Aloysius).

In 1982 Winning remarked that 'eight years as archbishop have taught me that looming at the dawn of each day is a crisis in education'.[42] He was bound to be aware that the number of RE teachers who were supposed to be offering Catholicism not merely as a subject but as a guide for living were diminishing. Younger ones were often half-hearted or evasive in their approach if their own lifestyle did not comply with Catholic doctrine. In an age of growing uncertainty, Religious Education (RE) periods often proved the most boring part of the timetable due to the lack of genuine interest on the part of the pupils and teachers alike.[43] Fr. Thomas Chambers, the episcopal vicar for RE in the Glasgow archdiocese admitted in 1986 that the materials designed to acquaint children with religious values were low-grade, something that wouldn't change until the next century.[44]

In contrast to the long Cold War starting to break out between the British Catholic churches and secularist forces, dialogue on contentious issues was occurring between the two main Scottish Christian churches. Arguably, it would yield fruitful results.

From the 1970s Rome gave national hierarchies much greater autonomy in determining their attitude to a Catholic who wishes to marry a non-Catholic. In Holland and Switzerland, which like Scotland have a history of Protestant-Catholic rivalry, the bishops have long been happy to approve a marriage between a Catholic and a Christian of any other denomination. The Catholic church saw itself making few gains from these unions; indeed the number of conversions to Catholicism in Scotland hads fallen markedly since the 1950s. Well-grounded fears existed that these marriages would be the means by which it loses its presence in the working-class: nominal Protestants are most commonly found in the urban working-class and, since the Catholic community remains overwhelmingly working-class itself, a mixed marriage is highly likely to involve a couple where one partner does not share even the qualified religious conviction of the other.

By the start of the 1980s, the Catholic church was prepared to give its blessing to a wedding between an adherent and a committed Christian with the priest being ready to officiate at the service. However, it refused to approve a wedding involving one of its members and a nominal Protestant. The hierarchy and the Kirk's view of what constituted a 'nominal' Protestant were at variance. After 1982, ministers, church elders, priests and nuns came together to study a theme of relevance to the mission of the churches in the west of Scotland after agreeing to 'make our pilgrimage on earth hand I hand'.[45] These regular encounters led many church leaders to recognise that the major contemporary problems besetting the west of Scotland transcended religious barriers:[46] As a result, the churches spoke with an increasingly united voice on social issues like education, welfare and unemployment. The election of a Tory government in 1979 which only enjoyed minority support in Scotland proved to be a watershed. It went on to reject the pre-existing consensus about the need to protect full employment and devolve a certain amount of wealth and opportunity to the regions and nations on the periphery of the United Kingdom. Religious leaders came together to try and save car plants, shipyards and steelworks on which the livelihoods of entire communities were dependent; local authorities and the trade union movement welcomed them as valuable allies prepared to travel to London to plead for a less unfeeling attitude from a government which, in 1983, derived its massive majority largely from the southern third of Britain." Archbishop Winning threw his weight behind several campaigns in the 1980s to save jobs at a time when he feared that many of the social advances secured after 1940 were in danger of being lost. In 1986, when by an overwhelming decision, the General Assembly decided to repudiate the description of the Pope as anti-Christ and delete other anti-Catholic statements in the 1647 Westminster confession, its principal subordinate standard of faith next to the Bible, the move seemed like an anti-climax.[47]

But the authority of the Catholic church was waning owing to the decline of religious practice. In the large housing schemes on Glasgow's periphery up to one-third of the population was unemployed in the mid-1980s, perhaps half of the young people having no real work to go to. In such bleak circumstances there is now little scope for the economic rivalry which once caused workers to distinguish themselves from other workers by erecting racial and cultural barriers. But nor was there room for complacency: even in the absence of denominational and economic rivalry, sectarianism could still prove a menace to community peace.

NOTES

1 Interviews with Right Rev. Andrew Herron, 8 July 1986, and the Rev. Donald MacDonald, 16 April 1986.

2 Sir David McNee, *McNee's Law*, Collins, 1983, p. 41.

3 Rev. Donald MacDonald.

4 See Graham Walker, *Intimate Strangers*, Edinburgh: John Donald 1994, chapter 6.

5 Stephen McGinty, *The Turbulent Priest: The Life of Cardinal Winning*, London: Harper-Collins, 2001, p. 163.

6 See Ian S. Wood and Andrew Sanders, *Time of Troubles: Britain's War in Northern Ireland*, Edinburgh: Edinburgh University Press, 2012.

7 See David McKittrick, *Irish Times*, 9 December 1975.

8 David McKittrick.

9 David McKittrick.

10 Steve Bruce, *No Pope of Rome: Militant Protestantism in Modern Scotland*, Edinburgh: Mainstream, 1987, p. 175, for McDonald's television interview and its aftermath.

11 *Glasgow Herald*, 13 December 1976.

12 'The role of the Grand Orange Lodge of Scotland towards Ulster', *Orange Torch*, February 1977.

13 *Irish Times*, 20 April 1984.

14 *Guardian*, 10 April 1981.

15 Interview with Hugh Brown MP, 26 April 1984.

16 Rev. Donald MacDonald.

17 Interview with Jean McFadden, leader of Glasgow District Council, 1979-86, 31 July 1986.

18 Interview with Fr. John Fitzsimmons, 1 August 1986.

19 Interview with Archbishop Winning.

20 Interview with Lawrence Boyle, then senior city administrator in Glasgow, 30 July 1986.

21 *IrishTimes* 17 May 1982.

22 *Scottish Catholic Observer*, 18 October 1985.

23 James Coffey, *Sunday Mail*, 19 May 1985.

24 Interview with Archbishop Winning.

25 *Irish Times*, 17 May 1982.

26 'How Glasgow may have saved the Pope's visit', *Times*, 29 May 1982. See also McGinty, *Turbulent Priest*, p.p.228-37.

27 *Glasgow Herald*, 15 April 1982.

28 *Glasgow Herald*, 28 February 1982.

29 Willy Slavin, 'Roman in the gloamin', *Cencrastus*, No. 11, 1983.

30 Allan Massie, 'Vive l'Ecosse libre', *Spectator*, 6 June 1982.

31 Massie, *Spectator*.

32 *Glasgow Herald*, 16 April 1982.

33 Private information.

34 Jack Brand, *The National Movement in Scotland*, Routledge, London, 1979, p. 152.

35 Henry Drucker and Gordon Brown, *The Politics of Nationalism and Devolution*, Longmans, 1980, p.50.

36 Interview with Hugh Brown MP, 26 April 1984.

37 *Scottish Catholic Observer*, 19 January 1979.

38 Simon Bain, 'Orange politician reveals his true colours', *Scotsman*, 3 July 1986.

39 *Glasgow Herald*, 13 September 1984.

40 Interviews with Helen Liddell, 20 February 1985; and Jean McFadden.

41 *Scotsman*, 8 February 1982.

42 *Scottish Catholic Observer*, 20 May 1982.

43 The view of a practising Catholic teaching in the denominational sector in the mid-1980s.

44 *Times Education Supplement for Scotland*, 3 January 1986.

45 Excerpt from one of the homilies delivered by Pope John Paul II on his visit to Scotland.

46 Interview with Fr. John Fitzsimmons.

47 *Tablet*, 3 May 1986.

CHAPTER 7
Sectarianism: An Unsettled After-Life?

THE 1990S SAW the end of full-scale violence in Ulster and the arrival of Scottish self-government. This chapter argues that no marked improvement in community relations occurred. Low-level communal suspicions and rivalry were still apparent in the economic realm, over education and, above all, in the world of football. The working-class was scarred by disruptive changes which it was ill-equipped to cope with and which deepened its introspection. Competition over limited opportunities and resources gave sectarianism continuing staying-power and was reflected, at times, in middle-class status anxieties that grabbed the headlines.

The recession of the early 1980s narrowed the distance between lower income Catholics in Scotland and the rest of the population. Working-class Protestants who had enjoyed relatively secure levels of employment in the engineering sector in the West of Scotland suddenly saw the bottom fall out of their lives as the sector took a huge economic hit. High interest rates and a high value for sterling crippled manufacturing firms relying on an export base. Companies requiring sheltered economic conditions found themselves drowning in the maelstrom Mrs Thatcher stirred up in order to usher in a more competitive and entrepreneurial business environment. In many instances, the children of workers who lost their livelihoods in the 1980s were in very bad shape over the next thirty years.[1] They included the children of Protestant workers made redundant in much greater numbers than in previous post-war recessions.

The Thatcher governments' determined but incoherent attempt to liberate society from state control had some benefits. There was a surge of entrepreneurial energy which was visible even in parts of Scotland. But communities dependent on industries which folded in the 1980s witnessed a deterioration in social conditions. Scotland would acquire some of the worst statistics for consumption of illicit drugs, under-age drinking, and teenage pregnancies anywhere in the western world. Thatcher and her advisers had no understanding of how harmful the impact of neo-liberal policies would be on the standards of family life in many working-class areas. Mainly leftwing social planners had already been disdainful of the positive role often exercised by stable families in preparing youngsters for a fulfilling and responsible adult life.

Archbishop Winning of Glasgow was aware of the immense social damage being caused by such economic adversity. £1.6 million set aside for renovating St. Andrew's cathedral was diverted into poverty relief.[2] Perhaps it was no coincidence that it was religious leaders, particularly from the Church of Scotland who sought to give intellectual coherence to the nation's rejection of Thatcherite values. They would be one of the main driving forces behind the campaign for a Scottish parliament. One of its primary goals was to shield Scotland from an 'enterprise culture' centred on unfettered economic individualism that, according to the historian David Marquand, was abhorrent both to the Calvinist and Catholic traditions in Scotland.[3]

Devolution, with Scotland acquiring a parliament that would control most domestic policy, was accomplished in 1999. But the churches would not be among the interest groups which wielded influence in the new order. Scotland would be slow to witness any transformation of political ethics.[4] Centralisation, cronyism and low-level efficiency which had characterised large swathes of the unionist era, would not be replaced by a more innovative and participatory form of government. Ordinary Scots would have to acquire reserves of patience before London's partial retreat from Scotland saw a real difference in how they were governed.

Some historians of the future are likely to conclude that the biggest change seen in Scotland in this period of outward political transition was not political at all but social – and essentially regressive. The decline of heavy industry threw into sharp relief the absence of any meaningful role in life for a huge proportion of Scotland's men. The kind of jobs which many aspired to fill no longer existed thanks to de-industrialisation. For Sir Harry Burns, Scotland's chief medical officer, Scotland's history of economic and social disruption – and the consequent stress upon its populace – help to account for the psychological negativity that impacts on health and behaviour: 'Scotland never replaced the steel works and we have now had 50-60 years' worth of that – three generations of people who have not expected to be employed.' [5]

Speaking in 2009, he referred to the 'the Scottish effect'; a poisonous cocktail of economic and childhood turmoil that has been felt worse in parts of Scotland, such as Glasgow, than other parts of the UK. 'You had a hopelessness pervading the community. . . It was visible in the poor parenting skills of many mothers and fathers,' he said.[6]

Conventional families had not always been a bulwark against social breakdown. But half-a-century of evidence would arguably show that they had performed a stabilising role far more effectively than the looser partnerships legitimised by market forces and consumerism and also by the state in the way it organised the tax and welfare system. Women appeared to benefit from the greater individualism underpinned by state efforts to narrow the gender wage differential. But it was middle-class and better-educated women who were really best-placed to seize the new opportunities. In the absence of social restraints, and still facing educational and other disadvantages, growing numbers of girls from lower-income families made bad life choices. Unless it is assumed that individuals are manipulated at all stages by powerful institutions and social forces, the statistics for women's health and well-being in Scotland arguably make this a tenable claim.

The message from the media and market forces was that young people should go out and fulfil their material and emotional wants. Increasingly, in working-class communities there were no countervailing balances encouraging restraint, a longer-term perspective and wider social concerns. Poverty might no longer stalk the new communities hastily erected by urban planners but they were often soulless places. People with traditional values, such as the Christian clergy, found it hard for their voices to count unless the priest or minister possessed remarkable dedication like the Rev. John Miller who worked for many years in Glasgow's Castlemilk from the start of the 1970s.[7] Young people often lacked any secure anchor in family, education, or faith. But they were encouraged to assert their ego, sometimes in distinctly edgy and destructive ways. This increased the already worrying level of inter-personal violence with knives being reinforced by guns as weapons that were in increasing use.[8]

By 2011, the murder rate per 100,000 people for Scotland was 2.34 compared to a figure in England and Wales of 1.35. Ten of America's 50 states actually had a lower murder rate than Scotland despite the wide availability of firearms in the US.[9]

Men without a purpose had contributed to a series of ferocious wars occurring in the Balkans during the 1990s, after the collapse of communism led to a chronic shortage of jobs. The Irish demographer and social forecaster Gerard O'Neill argues that 'no civilised society can survive without the engagement and commitment and support of its young men'.[10]

Such a view is almost unheard of in Scotland. At conferences and fringe meetings on the future priorities of a devolved Scotland, it was usually young professional women (never men from any class) who boldly insisted that the process would be a sham unless it allowed Scottish womanhood to fulfil itself. Such advocacy led to the Labour Party ensuring that half of its MSPs (members of the Scottish Parliament) would be women. They were nominated for eligible positions on the candidate lists by small caucuses and many came from the state bureaucracy and quangos. Arguably, the limited amount of political talent to be found among women recruited through such a narrow selection process did not advance the feminist cause in Scotland. But even given knowledge about the social realities for inactive men in downscale communities, there was no equivalent demand for men to be fast-tracked into Holyrood. Gender gaps that are to the detriment of men, such as higher levels of unemployment, imprisonment, suicide, as well as the greater likelihood to be victims of violent crime, are played down by the media. In Scotland, more than elsewhere, its 'high end' is under the strong influence of columnists with a feminist world view.

Men also die younger and the proportion doing well in higher education is in fast decline. O'Neill provocatively remarked: 'many feminists talk about the glass ceiling, while conveniently ignoring the glass cellar that traps their brothers, fathers, sons and husbands. . . A Western culture sadly afflicted in the past by misogyny – the hatred of women – has now become one afflicted by a strident culture of misandry – the hatred of men. Both equally intolerable.' [11]

The Orange Order, with its annual marches in Lowland Scotland's urban centres, continued to defy fashion and assert a male working-class and Protestant presence. Its numbers were in decline but it continued to have staying power that was not bound up with events in Ulster. A loyalist sub-culture persisted in parts of Scotland long after the ending of the undeclared civil-war in Ulster during the mid-1990s. In April 2013, when banning a landlord from being in charge of a pub for five years, licensing chiefs in Ayrshire expressed dismay at 'the widespread and serious disorders' that had ensued when he held a 'Sash Bash' in Dalmellington attended by over a hundred people. [12]

Distrust of Roman Catholicism and its religious dimension, merging with the need to defend Reformation principles, still provided the official justification for the Orange Order's existence. But its colourful processions were the antithesis of Reformation austerity and it brought colour into plain lives. These public affirmations of faith and patriotism were seen as increasingly archaic and also offensive not just to Catholics but to secular liberals uncomfortable with overt quasi-religious displays. However, the Order was in tune with an age when people were encouraged to assert whatever their collective identity was.

Crude onslaughts on Catholicism may have remained a staple for some speakers at Orange parades but they were increasingly absent from the Orange press in Scotland. The Order increasingly emphasises its political role as a custodian of the British link.[13] In March 2007, tens of thousands of Orange men and women marched down the Royal Mile to Holyrood palace to commemorate the 300th anniversary of the Act of Union. Ever since the SNP took charge of the Scottish government in 2007, there has been energetic campaigning designed to prevent the SNP taking Scotland into a post-British future. The pages of its magazine, the *Orange Torch*, have witnessed some of the most biting criticism of Alex Salmond and his movement seen anywhere in the Scottish media, and in 2012, it hardly came as a surprise when Orange figures started to warn of government plans to legislate against Orange parades. The justice minister when asked specifically about the cost of policing Orange parades by Humza Yousuf MSP, indicated that he thought action against them was overdue.[14] He indicated that their presence was disruptive in contrast to 'innocuous' bodies like the Boys Brigade. Orange marshals had already been trained to enable the police presence at regular summer rallies to be scaled down.

But arguably the Order's high-profile in parts of the year is a challenge to the SNP's desire to establish its own public ascendancy in Scotland. The removal of the Union Flag from the iconic Belfast City hall led to weeks of disturbances in the winter of 2012-13 and resistance to any attempts to banish the Order from Scottish streets is likely to go all the way to the human rights court in Strasbourg. If Orangesim faces restrictions as the 2014 referendum approaches which are not ones that bear down on gay rights or pro-environment protesters, it could well provoke bitter controversy and even street-level tensions. [15]

A West of Scotland Catholic identity steeped in Irish traditions could be expressed more openly in the absence of violence in nearby Ulster in the name of a united Ireland. But there was still plenty of opposition to weaving distinctive Irish immigrant threads in the composite Scottish national tartan. Catholics continued to be identified by the schools that they mainly attended, and by often possessing Irish names or being Celtic supporters. Education inspectors have been unable to detect evidence that the schools inculcate a sectarian outlook despite their existence continuing to be a sore point in parts of the Scottish media. But they do promote a religious ethos which is bound to cause difficulties in a country where the drive towards uniformity (now secular in dimension) has always been a strong one.

Arnold Kemp, who edited the *Herald* during one of its most creative phases, noticed a keen interest in his religious affiliation after he moved from Edinburgh to Glasgow to be editor in the 1980s. He assumed that this interest in his ethnic origins was far from being an idle matter.[16] The accumulation of such information in the work context could be put to harmful use. Dr. Patricia Walls who, in the early 2000s, carried out numerous in-depth interviews across the communal spectrum partly in order to assess how separate identities could give rise to opposing attitudes and discriminatory practices, included one which revealed that self-identifying on religious grounds could also be a middle-class phenomenon.

A Glasgow Catholic related the experience of his Edinburgh-based daughter upon briefly returning to the city: '. . . my daughter had a very high-powered job and she. . . lives in Edinburgh. . . she had to come to Glasgow to see one of the senior management of the company and when she walked into his rather palatial office he came forward and said, ah Miss . . . pleased to meet you. . . that's not a Scottish name. She said, No it's Irish and Catholic. Now can we get on with business please? She was very angry because. . . [in] Edinburgh you don't get this nearly so much and she thought she had left it all behind.' [17]

Given the extent of religious identification in the West of Scotland, Walls wrote that 'leaving all that behind was something that was not within the power' of this management high-flyer and Catholic.'[18] Customarily, Catholics had not usually actively resisted slights or attacks in the workplace nor had their church counselled a robust response. Toughness and self-belief was often needed in order to scale the career heights.

The renowned historian Tom Devine is an example of a Lanarkshire Catholic very comfortable in his own skin who has not hesitated to complain if he feels that he has been denied the recognition that he deserves. In 2008 he assailed BBC Scotland for overlooking him in favour of Neil Oliver as the presenter for the ambitious 'History of Scotland' series shown in 2009.

Oliver, he complained, was a 'hapless long-haired presenter. . . physically in the old visual tradition of Braveheart and the Highlander movies,' to which Oliver responded: 'I could not be less interested in what a plump old man thinks about my physical appearance.' When fellow historian Christopher Harvie defended Oliver because of his excellent camera technique and other skills, Devine's response was a revealing indication that the competition over limited opportunities and resources (one that has intensified and prolonged sectarianism), certainly also existed in other dimensions of Scottish life:

> 'this series is about the post-1600 period, about which I have written 27 books and more than 100 academic articles covering the whole gamut of Scottish history. So it's extremely sad that Chris is questioning my credentials. Very sad and very Scottish.

'Scottish history is a snake-pit. . . The academic community is relatively small and people here in general are passionate about history. But there are a lot of Scots in their forties, fifties and sixties who are historically illiterate. It's not their fault but down to the failings of our school system. What angers me is that the BBC had a golden opportunity to address that educational deficit in a proper way. Why do they dumb down these things? Why can't they have heavyweights discussing heavyweight issues?' [19]

Unless they are unabashed extroverts like Billy Connolly, upwardly mobile members of West of Scotland's still most visible minority often prefer to play down their ethnic identity. A good case in point is the cultural bureaucrat James Boyle. He was a product of Holyrood school in Glasgow's Govanhill who became controller of BBC Radio 4, acquiring the reputation of being the most faithful executor of the will of John Birt, the Director-general who moved it in a free market and highly managerial direction in the 1990s.[20] He is perhaps the most influential arts administrator Scotland has produced in recent times. Now back in Edinburgh, his range of talents have enabled him to become head of the National Library of Scotland, but his otherwise comprehensive *Who's Who* entry gives no clue about his education before going to university. By contrast, Patrick Bosco McFadden, the Labour MP for Wolverhampton South-East and a member of the Privy Council appears proud to emphasise his attendance at a Catholic school which parents from Catholic and non-Catholic backgrounds across southern Glasgow remain anxious to enrol their children in. [21]

Writing in 2005, at a time of distancing from Catholic symbols and practices, the sociologist Patricia Walls, believed that: 'For Catholics, adherence to Catholic schooling may actually prove beneficial to health and a source of social capital'. She went on to claim: 'Attending Mass, and attending Celtic games, may likewise nurture the "trust, norms and networks" from which social capital emerges.' She further wrote:

'Those Catholics who retain links with identified sections of the Catholic community, having greater involvement in wider social networks, deemed crucial for good health. . . and more access therefore to social capital. . . may have an advantage over those without close links with the church, schooling and even football, over time. Being integrated into the Catholic community may offer social support which may remove the effect of other vulnerability to stressful life events. . .'[22]

For many Catholics, discrimination was unavoidably part of the stress and disappointment of life. Kevin McKenna, a veteran journalist (who had flourished in the Scottish media world), believed that after doing a *vox pop* of Celtic supporters following the 2012 liquidation of Rangers, the almost unanimous sense of pleasure at the event sprang from a feeling that the club symbolised their victimisation:

> 'Almost to a man and woman, they would have no qualms if Rangers FC were to go to the wall. To them, this is an opportunity of exacting a terrible cultural revenge for what they see as a century of being treated as second-class citizens in their own country.'[23]

As late as the 1970s, even in the absence of residential segregation, encounters between Protestants and Catholics could be as rare as those from people at opposite ends of the class divide. The Glaswegian comedian Frankie Boyle recalled:

> 'getting my tonsils out when I was a wee lad and I made friends with a Protestant boy on my ward. . . When my dad asked me what I'd done in hospital I said, "I spoke to a "Protestant". It just seemed much stranger than anything else that had happened.'[234]

The perception of continuing tensions underneath the surface were confirmed in survey data. In a 1997 study of electoral behaviour, younger people were far more likely to think conflict is serious than older people (53per cent compared with 30per cent).[25] In a first for a Scottish newspaper, the *Herald*, on 3 September 1999, published the findings a poll to test Scottish perceptions about the staying power of religious divisions. Interestingly, it was in the small communities and towns surrounding Glasgow and Edinburgh, that the highest incidence of those agreeing strongly with the persistence of tensions (20per cent) were to be found, compared with 14per cent in Glasgow itself.[26]

Entry into middle-class occupations, including those in the public sector did not necessarily mean that communal attitudes were being left behind. The BBC in Scotland has been accused of an anti-Catholic hiring policy by a veteran chronicler of Celtic football club's fortunes, Tom Campbell. He has written that the Sports department, under Peter Thomson's leadership in the 1970s, was an obvious example.[27] He has also written that Celtic's then manager, Jock Stein, made little attempt to hide his contempt for Thomson and his cronies and they frequently became targets for his biting wit: Thomson was instantly dubbed Blue Peter.

Campbell goes on to write that as 'a Lanarkshire man and a Protestant', Jock Stein, Celtic's manager, 'had a personal knowledge of the subject and was not shy about expressing it.' When he asked a later BBC Scotland sports chief, Archie Macpherson about how many Celtic supporters – or Catholics – worked for the BBC, his response as described in his memoir *Action Replays* was: 'I don't know anybody's religion'. MacPherson wrote that this was 'the stock answer' and it 'was a mistake. He laughed in disbelief and I remember he turned away and waved at me dismissively: "all right, I [MacPherson] added. I suppose none at a guess".' [28]

Suspected in different quarters because of their non-Scottish traditions and loyalties, Catholics with an Irish awareness channelled their identity through a footballing institution. Celtic had long been a surrogate Irish world, the club functioning as a socialising agent for a unique form of Irish cultural activity. The remark of the revered Celtic player and manager, Tommy Burns that 'When you are playing for Celtic, you are playing for a cause and a people' resonated deeply with many people.[29]

Placed in an enclave partly due to their own choice and the reaction of the elite in a conformist country to their presence, the expression of anti-establishment values came easily to hardcore Celtic supporters. It was sharply on display than during 'the Poppy controversy'. Uproar ensued when, in November 2010, a group of hardcore Celtic supporters belonging to 'the Green Brigade' displayed a banner at the home ground denouncing the poppy symbol being displayed on players' jerseys during remembrance weekend. The banner read: 'Your deeds would shame all the devils in hell. Ireland, Iraq, Afghanistan. No bloodstained poppy on our hoops.' The majority of Celtic fans distanced themselves from the poppy protesters and many online forums spoke of disgust at an extreme faction bringing 'shame upon the club'.[30]

The journalist and politician, Brian Wilson believes that Celtic's 1967 European Cup victory was the catalyst for broadening its base and acquiring some non-Catholic support; he didn't know any Celtic supporters in sedate Dunoon where he grew up but that later changed. [31]

Celtic managed to be framed more sympathetically in the broader media than Rangers. But the club faced impending disaster, at the start of the 1990s, after a long run of indifferent results. It was left with only 8,000 season ticket holders and when, in 1993, the Bank of Scotland refused to extend it credit, bankruptcy loomed. Fergus McCann, a shrewd, taciturn businessman known for his trademark cap, which gave him the nickname 'the bunnet', then appeared on the scene. He acquired control of Celtic in 1994 when it was £9 million in debt. He spent £41 million rebuilding the stadium at Parkhead and opening the club up to a massive share option, largely taken up by the Celtic fans themselves. The club had 53,000 season ticket holders when he sold up in 1999. He made a tidy profit but he had taken a considerable risk, spending £40 million on new players and left the club in a robust condition.[32]

This tourism entrepreneur was the son of the headmaster of a Catholic school. But he was ready to break with tradition by banning priests and nuns from collecting charity funds outside Parkhead. [33] He had a collision with Archbishop Winning who had a 'perception of the club as a secular extension of the institution to which he had given his life: the Catholic Church'.[34] This was over the Celtic owner's plans to hold weddings over the centre-spot at the club's ground. McCann was told by the archbishop that 'the only suitable place for a Celtic fan, and by his definition, a Catholic, was at the altar of a Catholic Church' but the Celtic's boss was unmoved.

He was also prepared to crack down on pro-IRA songs at away matches: 'Those songs are anti-Scottish, they have no connection with football. . . This is not a political organisation.' It was therefore no surprise that in 1996 Celtic were quick off the mark in trying to check expressions of sectarianism in its own ranks. The 'Bhoys Against Bigotry' campaign, was launched followed by 'Youth Against Bigotry' which, according to the then chief executive was meant to 'educate the young on having. . . respect for all aspects of the community – all races, colours, all creeds.' [35] By 2003, Rangers had launched its own anti-sectarian initiative.

Rangers had also faced mounting financial adversity at the time that Celtic had its near-death experience, but its day-of-reckoning was postponed due, in part, to the higher standing that it enjoyed within the Scottish establishment. The club entered a new era when Sir David Murray, whose fortune derived from property and metals, bought Rangers for £6 million in 1988. The Bank of Scotland was prepared to pump very big loans and additional equity into businesses which were facing severe adversity.[36] This enabled Murray to pursue an ambitious policy of expensive player signings so that Rangers could establish its supremacy in Scottish football which it did for a while. At one stage, the club had more Catholic players than Celtic because on the eve of the Murray era, the club sensibly ditched its Protestant-only signing policy. Club scouts wedded to this policy had missed out on impressive players like Kenny Dalglish and Danny McGrain. They were thought, wrongly, to be Catholics and went on to have outstanding careers at Celtic. [37] The club was prepared to repudiate some of the traditions that resonated with intransigent fans. In no small degree, this was due to the outlook of Graeme Souness, club manager from 1986 to1991.The Edinburgh born player-manager stated in 2009: 'Every manager politically would say yes (about signing a Catholic) but I actually meant it. I was married to a Catholic, my children were christened Catholics.' [38]

Relations between the rival clubs at management level were usually constructive ones not least because they both had a vested interest in ensuring their dominance over the rest of the footballing world in Scotland. Therefore it did not seem so unusual for insiders when, on 16 May 2008, Walter Smith, who succeeded Souness as manager, arrived at Celtic park to lay a wreath in honour of Tommy Burns, a Celtic player and the club's manager who was widely admired across football and had just died from skin cancer.[39]

But such expressions of mutual respect were dwarfed by ferocious rivalry and also suspicion – especially on the part of Celtic's following – about the even-handedness of match officials presiding over, and journalists reporting on, Old Firm duels. In 1999, Celtic actually suggested to the Scottish Football Association (SFA) that the referee Hugh Dallas should not be considered for the last Old Firm league fixture of that season. He has entered into the demonology of the Celtic faithful as possibly no

Rangers player or official has ever done for controversial refereeing decisions. At an Old Firm match in May 1999, after outrage was caused by his awarding of a penalty to Rangers, he was injured by coins throws from the stand and narrowly avoided assault from Celtic fans who invaded the pitch.[40]

Scottish journalists are usually sheltered from the fans' fury but they have been chastised by commentators supportive of Celtic for periodically complaining that the club has a vested interest in sectarianism or is 'too Irish' and therefore unwilling to back the Scotland national squad (the last claim having a strong basis in fact where many supporters are concerned).[41]

Before the twentieth century had ended, Dennis Sewell a BBC journalist in London, noted the readiness of the Scottish media to insist that 'there is little to choose between the two sides of the sectarian divide'. He warned in 2001 that unless it begins 'to recognise the level of provocation emanating from one particular quarter, they are in danger of perpetuating an unconscious, institutionalised bigotry of their own.'[42]

Correspondence with a senior BBC Scotland administrator in 2011-12 about the limited coverage of Scots of Irish Catholic background and descent produced a defiant reaction about the broadcaster's treatment of 'sectarian matters'. The official refuted claims that BBC Scotland has 'marginalised' Lowland Scots of Irish ancestry but was only able to refer to three full-length programme initiatives in a period spanning over three decades. [43] The official was prepared to stand by all BBC staff across departments and their treatment of communal tensions whereas a less embattled media manager might have been prepared to concede that there had been variations in quality, consistency and representativeness, welcoming stimulus from outside in order to boost the quality of coverage of a sensitive dimension of Scottish life.

It was not investigative reporting by the BBC but sporadic murderous violence which shone a light on the persistence of Scotland's sectarian demons. In 1996, Jason Campbell was convicted of the unprovoked murder of sixteen-year-old Mark Scott who was wearing a Celtic jersey although covered by a jacket when he met a terrible end following an Old Firm match at Parkhead in 1995:

'According to witnesses at the scene, at approximately half-past-five
on the afternoon of 7 October 1995, a man rushed up to behind
Mark, seizing him by the head with one hand, and with the other
drawing a knife across his throat with such vehemence that it cut
clean though the flesh as far as the spine. Mark staggered, spurting
blood, for more than twenty-five yards before he collapsed. Dozens
of people looked on, but no one tried to catch his assailant.' [44]

Despite witnesses being able to identify the killer, 'the jury took. . . an
unconscionably long time in their deliberations and had to be sequestered
for a night in a hotel before reaching a guilty verdict.'[45]

The killer's father, Colin and uncle, William had been jailed for life in
1979 for blowing up two Irish pubs in Glasgow which were full of people
on a Saturday night.[46] He applied to be transferred to the Maze prison in
Belfast, his lawyers arguing that he was entitled to be viewed as a political
prisoner. Remarkably, Scottish ministers, including Henry McLeish, then
minister for prisons indicated that they were considering his transfer.
Arguably it was an insensitive gesture that revealed a weary tolerance of
the acceptance of sectarian behaviour in Scotland. The sociologist Elinor
Kelly has written:

'On the streets, in football crowds, and within communities,
Campbell's status was enhanced, because he came close to
achieving the status he sought – loyalist icon within Scotland.'[47]

A close friend of Jason Campbell's, Thomas Longstaff, mimicked his
crime, in November 1996. On the same street in Bridgeton, he attacked
Sean O'Connor, a student supporter of Celtic who survived and was able
to give evidence in the subsequent trial. Longstaff was defended by Donald
Findlay, the lawyer who had led Campbell's defence. Findlay took great
pride in his position as Vice-Chair of the Rangers and in both trials, he led
the court into focusing on the 'mindlessness' of the act rather than on any
sectarian context.[48]

With nine Catholic civic leaders (Lord Provosts) in a row Glasgow was
seen as leading the way in integration at the top of its civic life. But there
was not much desire to emulate the comprehensive anti-discrimination
legislation being introduced in Northern Ireland in order to try and

consolidate the peace process. Glasgow Council race equality officers were not allowed to deal with sectarian issues, at least for much of the 1990s.[49] This was despite the fact that, in a 2003 survey commissioned by the city council, perceptions of ongoing sectarianism were found to be high and one-quarter believed it influenced job decisions in employment.[50]

Displays of public antagonism persisted that often had a religious dimension. In 1990, Glasgow's Catholic archbishop was ambushed during an ecumenical initiative in Perth. He had been invited to preach at St. John's in the city. For four centuries it had been a Catholic church until John Knox had invaded its pulpit to deliver a sermon against idolatory. He incited a mob to desecrate the sanctuary before it went on a rampage through the town. Such a fierce event made it an appropriate venue for a service of reconciliation. But as Winning was about to deliver his message of Christian fraternity, Pastor Jack Glass appeared. He 'flung down thirty pieces of silver for the Judases who had allowed an agent of the anti-Christ across the threshold of a Protestant church. Then he smashed a plaster bust of Pope John XXIII on the ancient flagstones. He was hustled out and decorum briefly restored. But as the *Daily Express* related: the service was all but ruined thanks to protesters planted among the congregation who rose up, shouting the Pope was the anti-Christ and Thomas Winning a wicked blasphemer.' [51]

In Glasgow itself, several Catholic churches have been subjected to regular physical attack. Twenty years after Glass's protest, the Sacred Heart of Jesus church in Bridgeton had original leaded windows smashed and a commemorative stained-glass window shot with airgun pellets. The attack came less than a week after the church marked its centenary with a Mass celebrated by Mario Conti, Archbishop of Glasgow. Fr. Stephen Dunn, the parish priest said Catholics, including himself, had experienced many problems in previous years.[52]

When territorial tensions surfaced in 2001, the international dimension brought embarrassment for Scotland, leading BBC journalist Fergal Keane to depict the country as 'a place where bigots can win the day'. Ireland's Prime Minister Bertie Ahern was due to visit a shrine to the victims of the Irish famine at the Carfin grotto in Lanarkshire; that is until the local MP, Labour's Frank Roy wrote 'trenchantly' (the word used by an Irish diplomat), urging him to stay away, stating that his presence might inflame sectarian tensions and provoke violence (a view not shared by Strathclyde police). Keane wrote: 'The logic of what Mr Roy has said is that Bertie Ahern's Irishness and his Catholicism would cause certain elements in his constituency to make trouble... So what does a brave politician do in such circumstances? You might think he stands up to the bigots... well actually no. The politician in this case issues dire warnings and embarrasses the Scottish executive' (which was then led by Henry McLeish).[53]

One year later, at least the Church of Scotland was prepared to peer into its collective soul and disown its own unworthy brush with sectarianism before 1945. In 2002, a report of the Church and Nation committee was approved by the General Assembly (part of which read):

> 'Sectarianism is not someone else's problem. In the years around the Great Depression of the early thirties of last century, the Church and Nation Committee campaigned intemperately against Irish immigration into Scotland. From a current perspective it is a matter of regret that the Committee and the Church should have taken such a position.
>
> '... we have to recognise that a demon in our society has been acknowledged and brought into the open... we are aware that the Orange Order is widely perceived to be a sectarian organisation ... We believe that those within the Church who associate themselves with the Order should reflect upon this and take this to heart.' [54]

But by 2011 it was clear that the momentum behind the replication of sectarianism was not down to any single body. In 2011, Charity Action for Children carried out a survey among 14 to 20-year-olds, across the West of Scotland. It showed that young people acknowledged its hold on parts of society. [55] A third of the sample said they had felt its effects and two-thirds believed it was not confined to football. Upbringing, and not religious belief, were seen by these youngsters as the main impetus behind its transmission across generations. 47% believed that tougher sentences will not bring an end to sectarianism, and to other forms of hatred in Scotland and placed an emphasis instead on education programmes in schools about sectarianism, different kinds of punishments and the greater use of football banning orders. The survey found most young people thought sectarianism was getting worse, and that it led to violence and knife crime. 36% had been treated badly or unfairly because of sectarianism, or some other form of hatred, and almost twice as many knew someone else who had been a victim of sectarianism. These were bleak figures which run counter to the established wisdom in academia about the prevalence of what James MacMillan had dubbed 'Scotland's Shame'.

NOTES

1 Philip Blond, *Red Tory*, London: Faber 2010, p. 115

2 McGinty, *The Turbulent Priest* p. 202; for the Church's role as a service provider, especially in the welfare sector, see Peter Lynch, 'Catholics, the Catholic Church and Political Action in Scotland' in Raymond Boyle and Peter Lynch Eds.), *Out of the Ghetto?: The Catholic Community in Modern Scotland*, John Donald, Edinbrurgh 1998, p. 47.

3 David Marquand, *Britain Since 1918: The Strange Career of British Democracy*, London: Weidenfeld & Nicholson, 2008, p. 336.

4 See Tom Gallagher, *The Illusion of Freedom: Scotland Under Nationalism*, London: Hurst & co 2009, from chapter 5 onwards.

5 Eddie Barnes, 'Harry Burns: 'Properly functioning families are the key to making Scotland healthier' *Scotsman*, 19 December 2009

6 Barnes, 'Harry Burns'.

7 See 'The poor look after each other', *The Herald*, 21 February 2007; also 'A man of God and the people', 7 July 2007.

8 See Carol Craig, *The Tears That Made the Clyde*, Argyll Publishing, Glendaruel 2011, especially chapter 14.

9 Richard Carey, *Libertarian Home*, 22 December 2012

10 Gerard O'Neill, 'The Future of Marriage', *Turbulence Ahead*, 4 March 2012, www.turbulenceahead.com

11 O'Neill, 'The Future of Marriage'.

12 *The Sun* 26 April 2013.

13 Interview with Ian Wilson, 23 July 2012.

14 BBC News, 28 June 2012 .

15 For long-term ties between Ulster and Scotland, see Graham Walker, *Intimate Strangers*, Edinburgh: John Donald. 1995; and Ian S. Wood (ed),

Scotland and Ulster, Edinburgh: Mercat Press, 1995.

16 See James MacMillan,' Scotland's Shame' in T.C. Devine, *Scotland's Shame*, Edinburgh: Mainstream, 2000, p. 20

17 Patricia Walls, 'The health of Irish-descended Catholics' in *Glasgow: A qualitative study of the links between health risk and religious and ethnic identities*, Ph.D, University of Glasgow, 2005, p. 182

18 Walls, 'The health of Irish-descended Catholics', p. 269.

19 Rob Brown, 'Blood spilled on historic battlefield', *Scotland on Sunday*, 29 November 2009.

20 Michael Vestey, 'Boyle's legacy', *Spectator*, 29 January 2000.

21 In January 2013 Holyrood secondary school confirmed James Boyle's attendance as a pupil.'

22 Walls, 'The health of Irish-descended Catholics', p. 195.

23 Kevin McKenna, 'Don't be too quick to gloat at the plight of Rangers', *Observer*, 19 February 2012.

24 Frankie Boyle, *My Shit Life So Far*, London: Harper Collins 2009, p. 21.

25 Michael Rosie and David McCrone, 'The Past is History: Catholics in Modern Scotland', in T.M.Devine, *Scotland's Shame: Bigotry and Sectarianism in Modern Scotland*, Edinburgh: Mainstream, 2000, p. 205.

26 Tom Gallagher, 'Holding a Mirror to Scotia's Face', in Devine, *Scotland's Shame*, p.p. 46-7.

27 Tom Campbell, *Celtic's paranoia. . . all in the mind*, Fort Publishing, Ayr 2004, p. 191.

28 Campbell, *Celtic's paranoia*, p. 192.

29 James MacMillan in Richard Purden, *We Are Celtic Supporters*, London: Hachette Scotland, 2012, p. 16.

30 See James MacMillan, 'Celtic fans need to ditch their shady, pro-terrorist sympathies and return to their Catholic roots', *Daily Telegraph*, 26 August 2010.

31 Harry Reid, *Outside verdict: An Old Kirk in a New Scotland*, Edinburgh: Saint Andrew's Press, 2002, p. 128.

32 Andrew O'Hagan, 'The final whistle for God's squad?', *Guardian*, 27 February 1999.

33 'Rangers: is this the end of Scottish sectarianism?' *Catholic Truth*, 15 February 2012, www.Catholictruthscotland.com

34 Stephen McGinty, 'Winning ways are over in Paradise', *Scotsman*, 10 March 2011.

35 Brian McGuirk, *Celtic FC, The Ireland Connection*, Black and White, Edinburgh 2009, p. 89.

36 Alf Young: 'Funny business of a football club', *Scotsman*, 18 February 2012.

37 *Daily Record*, 3 August 1999.

38 *Daily Record*, 7 July 2009.

39 *Daily Mail* 21 May 2008.

40 See Campbell, *Celtic's paranoia*, p.p. 171-2, 159-60.

41 Dennis Sewell, *Catholics*, London: Penguin 2001, p. 120; Bradley, *Ethnic and Religious Identity*, p.p. 45-6, note 31.

42 Sewell, *Catholics*, p. 129.

43 Private correspondence.

44 Sewell, *Catholics*, p.118.

45 Sewell, *Catholics*, p. 118.

46 *The Herald*, 28 May 2011.

47 Elinor Kelly, Challenging Sectarianism in Scotland: the prism of racism', *Scottish Affairs*, no 42, winter 2003, p.8.

48 Kelly, 'Challenging Sectarianism', p.9.

49 Walls, 'The health of Irish-descended Catholics', p. 218, quoting Hickman and Bronwen Walter, *Discrimination and the Irish Community in Britain: A Report of Research Undertaken for the Commission for Racial Equality*, Commission for Racial Equality, London 1997.

50 Nil by Mouth, *Newsletter* 2, Spring 2003.

51 Donald Stewart, 'Glass shatters week of unity for the church', *Daily Express*, 22 January 1990.

52 Cate Devine, 'Fury over sectarian vandalism at church', *Evening Times*, 19 Jun 2010

53 Fergal Keane, 'The bigotry that still beats in the heart of Scotland', *Independent*, 10 February 2001

54 Kelly, 'Challenging Sectarianism', p. 7; the most detailed account of the Presbyterian campaign against first Irish immigration and later attempts to encourage the marginalisaton of the Irish community can be found in S.J.Brown, 'The Scottish Presbyterian Churches and Irish Immigration, 1922-1938', *Innes Review*, vl. 42, 1991, .p.21-45.

55 Stewart Paterson, 'Divided we fall', *Evening Times*, 28 September 2011.

CHAPTER 8

Scotland's Shame? What Shame!

IT WAS AGAINST a background of sporadic sectarian killings, and continuing assertions that Catholics were engaged in a rapid process of integration and were thus no longer discriminated against, that James MacMillan, a 40 year old Catholic from Kilwinning in Ayrshire, delivered a keynote address at the start of the Edinburgh Festival on 9 August 1999. He challenged some well-worn assumptions. His reputation as Scotland's most prominent composer gave him such a sought-after platform. In a lecture entitled 'Scotland's Shame', he described his native land as 'Northern Ireland without the guns and bullets' and sought to explain why he thought ongoing anti-Catholic bigotry was hampering Scotland's ability to evolve into a modern nation.[1]

His unsettling portrayal of contemporary social realities made it easy to dismiss him as an obsessive which could well have proven to be his fate but for his renown as a composer. His analysis was a challenge to the near-orthodoxy, as defended by Professor Steve Bruce, a sociologist at Queens University, Belfast and later the University of Aberdeen that inter-marriage was rapidly bringing about assimilation and, were it not for Catholic schools, little or nothing would now distinguish the descendants of the Irish from native Scots.[2] An academic rival, Professor Tom Devine would also in time draw closer to the Bruce perspective by arguing that structural discrimination was disappearing, leaving behind it the attitudinal variety.[3]

As recently as February 2005, both men had debated the issue in public at the University of Aberdeen, Bruce denying the existence of systematic discrimination and Devine insisting that sectarianism remained a trouble-some issue. [4] Ironically, public disagreement among academics on the subject has been more forcefully expressed than between traditional foes like the Catholic church and the Orange Order. One Orangemen who at the time was Grand Master of the Scottish institution expressed the hope that, one day, someone like Archbishop Mario Conti could stand in Glasgow's George Square and review an Orange parade.[5] But it is hard to see such common ground emerging among academics where the struggle to buttress reputations as authorities on the subject and acquire funds for research programmes can appear all-consuming.

As well as a survey by the *Herald* which indicated widespread perceptions that sectarianism was a continuing problem, MacMillan's address prompted Catholic professionals to publicly relate some of their experiences. Joseph Beltrami, a leading Glasgow solicitor, described in the *Daily Record* how:

> 'When I started in the law in 1950, I was sent to about 30 firms for interviews for the apprenticeship.
>
> 'I was late in starting my apprenticeship because of the difficulties I had. You would go to a firm and they would take your particulars, ask you which school you were at and then you would hear nothing.
>
> 'I was naive and didn't think of bigotry. No one wrote back telling me I was not starting with them. I was constantly knocked back without any reason being given and I did, eventually realise what was happening. . .' [6]

More than a generation later Brian Fitzpatrick, who worked closely with Donald Dewar in the initial stages of the Holyrood Parliament, described a situation that had not fundamentally changed:

> 'As a young would-be lawyer it raised its head in having umpteen applications for interview declined while less provocatively surnamed and less qualified contemporaries clocked up interviews with blue-chip firms in Glasgow and Edinburgh. It is no surprise that the Scottish Bar, where advocacy and brains now mostly outrank connections, is home to a disproportionate number of advocates with Irish ancestry, in marked contrast to those same blue chip solicitors' firms.' [7]

In response to a 2011 article in the *Guardian* entitled 'Scottish sectarianism? Let's lay this myth to rest', in which Steve Bruce argued that Scotland was disgraced not by bigotry itself but by the unthinking way that its existence was assumed, an architect sought to counter his argument 'with a little realism':

'I am a 40 year old, professional architect. I was born and raised a Catholic in Cambuslang, Rutherglen, and . . . in order to counter Mr Bruce's argument. . . I'd like to reflect on a few key 'myth-like' moments in my life:

'1. 1982. I'm 12 years old. I'm doing a paper round, as we all did in those days, and because it's a Sunday I started a bit later than we usually would. It's now 11am and I pop up a close to deliver papers and when I hit the road outside I walk into an Orange Walk procession. I've made the heinous crime of wearing a Celtic shirt and I am spat upon, beer cans are thrown at me and I hear, for the first time, that 'I'm a dirty fenian bastard', and this from people in suits and bowler hats. I run home in tears.

'Is this myth?

'2. 1988. I'm doing my Highers. An independent careers adviser interviews me.

'I'm told, without irony, that I should never consider banking, accountancy, or the police as a career as we know "as a Catholic you'll just never get in".

'This is fact.

'When I express an interest in architecture, my career adviser expresses, without irony, "you may have a chance there, I don't know", that's not on our 'can't do' list".

'Is this 'Myth?

'3. 1994. upon graduation, I have an interview with a large and very successful architect's practice in Glasgow. I get the job – so happy days.

'One Monday, 3 weeks later, I walk in and express delight at Celtic winning that weekend. There's a deathly silence and I am actually summoned to the boss's office.

'He's outraged: "Whit? You're a fukkin Fenian?"

'I explained that, indeed, I was a Catholic.

'My boss explained, without shame, that "I would never have hired you if I'd known you were a Fenian" and expressed shock that I slipped through the cracks. It transpired I only ever had the opportunity of an interview because I attended a school called

'Trinity', as opposed one with the prefix of 'St' whatever.

'My boss was disgusted, and I knew that, because of my Catholicism, I had no place there. Let me remind you that this was in 1994. That's not that long ago.

'Again is this story 'myth'?

'Mr Bruce, I left Scotland soon after to escape this nonsense, and I've never come home again. You describe modern sectarianism as a myth – perhaps a convenient crutch for us troublesome types? You fail to recognise it's still going on. I left Scotland in 1995, 6 months after discovering I was indeed a "fenian bastard" and had, as such, no future in such an "enlightened" society as Scotland. I now live half a world away from Glasgow, and friends here just cannot comprehend these stories.' [8]

In 2013, when sections of the Scottish media had rounded on Peter Kearney, the head of the Scottish Catholic media office, for also allegedly exaggerating the issue, an MSP spoke up about the continuing realities of sectarianism and how it had impeded him. The journalist Judith Duffy relates:

'The idea of refusing to be in the same room as a colleague because they are Catholic seems outrageous in the modern workplace.

'But Labour MSP Michael McMahon, who grew up in Lanarkshire and worked for over a decade as a welder from the late 1970s, cites it as an example of the bigotry he once faced because of his faith. He said: "When I worked in a factory the personnel manager wouldn't attend meetings I was taking part in, because he didn't want to attend a meeting with Catholics".' [9]

Harry Reid, a past editor of the *Herald*, writing in the wake of MacMillan's Edinburgh salvo, insisted that a lesson learnt after decades of mixing with 'highly educated and professionally successful Protestants and Catholics, was that sectarianism is not simply the solace of an underclass':

'[Among] the civic cream if you will – there still sometimes lurks atavistic bitterness and loathing. And worse, this loathing is carefully nurtured, so that it is handed, alive and warm, from generation to generation.' [10]

Just prior to MacMillan's foregrounding of communal antagonism, post-match singing had brought notoriety to Donald Findlay, one of the most successful courtroom lawyers in Scotland. The journalist Dennis Sewell describes what happened :

'On the last Saturday in May 1999, Rangers beat Celtic 1-0 in the Scottish Cup Final. . . After the match, the Rangers team returned to Ibrox to attend a celebration party. Late in the evening. . . Donald Findlay stepped forward to the microphone to congratulate the players. . . adopting a heavily ironic tone, he said, "You know, at Ibrox we don't have anything to do with this sectarian stuff anymore. . . if you promise not to tell anyone, join in. . ." With that he launched into a medley of anti-Catholic ditties, most of which were of the usual crude "Fuck your Pope and the Vatican" variety.[11] But . . . one particular jingle Findlay sang that evening demand[ed] special consideration. "The Billy Boys" is arguably the nastiest number in the Rangers repertoire. It contains the line "We are up to our knees in Fenian blood. Surrender or you'll die for we are the Bridgeton Billy Boys".'[12]

Sewell subtly observed that Findlay's impromptu Ibrox cabaret was more postmodern than sectarian, a 'teasing allusion to the place of sectarianism in the sub-culture of Rangers FC specifically, and maybe society at large. It was a half-ironic tribal dance, a reckless play of emotive cultural signifiers.'[13] But on the same page as the *Daily Record* exposé of Findlay there was another headline. ONE DEAD, ONE SHOT, referring to Thomas McFadden a young Catholic teenager, wearing a Celtic top stabbed, butchered to death shortly after the Old Firm cup final, and to Karl McGroarty, a Catholic student again in a Celtic jersey, shot in the chest by a bolt fired from a crossbow as he returned from the same match.[14]

Under pressure, Findlay resigned his position as Vice-Chair of the board of Rangers Football Club. He was disciplined for his behaviour by the Faculty of Advocates. The honorary degree he was due to receive from St. Andrews University, where he had served as Rector, was withdrawn. One of the few to argue the punishment was too harsh was the Catholic philosopher John Haldane who wrote in the *Herald* that 'the university ought not to revoke the decision to award the degree, at least not without seeing whether Findlay might embark upon a course of social reparation.'[15]

The top advocate indeed seemed to undergo a period of reflection and, in October 2001, he gave a newspaper interview in which he stated 'we have now reached the stage where we have to say "yes, you are entitled to adhere to your Protestant or Catholic tradition. But the way you express that has to change".' [16]

The Findlay affair was obviously a defining metaphor for MacMillan and, in his 1999 address, he stated that 'our professions, our workplaces, our academic circles, our media and our sporting bodies are jam-packed with people like Donald Findlay.' [17] But his speech did not result in any prolonged soul-searching. Tom Devine who later edited a series of papers in which academics debated the validity of his claim, himself appeared to suggest that his alarm and indignation were decades too late. He wrote in the *Herald* on 10th August 1999: 'James MacMillan has gone slightly over the top. What he fails to realise is the enormous change of status of Roman Catholics in Scotland over the last 20 or 30 years.'

The media quickly parked the issue of the sectarian divide rather than engage in a long-running examination of the theme, something that had occurred around English racism after the killing in London in 1993 of the black teenager, Stephen Lawrence. This was hardly surprising in retrospect. For years, the press corps had shrunk from launching a genuine crusade, reinforced week after week in print, on radio, or on television to end football's role as a channel for communal hatred. In war-torn Northern Ireland, the media had at times played a brave and distinctive role in mobilising citizens impatient with the mindless nature of aspects of the long-running conflict there and the BBC had been a force which, by its programme output, had kept alive a sense of common Northern Irish identity. In Scotland, by contrast, there was little sign of the media trying to galvanise civic feeling in this way.

In 2012, the film specialist Ian Hoey observed, 'the televisual and cinematic arts of Scotland had also found it very easy to turn a blind eye to the massive social divide that has been present for generations. Where is the cultural spotlight on this cause of so much conflict?' [18]

Over a generation ago, television broadcast two dramatic works on Protestant/Catholic tensions both of which were written by Peter

McDougall. 'Just Your Luck' explored the dilemmas caused by a mixed marriage in working-class Scotland with the groom from a Catholic family and his bride from a strong Protestant background. It showed the common interests that seemed to transcend the sectarian divide but were too frail to prevent the reversion to negative attitudes.

'Just Another Saturday', filmed in 1974, focussed on rawer group tensions that spilled over into organised violence. Glasgow's chief constable warned that it would 'cause bloodshed on the streets in the making and the showing' and he advocated that both its filming and screening be prevented.

'Just Another Saturday' won the coveted Prix Italia for Best Drama and according to Hoey it and 'Just Your Luck' stand up to viewing today with the former especially 'lacking none of its original punch or, depressingly, relevance'. And yet, for the next four decades, the cinema has remained silent on the social fault-line that originally caused these plays to be made. Hoey, writing in 2012, considers it 'an astounding fact that something so socially and culturally relevant can be largely ignored. It's hard to foresee an end to ingrained bigotry when people are so afraid to address it.' [19]

In 2004 along with Tony Glendinning, Iain Paterson and Michael Rosie, Steve Bruce published *Sectarianism in Scotland* in which it was argued that disadvantage and discrimination had long been vanishing problems for Catholics thanks to progressive social change and the inroads of secularism. Religion was also a rapidly shrinking marker for Catholics which further undercut the grounds for sectarianism.[20] A lot of the book's arguments and claims were based on an exploration of quantitative data that indicated a steady retreat in structural discrimination. However, the book failed to give active consideration to attitudinal discrimination or bigotry. Early on it defined bigotry as 'a widespread and shared culture of improperly treating people in terms of their religion'. [21]

But as Elinor Kelly, in a detailed review essay, pointed out, there was a failure to consider the continuing role of ethnicity. Bruce *et al* asserted that religion (or the ethnicity of one's ancestors) is no longer a major consideration in the lives of most Scots.[22] But incidents continued to occur which suggested that boundaries were adapting to social change rather than crumbling in its wake.

In 2005, Patricia Walls produced a Ph.D using different methodological tools in which she argued that religious antagonisms could enjoy a vigorous afterlife even in the midst of intermarriage.[23] This finding was based on data from 72 qualitative reviews with people in different religious/ethnic, gender, class and age groups. She argued that the private choices of couples were not indicative of a lack of bigotry in families nor could intermarriage prevent religion still acquiring a negative social significance.[24]

Her evidence, over time, indicated that intermarriage in Scotland was having a contrasting impact on the religious balance in society. She found:

> 'Catholics born in 1932 who entered into mixed marriages continued in most cases to identify as Catholics, this identification being displayed through religious practice and the schooling of their children. It was the norm for Protestant-born women to conform to the religious beliefs and practices of their Catholic husbands.'[25]

She found evidence that 'this pattern persisted for another thirty years: this involved the Protestant mothers supporting Catholic schooling for their children and ensuring attendance at mass.'[26]

However, by the 1970s, it was much more likely that in the mixed marriage context, Catholic women broke with their previous identity just as Protestant women had done. But there was a gender differentiation. While Catholic-born women could, in effect become 'secular Protestants' after marrying outside the community, it was less likely to occur for Catholic men entering the Protestant milieu: while 'Catholic spouses of Protestant men could encounter hostility which often faded in due course. . . Catholic men encountered deep-seated hostility within families due to being seen as interlopers';[27] regardless of lack of religious practice, they neither perceived themselves nor were seen by their spouse's family as capable of becoming cultural Protestants. [28] Indeed, this was a dilemma central to the plot of Peter McDougall's 'Just Your Luck'.

Mixed marriages still exhibited the capacity to create waves in Scottish society. The association between Rangers FC and Sir Alex Ferguson, when the football manager was a young man, indicated the tensions keeping alive a sectarian divide, albeit a weakening one. Although his mother was

Catholic, he had a Protestant upbringing in Govan, which allowed him to sign for Rangers, which has its stadium in this district of Glasgow. But in an autobiography, he claimed that hopes of progressing with the club were dashed owing to his marriage to a Catholic in the 1960s. In the eyes of the influential PR chief of Rangers, the late Willie Allison, this rendered him unsuitable for continued service with the club which eased him out. [29]

A generation later, a top Scottish politician, Jack McConnell, a Protestant from the isle of Arran married to a Catholic, was disturbed to find that UVF, the initials of a loyalist paramilitary group, had been daubed on his new Lanarkshire home and IRA on a nearby pavement after being elected MSP for Motherwell and Wishaw.[30]

After 2003 the police kept records on religiously-motivated crime and Lanarkshire was one of the worst-affected areas. Four hundred and forty Scots were convicted of religiously motivated verbal and physical assaults between 1st January 2004 and 30th June 2005, 726 cases being involved. In 64% of cases the abuse or assaults were motivated by hatred against Catholics, and by hatred against Protestants in most of the remaining cases.

In an insouciant response, Steve Bruce said according to the *Guardian's* Scottish correspondent that, as nearly 90% of the offences involved verbal abuse and breach of the peace, this suggested that religious intolerance was a minor problem. The figures, he said, showed that religious intolerance was evenly shared among Protestants and Catholics, as the two-to-one ratio of incidents was roughly the same as the size of those populations in the west of Scotland. 'I'm pleasantly reassured that 90% of these cases didn't involve violence,' he said. 'That puts it far, far below wifebeating, racial attacks and below gay-bashing.'[31]

Nearly a decade worth of figures on religiously-motivated crime would show no diminution of such crime and would be accompanied by new evidence pointing to a sharp awareness of religious tensions, particularly among younger age groups.

Gradually, public institutions began to acknowledge that sectarianism continues to be a major problem facing Glasgow and the West of Scotland. This admission was formally made by Glasgow City council on 22nd February 2001. [32] But, at a time when many cities saw the tourist potential or public relations value in presenting even a turbulent urban history to a wider audience, hesitation remained in Glasgow about how to incorporate people of Irish descent in the city's official narrative. It was only in 2012 that steps were taken to commemorate the human catastrophe, the Irish famine of the 1840s, that brought so many of their ancestors to the West of Scotland. This was largely thanks to Feargal Dalton, an Irishman and SNP councillor who had served in the British navy, and the Glasgow-based Irish Heritage Foundation. [33]

The devolved state already had a track record of working with Nil by Mouth, an organisation with a pro-active approach to challenging sectarianism which had been founded by Cara Henderson, the girlfriend of Mark Scott, after his murder. A trainee lawyer, she returned to Scotland, after graduating from Oxford in 1999, putting her career plans on hold. She said that the video of the lawyer who defended Mark Scott's killer, caught singing sectarian songs had been a defining moment for her.[34] Nil by Mouth's chief aims were to overcome fear and complacency about sectarianism and be a catalyst for overdue changes in Scottish society in which bigotry would no longer have a place.[35] Steve Bruce and his colleagues devoted much space in their 2004 book to challenging Nil by Mouth's assumption that Glasgow had disturbing levels of violent crime that could be traced to sectarianism, arguing that it was a cliché without a foundation in social reality.[36] As for Nil by Mouth, its vocal stance stemmed from one simple fact: 'It is a campaigning organisation that will exist only as long as it persuades funders that there is a huge problem it can help solve; its staff have a career interest in finding sectarian violence.'[37]

Nil by Mouth has always been a low-overhead body with a small staff; much of its funding has been ploughed into practical endeavours: its £402,000 grant from the Millennium Commission in 2001 (its biggest) was used for locally-based anti-sectarian projects.[38] Funding from Scottish official sources has been sporadic and in February 2009, with the SNP in office it looked as if this would come to an end. Stewart Maxwell, the communities minister, adopting the perspective of the Bruce school of sociology, insisted that sectarianism was no worse than other problems such as racism or obesity so it need not be singled out for special treatment.[39]

In the devolution era, political forces have oscillated from displaying complacency about the issue to being occasionally stirred into action. The immediate post-2000 period was one that witnessed a temporary mobilisation also involving the main Presbyterian and Catholic churches. At the urging of Nil by Mouth, they formed a 'Sense over Sectarianism' initiative in October 2001 and obtained more tentative involvement from parts of the media and the Old Firm clubs.[40]

A success had been registered in January 2000 over a census question about religious observance; despite such a question being included in the English census. Justice Minister Jim Wallace had initially indicated that there wouldn't be one. Through pressure exerted by the parliament's Equal Opportunities Committee and academics like Tom Devine, he was forced into a U-turn: 'an important opportunity to quantify and trek the religious diversity of Scotland was almost lost. This would have denied the base-line for those who wished to conduct in-depth empirical research into the subject of religious intolerance in Scotland.'[41]

A major breakthrough occurred in 2003 when the Scottish parliament agreed that courts should have the option to treat existing criminal offences more seriously if there was a sectarian dimension to them. Under Section 74 of the Criminal Justice (Scotland) Act 2003, the justice system added the concept of 'statutory aggravation for offences motivated by religious prejudice' and courts were required to take account of that factor in sentencing.[42]

The initiator of the bill was not a Catholic MSP but a Liberal Democrat, Donald Gorrie who was firmly secular in outlook. This former Edinburgh teacher only became aware of the depths of the sectarian problem upon becoming an MSP for his party for the Central Scotland region. He was prepared to grab a hot potato but he had few enthusiastic backers in a hesitant parliament. Interestingly, there was no vocal support from Catholic MSPs, some of whom may have been on their guard because he had initially indicated his belief that the best way to overcome the culture of bigotry was to wind up Catholic schools.[43]

The First Minister, Jack McConnell was an enthusiastic backer. He launched a series of 'anti-sectarian summits' to try and deter complacency about the issue and encourage influential leaders from across society to take it seriously. After he left office, he went on record to express his regret that his own 2001-7 government had not been more active with legislation designed to counter sectarianism. [44]

Sporadic engagements with the sectarian issue have emanated from official Scotland. It is still hard to point to any landmark speeches, laws, or initiatives from the world of politics or the civic professions. Nil by Mouth stands out as a grassroots body (whose impact has, perhaps unsurprisingly, faded over time). If sectarianism has receded it is due to changes in society rather than a pro-active stance by the state; yet the forces of inertia remain tenacious enough in the selfsame society to allow low-level intolerance to remain an inter-generational phenomenon in Scotland.

Academics, intellectuals and assorted campaigners have attracted the scorn of Steve Bruce and others who prefer to claim that that it is the harping on about sectarianism rather than the prevalence of the phenomenon itself that ought to be the cause of dismay in Scotland. Much of his co-authored 2004 book, is a critique of exponents of what he would view as an artificial sectarianism industry.

One force that is not open to criticism in the book is the Catholic Church even though it was written shortly after the era of the combative Thomas Winning had ended. The church rarely spoke out about the issue, at least then. Before the passing of the 1967 Abortion Act the church reserved its vigilance and occasional outspokenness for combating communism and defending state-funded Catholic schools. The denominational education system was a kind of sacred ark. But it gave surprisingly little thought to the fate of those who completed a Catholic education only to find that they were blocked in the labour market. Arguably, the Catholic Church's difficulty in maintaining a mass base of adherents in Scotland stemmed to some degree from the failure of enough people in the community to break free from poverty and marginalisation as adults. There were exceptional figures of authority prepared to speak out against economic injustice.

One was James Breen, a head-teacher in Coatbridge which, with five Catholic secondary schools, in the 1980s was the Scottish town with the largest proportion of Catholics among its inhabitants. But it was hard for Catholics to get a job in any of its banks. For many years Breen, the headmaster of a selective entry school with a good academic reputation grew increasingly exasperated until, in the early 1960s, he decided to personally confront Coatbridge bank managers about the situation. Several of those that he saw informed him that they recruited new staff on the recommendation of existing employees and that there was no conscious policy to exclude Catholics. But when Breen said to one manager, 'I know for a fact that you contacted Airdrie High School about suitable recruits,' all he could say was, 'Oh, I forgot to approach your school.' Another manager, reacting positively to Breen and perhaps not realising the significance of what he was saying, said, 'I will phone head office in Edinburgh to see if the ban [on Catholics] is still in place.' [45] The headmaster had discovered an unspoken embargo and the chances are that it was duplicated in other Scottish towns; in time Catholics began to be taken on as bank employees in Coatbridge but it was a slow process.

The only priest whom I have come across prepared to intervene after one of his parishioners was subjected to blatant prejudice, resulting in being put out of work, was Fr. Joseph Chambers. He later headed the Catholic Education Commission, but, in 1967, as a young priest based in Clydebank he was prepared to champion a young churchgoer victimised on the grounds of her religion. In an interview with the academic Dr. Stephen McKinney, he described what happened:

> 'I remember as a young priest coming to Glasgow in 1967, a little girl leaving school in St. Thomas Aquinas went for her first job in a shop in Clydebank and the lady in the shop was giving her the job, told her to start tomorrow morning. And when she went to the shop at 8.45am or whenever it was, the lady said to her, I forgot to ask you what school you went to, and she said, oh I went to St. Thomas Aquinas . . . and I liked it, it was good. And the lady said well that job that I had, I haven't got it any more. I will phone you in a day or two and sent her away. The little girl came back and told me about it.
>
> 'I went to the shop the next day, it was a lady's dresswear shop, and I ordered two pairs of nylons across the counter and the lady looked at me kind of strangely but served me. And then as she was about to wrap them up and give them to me, I was paying for them, I said to

her by the way what religion are you; she said that has nothing to do with you. I said no you are dead right it hasn't, but there was a wee girl came in here yesterday for a job and because she was Catholic you took the job off her.' [46]

Such rejections are likely to have had a marked impact on the self-esteem of at least some young people struggling to make their way in life. It would not be foolhardy to conclude that a lot of the people from urban Scotland who found themselves as down-and-outs in London and other English cities during the twentieth century were not just victims of economic circumstance or personal weaknesses that they could not master, but were those who encountered such inhumanity at a very impressionable stage in their lives.

Yet the clarion call for action about sectarianism would come not from Catholics or their leaders but more often than not from people well outside their community such as Cara Henderson or Donald Gorrie, or Catholics who had moved somewhat apart from the community enclave such as the composer James MacMillan. As Dr. Patricia Walls found in her in-depth attitude surveys on sectarian attitudes, it was West of Scotland Protestants who were able to cite in the most substantial detail, how discrimination was arranged in the workplace.

The naturalness of excluding Catholics, and the absence of the need for concealment, came across in the lengthy account of a director of a large company, which maintained a policy of excluding them from all but the most undesirable of jobs, at least until he retired in 1986. She relates that 'as a director, he had the power to change anti-Catholic policy. However, he felt his power to intervene was constrained by the greater power of tradition':

'The firm I worked for forty years, there was never a Catholic employed in the office. If you went up and said, "which school did you go to?" "St. Mark's," they would say, "thanks for coming but, no thanks."

They never employed any?

Never at all, but nobody said to do it. . . there were no Catholics in the office at all, none at all, none of the directors, none of the officials, none of the clerks were ever Catholics, or typists. But the works had them.

The works?

The works where we made the batteries, they had them. Oh yes, poorer jobs. . .

So you didn't feel it was an active move on the part of the organisation to keep them out?

Oh no, no, no, it was a Glasgow trait, it was a Glasgow firm, and I think the people had grown up just as I grew up. I wouldn't have broken the mould latterly. I never employed anybody that was a Catholic, not that there were many Catholics applied.

But if one did apply?

. . .its hypothetical, but had somebody applied and they were a known Catholic, they wouldn't have got a job.

I'm not trying to go on about this but could you just sort of explain why that would be?

Because that's the way it's always been done.

Just that's the way?

Yeah, tradition, it was more tradition.'

(66 year-old Protestant male who became director of the large company he worked in until 1986).[47]

Walls claims that her survey establishes the *fact* of discrimination but not its prevalence. Given that in the absence of direct evidence of discrimination, Catholics were loathe to claim they had suffered from it, she believes that the experience of discrimination may have been under-estimated.[48]

She also contends that the design of the study, which included the experience of both Irish and Scottish origin as well as Protestant and Catholic religious background, meant that clearer links between religious identity and ethnic origin could be made, showing that it was *Irish Catholic* origin which was the focus of discriminatory practice.[49]

Arguably, the continuation of Catholic schools gave the community a heightened level of visibility which made discrimination easy to pursue simply by asking a job applicant to name his or her school. Perhaps recognition of this realty prompted some upwardly mobile Catholic families with definite ambitions for their children to shun the Catholic school system. Certainly plenty of Catholics were bound to figure among those Scots who wished the system of state-funding for those schools to be abolished. The *Sunday Times*, on 21st January 2007, reported that 70% of Scottish voters believe that 'denominational schools contribute to sectarianism' and that they should no longer be state funded.'[50]

There has been an unwillingness to acknowledge that the existence of these schools might actually be a social gain for a country which, by western standards, is plagued by high levels of inter-personal violence – that perhaps these schools, given their ethos, might be helping to improve the standards of behaviour of children and young people and impede delinquency and violence (much of which is territorial and without evident sectarian features). The SNP could be expected to endorse an institution which had a civilising impact on Scotland and after the survey, Alex Salmond, its leader, was the only prominent politician to offer them vocal backing. Four months before his party was able to form a government in Edinburgh, he defended them in print and refuted any connection with sectarianism. [51] But long-term polling indicates that he is out-on-a-limb on this issue (especially within his own party). The bulk of Scots appear to line up with Professor Steve Bruce that separation of children, once they reach school age, consolidates a sense of difference through which presumably small pockets of sectarianism are able to renew themselves. [52]

Within the Scottish state, there is little evidence that backing exists for in-depth research into the long-term treatment of working-class Catholics in Scotland. It was noteworthy that, after mid-2005, both the Scottish Government and the Crown Office discontinued the practice of offering a breakdown of the character of sectarian crimes and refused repeated requests to return to it. The Crown Office continued to publish the total number of convictions under Section 74 every year but, until 2012, it refused to reveal how many crimes were anti-Catholic, anti-Protestant, anti-Semitic or anti-Muslim. [53]

NOTES

1 *Guardian*, 9 August 1999

2 Steve Bruce, 'Inspection of the facts points to a ready assimilation', *The Herald*, 10 August 1999

3 See Chris Watt, 'Professor: Catholic Church's attack on bigotry is historic', *The Herald*, 29 November 2010.

4 Joseph Bradley, 'One Scotland Many Cultures', *Irish Studies Review*, Vol. 14, No 2, 2006, p. 202. note 15.

5 Ian Wilson, 'Rangers and the Orange Order', in Graham Walker and Ronnie Esplin, *It's Rangers for me: New perspectives on a Scottish Institution*, Ayr: Fort Publications, 2007, p. 169.

6 *Daily Record*, 10 August 1999.

7 *Scottish Review*, 31 May 2011.

8 'Jozicelt', *Guardian*, 24 April 2011. In early 2013, I traced the author of this post and corresponded with him: he practices as an architect in one of the largest cities in the southern hemisphere.

9 Judith Duffy, 'Civil rites', *Sunday Herald*, 13 January 2013

10 Harry Reid, 'Bad Blood & Bigotry', *The Ferris Conspiracy Forum*, 23 April 2006. www.Ferrisconspiracy.co.uk

11 *Daily Record*, 31 May 1999

12 Sewell, *Catholics*, p. 124.

13 Sewell, *Catholics*, p. 134.

14 T.M.Devine, *Scotland's Shame: Bigotry and Sectarianism in Modern Scotland*, Mainstream, Edinburgh 2000, 17-18 .

15 John Haldane, 'Growing Up', in Devine, *Scotland's Shame*, p. 93.

16 *Evening Times* (Glasgow), 23 October 2001

17 Sewell, *Catholics*, p. 131.

18 Ian Hoey, 'The Orange and Green Elephant In The Room', Reel Scotland, 23 March, 2012

19 Hoey, 'The Orange and Green Elephant'.

20 Steve Bruce et al, *Sectarianism in Scotland*, Edinburgh: Edinburgh University Press, 2004, p. 4.

21 Bruce et al, *Sectarianism in Scotland*, p. 4.

22 Elinor Kelly, 'Review Essay: Sectarianism, Bigotry and Ethnicity – The Gulf in Understanding', *Scottish Affairs*, p. 4 [electronic version].

23 Walls, 'The health of Irish-descended Catholics, p. 257.

24 Walls, 'The health of Irish-descended Catholics', p. 257.

25 Walls, 'The health of Irish-descended Catholics', p. 91.

26 Walls, 'The health of Irish-descended Catholics', p. 96.

27 Walls, 'The health of Irish-descended Catholics', p. 169.

28 Walls, 'The health of Irish-descended Catholics', p. 101.

29 'Fergie stirs up the ghosts of old Ibrox', *Daily Record*, 3 August 1999.

30 *Daily Telegraph*, 16 October 2002

31 Severin Carrell, 'Catholics bear brunt of Scottish sectarian abuse', *Guardian*, 28 November 2006

32 See *Sectarianism in Scotland today: A Report for the Church of Scotland General Assembly*, Edinburgh: Church of Scotland, May 2012.

33 *The Herald*, 1 September 2012.

34 Kirsty Scott, 'A game of two halves', *Guardian*, 15 May 2001.

35 Nil by Mouth, *Newsletter* 1, Summer 2001

36 Bruce et al, *Sectarianism in Scotland*, p.p. 140-9.

37 Bruce et al, *Sectarianism in Scotland*, p.146.

38 Nil by Mouth, *Newsletter* 1, Summer 2001.

39 Hamish Macdonell, 'Jack's legacy is the loser in the great game of politics', *Scotsman*, 31 December 2008

40 Nil by Mouth, *Newsletter* 2, Spring 2003.

41 James MacMillan, 'I had not thought about it like that before', in Devine, *Scotland's Shame*, Mainstream, Edinburgh 2000, p. 268.

42 Scottish Parliament debates Section 59A, 'Offences aggravated by religious prejudice', 19 February 2003.

43 Interview with Michael McMahon MSP, 5 February 2013.

44 *The Herald*, 15 May 2009.

45 Conversation with retired headmaster, James Breen, 4 July 1986.

46 Stephen John McKinney, 'Catholic schools in Scotland: Mapping the Contemporary Debate and their continued existence in the 21st century', Ph.D thesis, Faculty of Education, University of Glasgow, 2007, p. 213

47 Walls, 'The health of Irish-descended Catholics', p.p. 202-3.

48 Walls, 'The health of Irish-descended Catholics', p.214.

49 Walls, 'The health of Irish-descended Catholics', p. 214.

50 McKinney, 'Catholic schools in Scotland'. p.p. 91-2.

51 Alex Salmond, 'Lets Learn from Catholics', *Sunday Times*, 21 January 2007.

52 McKinney, 'Catholic schools in Scotland', p. 91.

53 *Sunday Herald*, 24 April 2011

Chapter 9
Football, Religion and Nationalism

IN EXISTENCE since 1934, it would take eight frustrating decades before the Scottish National Party (SNP) would taste power. Its time in the wilderness was prolonged by working-class voters, particularly in west-central Scotland, who refused to discard quasi-religious loyalties. These were ones which, in the party's eyes, created a false consciousness that prevented voters in these mainly Labour strongholds from embracing pro-independence views.

The SNP's belated rise to power coincided with a double crisis in Scottish football, centred mainly on the inveterate rivals, Rangers and Celtic. Rangers were banished to a lower league and the club's long-term survival prospects placed in doubt, due to facing the threat of financial insolvency. On the eve of this crisis, in 2011, some of the worst clashes, extending from players to fans and managers, prompted the state to rush through measures designed to impose decorum on a disorderly game. The conventional media often struggled to adequately explain the pace of events. The information vacuum was filled by blogs which at times themselves played a critical role in the story and are thus examined here.

This chapter reflects on a period of unprecedented turbulence in Scottish football and the newly ascendant political and social forces which tried, with varying success, to manipulate the game for a variety of ends. It argues that Glasgow's footballing rivals fell victims to a re-definition of tolerance so that words and chants deemed hurtful were henceforth proscribed by a heavy-handed state. But first it begins by setting the political context, charting the growing appeal, especially among Catholics of a party committed to supplanting enclave identities with emphatically nationalist ones.

For decades, since the SNP's first inconclusive electoral breakthrough in the mid-1970s, opinion polls often showed that more voters were attracted to the independence option than were prepared to vote for the

SNP. A surprisingly high number of Labour voters in the pre-devolution era indicated to pollsters that they were for independence. It is quite likely that lower-income Catholics figured prominently among them: the arrival of Thatcher and more distant Irish sympathies made them sceptical about the British link, but unless they moved in a secular direction, plenty sensed that their Catholic identity did not easily blend with Scottishness.

Some Protestants regarded being 'Protestant', even in the absence of religious practice, as a key aspect of Scottish ethnic identity. [1] This perspective was shared by some Catholics, particularly more embattled followers of Celtic.

It will seem fanciful as well as offensive to some, but the profile of Alex Salmond, the SNP's leader may well have deterred some Catholics from embracing the party. This confrontational rule-breaker was the type of pushy and outspoken figure, one exploiting an ethnic appeal, who had sometimes made life awkward for them in the workplace.

Thanks not least to the undimmed appeal of Celtic Football Club, enough cultural Catholics exist who are completely at home in living isolated lives in an enclave. It is one that detractors would see as an absurd kitsch existence in which the rituals around worshipping Celtic have placed lots of these Scots in a pre-modern time-warp.

In 1999, Jack O'Sullivan introduced this tribal Celtic worshipper to the readership of a major British newspaper when he profiled J.J. McPhee, 'a 47-year-old Catholic man. . . born and bred in the East End of Glasgow. So were his parents and his grandparents. He has never been to Ireland. . . Yet he is decked out in green shirt and hat in a pub with a green bar and images of John F Kennedy and Irish memorabilia. I am bemused by this and ask him what would he call himself?'

> 'I am Scottish, but only by birth. I would rather have been born in Ireland,' he says, pointing at the image of a phoenix (a republican symbol) on his shirt.
> 'Scotland is a Protestant country and they seem to think they own it. I'm not proud to be Scottish. There are places in Scotland where Catholics are hated.'
> So how does he feel about the great new Scottish Parliament?

'I don't like the idea of home rule,' he says. 'I don't think Catholics will get a fair crack of the whip.'

It is an extraordinary statement of political disaffection. Others in the bar feel the same way. And these are not a disaffected minority. All this must be confusing to those who think that the disaffected in Scotland are simply fed-up with the English. But it is becoming clear that some of them are also fed-up with the Scottish.

I ask JJ McPhee if, given the importance of being a Catholic, he goes to Mass.

'Oh no. I don't believe in religion much. I'm Catholic in a football sense, not a religious sense. You could say Celtic is my religion.'[2]

But in 2011, just over 43% of those Catholics who voted in the Holyrood election, backed the SNP. For the first time the SNP had gained the largest share of Catholic votes in a national election. David Kerr thought that the introduction of a proportional voting system for local government in 2004 had been a key event loosening Catholic ties to Labour in working class districts. Most now had an SNP councillor and very often they offered better service, thus subverting Labour's patronage networks. [3]

A rare SNP perspective about how districts mired in sectarian rivalry and in which Labour prevailed by playing the role of neutral umpire, were at last starting to change was provided in 2011; it was in response to a satirical piece written by the author on the day it was announced that the inexperienced 28-year-old Kim Jong-un was succeeding his father in North Korea as leader of the hyper-nationalist and secretive regime. Tongue firmly placed in cheek, I argued that Alex Salmond could be the ideal tutor to coach this untested leader in the basics of political nationalism. For my sins, I was dismissed as a Labour stooge by Dave Coull and part of his response may be worth quoting in order to show how a SNP activist living in a polarised community believed the party dynamic enough to gradually banish sectarian differences from Scotland:

'Living in the west of Scotland in what I would describe as a particularly sectarian and divided town I am ashamed to say that I have met many Tom Gallaghers. Thankfully most of them are in their twilight years and are slowly disappearing.

'Many of them, despite wallowing in victim status, have done very well out of the Labour/Unionist machine by obtaining good jobs with high salaries (some deservedly, others not). . .

'They have been guilty of the very worst tribalism that has kept
Scotland down for decades. The new generation of (Irish) Catholics
growing up in the west of Scotland are (thankfully) showing signs of
abandoning that nonsense.' [4]

But Dave Coull ended on a sombre note: 'the real and durable
opponents to Scottish independence will come from the Orange mob, with
their irrational allegiances to the monarchy and the British state. I am
pessimistic regarding that lot, I'm afraid.'

Perhaps in his short and eventful life, the energetic and outspoken
Scottish lawyer, Paul McBride (1964-2012) highlighted some of the changes
which were altering the composite political identity of at least middle-
class Catholics. He expressed concerns in 2011 not unlike those once held
by Cardinal Winning about Scottish self-rule:

'I think there are legitimate concerns on the part of Scotland's
Catholic community that if Scotland were ever to become
independent, and these prejudices remained as deep and wide as
they evidently are, it could result in very serious consequences when
it comes to social cohesion and related matters. . .

'We must not delude ourselves that this isn't the most serious
social issue in the country today. If we do, if we continue to treat it
with the collective myopia it has been traditionally treated with, we
will only succeed in failing future generations.' [5]

But in the months before he died in March 2012, he had become
increasingly supportive of SNP legal efforts to crack down on soccer
troubles with a religious tinge and Alex Salmond was the main political
figure at his funeral.

The SNP leadership had reached out to the Catholic community by
endorsing denominational schools despite 64.4% of the party membership
being opposed to their continuation in one 2012 poll.[6] Hostility to religious
views influencing state policy and even the attitudes of state employees
was not hard to find in the SNP. In the 2011 local elections, the party
received a setback in Lanarkshire when one of its candidates there, Lyall

Duff, branded two Catholic midwives, Mary Doogan and Concepta Wood as a 'a pair of money-grabbing old witches' as they fought for the right not to supervise abortions at the hospital where they worked in Glasgow. He was suspended, but he still campaigned for the SNP as the date of local elections approached.[7]

Writing in 2000, Peter Lynch, an academic close to the SNP, appeared to share the view that the dimensions of sectarianism remained sufficiently large to justify initiating a 'truth and reconciliation commission' in order to bring feelings out into the open and hopefully speed the closure of the problem, but his views did not find an echo in the political sphere or the media.[8] Instead, the SNP emphasised that it was in politics to bring social justice to lower-income groups, among whom Catholics enjoyed prominence. Salmond's 2013 vision of a constitution that would be full of guaranteed entitlements in the economic and educational spheres, appeared designed to tempt more Catholics to spurn their Labour allegiances.

Social justice was at the core of Catholic thought on how best to manage society and, ever since he had waved a Saltire flag above his head in St. Peter's Square on being made a cardinal in 2003, Keith O'Brien, the Archbishop of Edinburgh, had been expressing pro-SNP sympathies. In 2007, speaking to a large gathering in Glasgow's George Square, O'Brien, standing alongside Alex Salmond, re-iterated the Catholic Church's opposition to the renewal of Trident nuclear weapons.[9]

Fifteen years of dramatic economic expansion in Ireland at the turn-of-the-century enabled the SNP to argue that Scotland's own bid for independence was not utopian. Ireland went from being a mocked land of 'tattie-howkers' to the dynamic 'Celtic Tiger'. Salmond proclaimed that both countries could be part of an 'arc of prosperity' even when many of the economic gains made in Ireland were wiped out by the long-running economic crisis after 2008, and high-levels of emigration returned.

Edinburgh-based Irish historian, Owen Dudley Edwards used his popularity in the broadcasting media to argue that Scotland need not be deterred by Ireland's chequered experience of self-government. But for Cardinals Winning and later O'Brien it was alarm about the cross-party consensus at Westminster on the acceptability of lifestyle choices that could have equal validity with Christian marriage and support for liberal abortion policies, which drew them steadily closer to the SNP. Winning would have no way of knowing that exactly a decade after his death, the SNP would include a pledge to introduce gay marriage in its 2011 electoral manifesto.

Thereafter, O'Brien made fewer statements on issues that could be seen as pro-SNP. Arguably, both men were more naive than predecessors who were wary of political parties and dealt with them on a strictly instrumental basis, pledging public support as long as Christian principles were not under threat. But after Irish self-government in the 1920s and with a decline in anti-Catholic feeling at the top of the political elite, Catholic leaders had dropped their guard and their political antennae grew rusty.

Nobody wielding influence in the church saw the need to warn the party of Scottish radical change of the desirability of having a Christian understanding of human nature. This meant being actively aware of their own limitations and the weaknesses of the wider society. But warnings against rash conduct and the belief that as post-British revolutionaries, they could dismantle institutions and build afresh, might well only have fallen on deaf ears. The dominant Scottish Left, split into nationalist and unionist camps, was nevertheless united in possessing an increasingly dismissive view of Christianity not unlike that held by radical continental theorists of the nineteenth and early twentieth centuries.

However, audacious and perhaps even laudable its goals, the talent at the disposal of the SNP was meagre as people of vision and energy increasingly shunned politics in Scotland, just as in much the rest of Europe. It was becoming increasingly clear to some as the party's hold on power tightened, that the people whom it relied on to create a new Scottish commonwealth, were not only of highly mixed ability but morally varied greatly in character. In the 1790s, the philosopher Edmund Burke had reminded Britons, looking on in horror at the French revolution, that it was obedience to a moral law shaped by the forces of custom and habit that placed restraint over those active in the public realm. But in a contemporary era of retreating Christian influence, laws determining the contours of morality were in a state of flux, often under the influence of radical lawyers of similar temper and outlook to those who had welcomed the French revolution.

Few church leaders were able to grasp that nationalism, in the wrong hands, could all too easily become an inverted religion or a secular cult; nationalism is highly adaptable and it is not just the totalitarian versions which have displayed impatience with the Christian doctrine of salvation through grace in death if it gets in the way of earthly forms of salvation that can be achieved primarily through top-down political change.

Catholic authorities, while troubled and outspoken about individual policies, failed to advance a vision for the exercise of authority in the secular realm. It is not just Catholics who were silent. In the last years of the twentieth century, the Rev. William Storrar of the Church of Scotland had detected a 'civic' Calvinist influence in the recent mobilisation of Scottish society in support of self-government. [11] But after 2000 the influence of the Kirk was increasingly harder to detect in political life.

With the eyes of Scots supposedly focussed on their country's constitutional future, a series of events occurred in 2010 and 2011, suggesting that sectarianism still had plenty of staying power.

Attention first focussed on the Scottish Football Association (SFA). On 20th November, it sacked its development officer Hugh Dallas, who had previously been Scotland's most senior referee. In September 2010, on the day of the Pope's arrival in Scotland, he had sent an email to other SFA staff from his work computer. It showed a road sign of an adult holding a child's hand. It was captioned: 'Caution: the Pope is coming'.[12]

Nothing happened for several months until the incident got into the press. At that point, Peter Kearney, head of the Scottish media office of the Catholic Church wrote to the SFA, expressing the church's deep concern. Contrary to later press reports, Kearney insisted that he had not called for Dallas's head. He asked the SFA to apply its rules on 'appropriate use' of the electronic web for its staff. On 26th November 2010, the SFA announced that he had resigned for family reasons;[13] only later did it emerge that he had been dismissed.

From that point on, the story centred not on Hugh Dallas but on the Catholic church and particularly its media spokesman. Professor Richard Dawkins, the Oxford biologist and noisy foe of organised religion, on his website denounced Kearney as a 'nasty little weasel' who was stirring up hate:

'The fact that sectarian Christianity even manages to infect football, in places such as Glasgow that have imported Irish political strife, should not lessen our contempt. Kearney was cynically exploiting Glasgow's traditional sectarian enmities in order to further his Catholic agenda and ruin a man's career.' [14]

Dallas retained a Trappist-like silence after the affair broke. But Dawkins assumed that 'he was as revolted as all decent people are by the Pope's illegal protection of Catholic child-rapists.' The best-selling author of books like *The God Delusion*, encouraged his followers to 'make this joke go viral, beginning by sending hundreds of copies of it' to Kearney's office (and also to the SFA) and any 'funnier jokes along the same lines' that could be devised.[15]

The leading atheist's assumption that the Catholic Church had no grounds for expecting special consideration because of clerical abuse scandals swirling around its head was one shared by many people. A UK-wide poll carried out for the English Catholic Church on the first anniversary of the Papal visit to the UK showed that Scots had the least favourable opinion of the Catholic Church of any British citizens. Scotland registered the highest level of scepticism over the Pope's actions to curb clerical sex abuse, over whether religion and morals should be taught in schools, and whether the Catholic Church ought to take a moral lead in British society over issues such as abortion and euthanasia. 51% of the Scottish sample disagreed with the claim that the Catholic church was a force for good and the figure supporting the claim was the lowest anywhere in the UK.[16]

Kearney's office was inundated with mail which ranged from the abusive and threatening to the disparaging and mocking, especially because of the church's self-righteousness and apparent lack of humour.[17] He had already been the target for criticism by drawing attention to the anti- Catholic origins of the popular song 'Doing the Hokey-Cokey'.[18]

Kearney showed no sign of retreating in the face of widespread criticism. He wrote that the widespread anger over his letter to the SFA 'has proved beyond doubt that Scotland has become completely inured to the corrosive effects of religious bigotry and may even have lost sight of what constitutes it.'[19] It would be wrong to characterise Kearney as completely absorbed with defending a religious cause. He had spent many years in the SNP and had even stood for the party in a British general election. It is perhaps not far-fetched to say that his readiness to spring to the defence of his faith is comparable to the tenacity shown by the newly-founded religious orders of the sixteenth century or else the religious figures who took on communism as it spread across Eastern Europe. He has no illusions that he is a deeply unfashionable figure in a Scotland where only a few causes outside politics and sport are seen as worthy of respect, with religion not one of them.

At the height of the storm, he himself wrote that 'over the course of a single generation, Scotland's political, academic and media elite have almost completely lost contact with religious practice and belief. This derogation from universally held objective moral standards supplanted by the embrace of subjective secular fashions has brought with it catastrophic consequences.' [20] This was perhaps a tacit admission that many Scots would have seen his response to the Hugh Dallas affair as harsh and unwarranted. Indeed, in a press article, Mark Smith, a Catholic from the east of Scotland complained that his church had over-reacted to something that was 'not deeply offensive'. [21] This was perhaps an example of the willingness (as Kearney saw it) for many Catholics to internalise attacks on their faith rather than reacting with vigour.[22] But he claimed that younger Catholics were now far less inclined to soak up punishment.

Paul McBride, the high-profile advocate might have been viewed as one of them. Legal action appeared imminent after he had branded the SFA as 'biased' towards Rangers in 2010.[23] But he ended the quarrel in 2011 by expressing regret for the offence caused to the SFA and its staff by his remarks and offering praise for the SFA chief Stewart Regan: 'Under his leadership I anticipate many reforms which will be welcomed across Scotland'. [24]

The affair had shown that in the world of Scottish football, religious controversy was not the monopoly of two notorious Glasgow soccer rivals. Even senior referees had gone on strike at the height of the 2010 controversy over what they saw as a rising tide of abuse from managers and players, to the point where their integrity is being queried and their personal lives affected.[25]

A year after the Dallas affair, the Scottish parliament was debating a new law that would create two offences relating to football disorders. Behaviour deemed to 'incite religious, racial or other forms of hatred' in and around football grounds and also online would become a criminal offence with those convicted facing the possibility of up to five years in prison and a lifetime's banning from football grounds.

On 20th February 2011, a midweek Old Firm encounter resulted in more than 300 arrests. The arrest total at a fresh duel on 3rd March saw only 34 arrests but thirteen bookings and three Rangers players sent off. What made the headlines was a furious confrontation between Celtic boss Neil Lennon and Rangers assistant manager Ally McCoist at the end of the game. Stephen House, then Strathclyde's high profile chief constable immediately complained about the public disorder imposing an unacceptable strain on his force. He called for a summit to tackle the problem and he won the support of First Minister Alex Salmond. 'Enough is enough,' they agreed. [26]

By May of 2011 a hastily drawn up bill had been laid before parliament which it was hoped would be law by the start of the football season in August 2011. It focused not on actions but on language. The police were required to decide when songs and chants were offensive. But there was no list of proscribed songs. If one had been compiled and it had included songs like Paul McCartney's hit, 'Give Ireland back to the Irish', it would have invited ridicule.[27] When asked if singing 'God Save the Queen' could lead to a jail term, the minister overseeing the bill, Roseanna Cunningham replied: 'The glib answer would be No but it depends on the circumstances.' She said:

> 'I have seen hundreds of Celtic fans making the sign of the cross in what can only be described as an aggressive manner at Rangers fans.

Making the sign of the cross is not, in itself, offensive but it all depends on the circumstances.'[28]

The suspicions of Rangers and Celtic had been fuelled and they issued separate statements criticising the provisions of the bill. Their dismay and the growing number of other bodies voicing concrete objections soon meant that the SNP was the only party in Holyrood supporting the bill. Michael McMahon MSP had bluntly stated at a Labour group meeting that if Labour capitulated to the SNP on this issue, he would defy the whip.[29]

Divisions existed among prominent figures linked to the police. Graeme Pearson, a former deputy chief constable of Strathclyde who since 2011 had been a Holyrood Labour MSP quoted Cicero, warning that 'the arrogance of officialdom should be tempered and controlled.'[30] He stated baldly that in his experience the police didn't like football crowds. This claim appeared to be confirmed as Les Gray, the head of the police trade union, Scottish Police Federation, called for Old Firm matches to be banned as they caused 'murder and mayhem', or at least for them to be played in empty stadiums.[31]

Michael Kelly feared that what were essentially folk songs were on the way to being proscribed. This is how he classified a song extolling the deeds of Irish freedom fighters of a century ago; he believed that 'The Boys of the Old Brigade' and 'Here Lies a Soldier' should be classified as folk songs like 'The Massacre of Glencoe' and what he described as 'the grossly offensive' but condoned 'Flower of Scotland'.[32]

Iain Macwhirter pointed out that the singing of 'Flower of Scotland', which celebrates violent behaviour against English people, will be illegal at Hampden but not at Murrayfield simply because they play rugby there. 'Why on earth should a song be offensive at one sporting event and not another?'[33]

Proscribing a song at what is the supremely working-class spectator sport could easily be seen as a class issue; certainly it is an argument taken up by the academic Stuart Waiton. He wrote:

'The elevation of the incorrect use of language, as a political and sometimes criminal issue, automatically puts sections of the working class at a disadvantage, especially young men who are more often crude and rude than their middle-class contemporaries.' [34]

Chanting at football matches is political in nature according to Michael Kelly and others. Lower income groups have relentlessly been deprived of influence in a political world dominated by narrow social groups and coteries. 'You can't take politics out of football without killing it,' according to the English football writer David Goldblatt. [35]

Alex Massie, writing from Scotland, argued that a robust self-confident society needed to cope with Old Firm mayhem rather than pursue ill-judged and simplistic plans to suppress it:

'the plain fact of the matter is that a civilised society must tolerate behaviour it finds distasteful. . .

'Implicit in all this is the suggestion, lurking even in the recesses of the prohibitionists' minds, that "political" speech probably ought to be kind of, sort of, more or less protected in some way. No such quarter need be offered to anything deemed "sectarian". That's fair game.

'Unfortunately, a football competition is definitionally a tribal, and thus sectarian, thing. Concentrating on the songs is, at best, to look at symptoms not causes . . .the causes of all this trouble cannot credibly be addressed by arresting men for singing the wrong kind of song.' [36]

The football writer Rob Marrs warned about the motives of politicians:

'We will hear calls for the removal of politics from football by politicians who, by and large, do not understand the issues at stake and who, when needs be, will arrange summits about the Old Firm to make themselves look better in the national press. Politicians want politics in football when it suits them and want politics out of football the rest of the time. Let's not listen to them uncritically.'[37]

On 23 June, Alex Salmond took many by surprise, including his own minister Roseanna Cunnngham, by announcing that a bill due to be law in time for the new football season, would instead be delayed for further consultations. [38] There had been few prominent supporters, other than the police and the civil service.

Events in the previous months had shown that Scotland could exhibit dangerous levels of sectarian intolerance far beyond the football stadium. In April 2011, what at the time appeared to be parcel bombs aimed at killing or maiming whoever opened them, were sent to three high-profile supporters of Celtic FC. Besides Paul McBride QC and Neil Lennon, the Labour MSP, Trish Godman got one on the strength of wearing her Celtic top in parliament for charity on her last day as an MSP.[39] Three weeks later, on 12 May, Trevor Muirhead and Neil McKenzie, men in their forties, were arrested in dawn raids.[40] At their trials, it was decided that the devices sent were unviable and the original charge of conspiracy to assault and murder was reduced to plotting an assault for which they each got five year jail sentences.[41] In an editorial, the *Herald* argued that 'a malevolent streak of sectarianism still lurks in elements of Scottish society, in defiance of considerable efforts to be inclusive and outward-looking'.[42] But on the same day, the *Scottish Daily Mail* carried a 1,200 word article making no mention of any anti-Catholic motives and describing the crime as 'an attack on Scottish Society'.

Arguably such an approach highlighted the 'failure of the Scottish media to engage with the subject of anti-Catholic hostility and debate the problem in any depth or detail.'[43]

The situation Neil Lennon found himself in during 2011 was a familiar one for him. He had needed police protection since physical attacks in successive years. In May 2003, after dining in the west end of Glasgow, he was chased to his car by a law and medical student, the former headbutting the then Celtic player.[44] Both were later fined and in February 2004 he discovered the anger his appearance in public could cause when a motorist cut in front of his car in the centre of Glasgow, rolled down the window, made a series of gestures and hurled obscenities at him. Car salesman Thomas Ferrie was later convicted and fined £500. Each of Lennon's tormentors were in white-collar jobs, or else probably destined for them. At his trial Ferrie told police, 'I did it because I'm a Rangers fan and he's a Celtic player, but I'm not a bigot.'[45]

A similar argument was accepted by an eight man and seven woman Edinburgh jury when John Wilson, an unemployed labourer, came before them after being involved in an incident at Edinburgh's Tynecastle stadium on 11 May 2011 in front of 16,000 supporters. At his trial, Wilson admitted that he had lunged at Neil Lennon, striking him on the head. The jury was told by a steward that he had heard Wilson call Lennon 'a Fenian bastard' as he approached him.[46] But the jury preferred to believe the defendant and deleted the allegation that the offence was aggravated by religious prejudice. He got eight months in jail but he walked free having served more than half that period on remand.

Celtic's chief executive Peter Lawwell described the not proven verdict on sectarianism as an 'extraordinary outcome'.[47] Paul McBride was less circumspect:

> 'What does this say about this country? . . . It sends out signals to thugs that they can get away with it. The whole world saw the video of the incident. The whole world heard his counsel admit the assault in court. And now the whole world has seen the jury let him off. . . [it] is a terrible message about how this country is seen by the rest of the world.'[48]

The jury's verdict appeared to sit strangely alongside surveys, such as the one showing that 89% of Scots found sectarianism offensive and unacceptable at football grounds while 85% believed it should be a criminal offence.[49] The views that some people give to pollsters may not be an accurate guide to their true beliefs (which was certainly the case in Northern Ireland where the popularity of moderate views was rarely translated into electoral success). This trial outcome is unlikely to have dented a sense of alienation towards Scotland and some of its social mores which was expressed on electronic Celtic sites after it was over.

Given his difficulties in settling into Scottish society, Lennon might be forgiven for displaying a stern attitude towards Rangers when it later plunged into financial difficulties. In 2012 he told the media that he thought Rangers should forfeit trophies won during a period when it was claimed to have been involved in serious financial irregularities. [50]

Richard Wilson, author of a well-received book on the Old Firm, asked in 2012, 'What is it about the Celtic manager that invited an aggressive reaction, a suggestion, nothing more, that he may have been responsible for a small part of his own misfortune.' He described Lennon as a 'high profile, brash, assertive figure, a Catholic from Northern Ireland who is unabashed in his feisty crusading on behalf of Celtic.' [51]

But in the words of the most belligerently anti-Rangers blogger, Phil MacGiolla Bhain, the problem with Lennon is that he is 'an "uppity Fenian" from central casting. . . A Catholic from Lurgan. . . he is the *Punch* cartoon figure of the Irish ape with the bomb.' [52]

West of Scotland Catholics were not united in their response to the proposed 2011 law. Pat Nevin, born not far from Celtic Park but never a player for Celtic, told MSPs in 2011 that he had turned his back on Celtic because of sectarian songs and he welcomed the state initiative to curb them. [53]

Writing towards the end of a tumultuous year in which sectarianism pushed right to the foreground of Scottish life, the Celtic historian and Labour politician Brian Wilson was in no doubt about the grip it still maintained:

> 'My own view is that bigoted, sectarian attitudes are buried deep in Scottish society. They are directed mainly against minorities, principally – as statistics confirm – the Catholic minority. That is a problem worthy of the Scottish Government's attention.'

'It is not too late,' he argued, 'for the Scottish Government to step back from this legislation and accept it is attacking symptoms rather than root causes.'[54] The Lord Advocate Frank Mulholland, a Coatbridge Catholic, believed the legislation could produce a 'transformational attitude' equivalent in the footballing sphere to the impact of laws curbing racism and drink-driving.[55]

But figures released in late 2011 showed that not only had offences with a sectarian dimension reached a four-year high, but the majority – 88% – were recorded away from football stadiums; this, according to James Kelly, Labour's justice spokesman, 'exposes the SNP's naive and dogmatic belief that sectarianism is solely a football problem.'[56] By way of an illustration, his colleague Michael McMahon MSP related that at the Scottish Trade Union Congress's annual anti-racism rally in 2008, an Irish group joined the march carrying the Irish tricolour only to be roundly booed by the audience with the police standing by.[57] There is in-built reserve about acknowledging the Irish strand to the Scottish cultural tartan. The academic Joseph Bradley has argued that 'significantly, and with few exceptions, the Irish or Irish Catholic experience in Scotland is largely absent from research, novels, histories and stories concerning modern life in Scotland.'[58] He thought the absence of any serious treatment of the massive Irish immigration to Scotland in an exhibition at the Scottish Records Office during the 1990s, recounting the history of immigration to Scotland, to be a significant omission (as did James MacMillan).[59]

In 2011, the quanqo Show Racism the Red Card (SRTRC) was criticised for its slowness to engage with anti-Irish racism in Scottish football. Kieron Brady, an ex-SRTRC employee in England, pointed out that after years of activity, it was only in 2009 that its national director attended his first Old Firm derby at Ibrox. Certainly anti-Irish racism doesn't fit the narrative of mainly non-white newcomers facing discrimination from the host society. Responding effectively to a longstanding cleavage in a faction-ridden society is also bound to require more commitment than some anti-racists working professionally in that field, are prepared to give.[60]

Given their lack of friends in the Scottish power structure, many fans vocal in social media believed that they would be the ones to chiefly fall foul of the SNP's law. Jeanette Findlay, of the Celtic Supporters Trust, said in 2012: 'This legislation is entirely aimed at Celtic fans. The existing legislation was entirely adequate, it was there and it could be used.' [61] Celtic Fans Against Criminalisation was formed to oppose the law, after it became clear that opposition from liberals and civil liberties groups was lukewarm or non-existent. Third sector groups, active in proclaiming the need for tolerance and respect for different cultures, were bound to be uneasy about a campaign to preserve songs and chants that many deemed as offensive.

Old-style and new forms of tolerance were in conflict here. In its original form toleration meant permitting other people's words and slogans, however unappealing they might have seemed:

'Children were taught that sticks and stones did not break their bones and individuals were expected to recognise the difference between words and actions. Words and their free use were considered important in a free society; name-calling might make children cry, but adults would teach them to deal with this and to grow up. . .'[62]

But some years ago, the sociologist Frank Furedi began to detect a new form that had powerful state backing. Tolerance was primarily viewed as being non-judgmental. It was wrong to challenge or question or offend different 'cultures' in any way. To judge was to be hurtful and we must offer respect unthinkingly towards 'difference' and 'diversity'. . .[63]

Stuart Waiton contended that in the new climate independently-arrived 'judgment was replaced by a formulaic unthinking respect of difference that is lifeless and not part of a culture of free contesting ideas and beliefs'. He identified a 'new moralising form of tolerance [that] has become a central framework around which the new Scottish elite and its institutions have organised themselves. . . With few ideas on how a future should be shaped, they embrace all ideas,' but insert various restraints to prevent their suitability coming under fire.[64]

Jackie Kemp, a social commentator, expressed not unrelated concerns. She saw the proposed law as an attempt to drive 'the hard, rough manners of old industrial Scotland' from places where they were still to be found such as football stadiums. It involved replacing a macho culture with a largely feminised world where 'discourse should be conducted at all times politely and with reference to the personal feelings of others. Shouting is always unacceptable, so is abuse'. [65] In her eyes, a dangerous Rubicon was being crossed:

'. . . making singing and chanting offences punishable by significant jail terms is an Orwellian response. What does tolerance really mean if it only extends to people with whom one agrees?'[66]

Even before the 'anti-sectarian bill' came into law, a disturbing case arose which indicated how far the criminalisation of speech could go. Stephen Birrell, a Rangers fan was jailed for eight months for expressing his hatred of Celtic fans on his Facebook page. 'Proud to hate fenian tattie farmers,' he said; there were no threats or incitement to hatred. Comedians frequently say far worse on television and radio but they are exempt from this law unless they decide to perform in the narrow spaces defined by the act. For the journalist Alex Massie, the jailing of Birrell was a thought crime, and 'a shameful moment that demeans the country far more than anything said, sung or written at or about any damn football match.' [67]

A virtually unchanged bill obtained its final reading in a debate held in Holyrood on 14 December 2011. Michael McMahon noted that some of the civil-servants who heard well-reasoned viewpoints from able people in his constituency about why this was a harmful law, too easily concluded that some of these Lanarkshire people were prisoners of backward views.[68] What placed apart a lot of civic-minded people in Lanarkshire from the bureaucrats and politicians in Edinburgh, according to the MSP, was that the former were often willing to base their approach to policy around a Christian perspective. It helped narrow denominational suspicions but it was at variance with the post-Christian world view that was increasingly entrenched at Holyrood.

On the day of the vote, supporters of Fans against Criminalisation were barred from taking their seats in the public gallery after it was discovered that they were wearing t-shirts that together spelled out 'Fans not Criminals' and 'SNP Shame on You'. Environmental activists had previously been allowed to display overt symbols of dissent. But the parliament's security chief was adamant that the Celtic visitors were going nowhere. It led to heated exchanges between several MSPs and their staff some of which I witnessed.[69]

All the opposition parties united to oppose the bill but it was passed thanks to the SNP using its overall majority to vote *en bloc* for the measure. Roseanna Cunningham saw one particular sport as the primary arena where action was needed against sectarianism because of her belief that 'it manifests itself in the context of football more visibly than anywhere else.'[70]

She was unmoved by the civil liberties concerns and showed little inclination to display equivalent vigilance in economic or other spheres. By early 2013, the police were starting to crackdown on the Green Brigade which had spearheaded much of the grassroots opposition to the law. This core group of fans, arguably most conscious of the club's history and Irish traditions, boycotted two matches due to the harassment it claimed to be receiving ; on 17 February 2013, in a statement it claimed:

> 'It has now gotten to the stage whereby members of our group live in constant fear of the police showing up at their homes or workplace with a trumped up charge, or to be told that they are banned from football matches as they approach the gates. . .' [71]

Several days later, the *Sun* reported that a policeman assigned to monitor Celtic fans had been moved to other duties after he 'had apparently bragged on Facebook that he works at 'Fume-a-Pest & Termite Control'. This led Stuart Waiton to claim that some of the main fears about the state's intentions towards football spectators were being confirmed: '. . . footy fans are viewed as scum by the Government and police. . . Through "over-the-top policing", they are being intimidated in a way that would be seen as unacceptable if carried out against any other section of society.' [72]

Much of this perspective has been endorsed by lawyers and also by the *Herald*. In an editorial, a year after the football legislation came into force, it contended that 'it has resulted in the surveillance and harassment of football fans who have committed no offence.' Such concern was expressed after studying cases which the newspaper believed 'amount to a draconian and unjust treatment of individuals. The law put in place by the SNP comes uncomfortably close to a new form of institutional prejudice against all football supporters, worsening relations between the police and the public.' [73]

Ironically, after 120 years of Old Firm duels, the main occurrence which the legislation was meant to oversee, vanished from the football calendar when Rangers was hit by an unprecedented calamity. On 14 February 2012, Her Majesty's Revenue and Customs (HMRC) moved to put the club into administration over an unpaid tax bill of £9 million; it was a debt that appeared to be owed to the tax authorities after the club had been hastily sold off to a hitherto obscure businessman, Craig Whyte in May 2011. [74]

Rangers were the reigning champions of Scotland and held the record for the number of domestic league titles won by any professional football club in the world when, suddenly, they confronted what appeared to be certain ruin. A widespread sense of loss gripped many fans, especially poorer ones with little else to occupy their lives, as Rangers suddenly crashed out of top-flight football.

The upheaval in Scottish football inevitably had reverberations in the world of politics. The most eagerly-awaited reaction was from Alex Salmond. In order to maximize support for independence, he had been arguing in early 2011 that a 'Social Union' would survive a formal split. Scotland would not move into a post-British future at all but through the crown, the armed forces, the BBC the National Health Service and now it seems a common currency, the pound sterling, there would hopefully be a durable social union. On 15 February, Salmond declared that Rangers was part of the 'fabric of the country' and HMRC must remain aware of this when pursuing its case against the Glasgow club. With regard to its chief rival,'he added, 'The most die-hard Celtic supporter understands that Celtic can't prosper unless Rangers are there. The rest of the clubs understand that as well.'[75]

Celtic's reaction to its rival's plight would help determine the severity of its punishment. However, its owners showed no inclination to delay or minimise the extent of Rangers's retreat from front-rank football. Soon, the SFA deemed that Rangers were disqualified from remaining in the Premier League due to thier failure to reach agreement with creditors and subsequent liquidation. But the club, under the control of a new company, Sevco Ltd, later to be renamed Rangers FC Ltd, was told in June 2012 by the SFA that it would be playing in the lowly 3rd division in the 2012-13 season. Celtic had enough clout to be able to minimise the extent of their rival's fall but Chief Executive Peter Lawwell showed the self-absorbed mood at the top of the club when he crisply told Salmond that their own future was not reliant on that of any other club:

'We are very disappointed with the First Minister's claims that Celtic "need" Rangers and that Celtic "can't prosper unless Rangers are there. . ." This is simply not true. In a series of interviews given just three days ago, we made it abundantly clear that Celtic has a well-defined strategy and a business plan independent of the fortunes of any other club.'

'We are extremely well-qualified to make our own position clear
and have no wish to see this being misrepresented for political
reasons.'[76]

It is unclear whether the Celtic business plan anticipated the sharp
fall-off in match attendance in the new season, with their old rival nowhere
in sight, and Celtic facing a series of monotonous fixtures against rivals
whom it should easily have outclassed but often failed to. At least one
journalist pointed out to Lawwell that a more prudent attitude would have
been to come to the assistance of its rival as had happened in Germany
recently when Bayern Munich had helped Borussia Dortmund out of a
tight financial hole. [77]

A sports media in Scotland that often appeared unduly reliant on the
patronage of Rangers, appeared to be disorientated by the demise of a
club which had been indirectly responsible for cash-strapped newspapers
hanging on to a large clutch of readers. The disarray of the conventional
press left the field open for new forms of online journalism to acquire
prominence by pursuing the Rangers story. The most notable new entrant
was a blog called RTC which started up in March 2011 and in 2012 won the
Orwell prize for journalism. RTC stands for 'Rangers Tax Case' and its owner
has studiously preserved his anonymity. In his inaugural post, he stated:

'My motivation to write is born out of the wilful ignorance of the
Scottish media on this story. While they reprint unbelievable PR
fiction related to Rangers as news, Scotland's Fourth Estate has gone
to great efforts to ignore the tax story. . .

'This blog will provide details on Rangers FC's appeals against tax
bills which the club has received for underpayment of tax going back
to 2001'.[78]

Stuart Cosgrove, director of diversity at Channel 4 but also a co-
presenter of BBC Radio Scotland's 'Off the Ball', hailed the appearance of
new media outlets offering a challenging fresh perspective on the troubles
of Scottish football. Writing in the 'Scottish Football Monitor' blog, he
explained the new media landscape with the aid of concepts borrowed
from 'French Marxist philosophy', even declaring that there had been 'a

fundamental change in the way we construct and receive knowledge'. [79]

Alasdair McKillop, one of the founders of *Rangers Standard,* a blog meant to offer serious discussion and analysis in order to prepare Rangers to overcome the stiffest challenges in its history, was unimpressed by the new forms of journalism. He believed that the mysterious release of restricted documents which were then dissected by people with knowledge of tax and legal matters, was part of an organised campaign to presume the guilt of Rangers and promote an atmosphere of condemnation and ridicule that would hasten its disappearance. He was also unimpressed by the ideological dimensions with the struggle being depicted as one between 'the establishment' and 'the people'.[80]

Mike Small, one of the most prolific journalists on the far-left of Scottish politics, claimed in July 2012 that Rangers' starting in the lowest league is 'a victory for fans over an inept elite. It means drastic cuts in Scottish football. Some clubs may have to close or downsize'. Remarkably, this doyen of the radical left asserted: 'This is no bad thing. We know we have too many clubs in this country. Endlessly chasing an utterly unsustainable model is failed economics.' This advocate of 'people's power' sounded more like a cold-hearted merger capitalist gleeful at the chance to 'rationalise' an industry that once had provided an important function for an entire community.[81]

Meanwhile, Gerry Hassan of the *Scotsman* felt able to argue that 'a wave of democratic protest' was changing the face of Scottish football: 'Over the summer, football fans across Scotland have come together, agitated and organised and overturned the time-honoured stitch-up which would have kept a newco Rangers in the SPL.'[82]

It is unclear why Hassan and Small assumed that depriving tens of thousands of mainly working-class fans of real sporting pleasure was a breakthrough for anything. The warriors for democracy whom Hassan named in his press piece were actually internet polemicists; the most uninhibited Phil MacGiolla Bhain may go down in history as someone who managed to open fresh wounds in the relations between Celtic and Rangers, at the level of popular culture, at a time when there was a real possibility of at least reducing the long-running enmity.

Alex Thomson, the Channel 4 journalist who wrote the preface for his book, admitted that: 'He wishes to see Rangers FC obliterated as far as I can discern' and 'he writes about Rangers' downfall with undisguised glee and mirth.' [83]

Perhaps not until the appearance of Phil Mac Giolla Bhain's articulate blog, implacably hostile to Rangers and its political sub-culture, has there been such an overt platform encompassing commitment to Celtic with passionate invocations of a heavily politicised Irish folk heritage.[84] This talented polemicist has thrived during the years of crisis for Rangers thanks to the unwillingness of an often sycophantic Scottish media to follow up stories that could have shed light on just how severe were the problems bearing down on the club. Resident in County Donegal and an activist in the National Union of Journalists, he has broken a number of stories shedding light on the dire state of the club's finances. I favourably reviewed a 2010 semi-autobiographical book, also called *Rebel Journalist,* in which he detailed his efforts to break stories that the established media preferred to overlook.[85]

But I soon developed second thoughts when he used his blog to launch a campaign to dehumanise Rangers supporters. This culminated in a notorious posting called 'the Incubator' in which 'Professor Struth' (presumably based on the legendary second manager of the club Bill Struth) creates a monster in his laboratory which proceeds to terrorise Glasgow.[86]

It was a palpable hit with the backwoodsmen among Celtic's following who finally had their deeply antagonistic feelings toward the dark enemy being articulated by an avenging angel.

After 'Jim' wrote in May 2012, 'The fascist club at Ibrox become more isolated by the day,' I warned about where this could be heading:

'Ever since the Ibrox club plunged into crisis, Phil has been busy trying to bury it and dancing on top of its grave when he thinks the job is done. Rangers is habitually described here as worthless, dangerous, a gonner in fact, so why not have a reader enlighten us with the gem that the club (and presumably its supporters) are "fascist" too.

'Phil is sowing dragon's teeth by allowing such ugly views the light of day and even encouraging them with his own highly-charged and often lurid interpretation of events. For any visitors to the site who are not Celtic ultras, the comments show that many among Phil's following are vindictive, petty and comically absurd in their perspective. It does not place the community they spring from in a terribly attractive light.'[87]

MacGiolla Bhain, rather than engage with these concerns, merely remarked: 'Tom, I refer you to Severin Carrell's excellent work on the presence of the neo-fascist right within the Rangers sub culture.'[88]

He appeared to be supremely unmindful about the impact his hard-edged campaign against Rangers and all its works might have on community relations in Scotland. As a trained social worker, he must have known how dangerous people in a fragile psychological state can become if what provides meaning in their lives is suddenly snatched away from them, and how innocent bystanders can quickly become the victims of their distress.

He was praised by Alex Thomson of Channel 4 news who wrote the preface for his book *Downfall*. Exactly 100 reviews had been posted on Amazon by 22 November 2012, two months after its appearance, 45 with 5 stars, 49 with 1 star and only 6 in between (indicating his genius at polarising opinion). He observed on 6 November 2012: 'Sure they won't even review THE bestselling Non Fiction book in Scotland this year. . . '[89]

On 5 July 2012, he wrote that 'Ibrox has been a culture dish for some very toxic societal pathogens for over a century.'[90] He had unpacked this argument in February of that year, confidently asserting that Rangers fans were 'The Trailer Trash of a dead empire'. [91]

In the left nationalist magazine, *Bella Caledonia*, he described himself as taking part in 'a culture war' against Britishness; without it being waged, 'Scots would remain happy with this early eighteenth century Anschluss' [the Union].

'I had grown up in a culturally Irish household that saw the predatory expansionism of the London state as a historical problem. Therefore I could spot the false consciousness issue quite clearly. The death of that football club could have positive unforeseen

208

consequences for those who wish to advance Scotland's claim of right.'[92]

But despite the unmistakable Marxist overtones in his interpretation of the Rangers crisis, it was the *Sun* newspaper which was ready to give the online polemicist the publicity which had hitherto been denied him in Scotland. A double-page spread promoting the author and the coming serialisation of his book appeared in the 1 September 2012 edition of the *Sun*. It described how Phil Mac Giolla Bhain had been given death threats for his role in uncovering the financial scandal that was to engulf Rangers. 'We knew he was a controversial figure, but it was clear from the book he had written that he had a story to tell.'[93]

By 3 September, the *Sun* had decided to scrap the serialisation after many Rangers fans contacted the paper. It reported the *volte-face* in this way:

> 'Most were reasonable, and wanted to point out some of the other material that the author carries on his website. Others. . .
> immediately engaged in the kind of disgusting abuse that sadly infects some of Scottish football's blogs and forums. . .
> Phil Mac Giolla Bhain is not one of our journalists and his blog undermines the entire industry.
> THAT is why we have decided not to carry the serialisation of the book.
> NOT because of the social media backlash.
> NOT because of the internet bullies.
> But because the author – previously unbeknown to us – is tarred with a sickening sectarian brush.
> We believed Phil Mac Giolla Bhain to be a proper and sound journalist. Channel 4 News chief correspondent Alex Thomson obviously agreed and wrote the foreword in the book. He was wrong and so were we.'[94]

MacGiolla Bhain, as quoted in the *Guardian*, declared: 'I think this is a dark day for journalism in Scotland when a major title can be forced into self-censoring in this fashion.'[95] But perhaps unavoidably, he is no stranger to censorship on his own principal media outlet. On 12 June 2012, he wrote:

'Today should put the officially sanctioned narrative of Rangers to bed for all time. HMRC will move to have the club liquidated. Their guys will carry out the liquidation. It will be a corporate execution on a digital scaffold to be viewed by all on Planet Fitba. Their humiliation will be total.'[96]

But in November an HMRC tribunal upheld Rangers' appeal which meant that its tax bill would be reduced from an estimated £74 million to around £2 million.[97] Mac Giolla Bhain's predictions about the complete destruction of Rangers were shown to be somewhat inflated. But he refused to publish a reply in which I exhorted him to give up his onslaught due to the harm being done to community relations. Its conclusion read:

'It is one thing to use your talents as a writer and agitator to expose the institutional wrongs at the heart of football in Scotland and the way it has been covered. But it is unkind, and I would contend rather unwise, to continue with this crusade against Rangers' continued existence. Rangers will return to big-time football and it is far better that the atmosphere at future Old Firm derbies will be free of new layers of rancour that should have nothing to do with the game.' [98]

In December 2012, when Charles Green, the new owner of Rangers managed to raise capital of £22 million in a successful share issue, it was difficult to persist with the narrative on hostile blogs about the club hurtling towards certain doom, but the commentary grew shriller. [99] This Yorkshire businessman appeared eager to engage with the media and supporters, the Rangers tradition of showing pride and aloofness to the outside world being discarded. On 28 February, the atmosphere further lightened for Rangers when Lord Nimmo Smith's tribunal ruled that the club would not be stripped of honours won during a period when his panel nevertheless ruled that it had broken players payments rules. The Gers' avenging internet angel raged about a club supported by 'a fascist underclass' who enjoyed impunity in Scottish football.[100] But Green's time at the Rangers helm was shortlived. He quit as CEO on 19 April 2013. He was linked, through financial transactions, to the discredited tenure of his predecessor Craig Whyte. Even worse in some eyes, he had been prone to indiscretions of speech that in some quarters amounted to racist language. [101]

Scottish football appeared a sorry spectacle by 2013.[102] The national side ranked seventy-seventh in world footballing terms. Celtic's performances were often lacklustre even against inferior sides. A spectre of insolvency hung over much of Scottish football, the historic Edinburgh side Hearts being threatened with closure by the tax authorities. In a febrile atmosphere, the Scottish Football Association was slammed in different quarters for poor leadership.

It remains to be seen if fans can put aside traditions of internecine rivalry to try and make sporting priorities, rather than those of corporate power, influence the direction of Scottish football. At the time of writing, the omens are not good. The rest of the Scottish fan base in the main welcomed the relegation of Rangers to a minor league in 2012 once alleged financial irregularities were taken seriously by the SFA and tax authorities. Even despite the success of a cerebral blog like the *Rangers Standard* revealing that there are plenty of passionate fans able to instill pride in the club without resorting to crude tribal metaphors, it remains isolated. Arguably, Celtic and Rangers both have a vested interest in joining the English premier league which would offer higher-quality opposition as well as financial rewards. David Cameron even indicated his backing for such an outcome, one that suited his unionist priorities. But Scottish football in general and the Old Firm duo in particular appear set to be apples of discord, beset by commercial troubles, eyed covetously by political forces, and occasionally rocked by sectarian tremors.

NOTES

1 Walls, 'The health of Irish-descended Catholics', p. 253.

2 Jack O'Sullivan, 'I'm Catholic in a football sense', *Independent*, 04 June 1999.

3 David Kerr, 'Charting the electoral winds of change', *Scottish Catholic Observer*, 1 July 2011

4 Dave Coull, www.our-scotland.org Forum Index -> UK and Ireland Politics (no date).

5 Andrew Whitaker, 'Catholic QC warns of bigotry after split from UK', *Scotsman*, 31 August 2011.

6 Ian Dunn, 'SNP quizzed over education stance', *Scottish Catholic Observer*, 17 February 2012.

7 *Scottish Catholic Observer*, 21 December 2012.

8 Peter Lynch, 'The Scottish Parliament and Sectarianism' in Devine, *Scotland's Shame*, p.p. 256-7.

9 *Independent Catholic News*, 26 February 2007 .

10 BBC News, 8 August 2010

11. Graham Walker, in Gerry Hassan and Graham Warhurst, *Anatomy of the New Scotland*, Mainstream Publishing, Edinburgh, 2002, p. 255

12 BBC News, 25 July 2011.

13 BBC News, 28 November 2010.

14 Roddy Forsyth, *Daily Telegraph*, 30 November 2010.

15 Forsyth, *Daily Telegraph*, 30 November 2010.

16 'Papal Visit', Online Fieldwork 9-11 September 2011, prepared by ORB (Opinion Research Business).'

17 I have seen many of these E mails.

18 *Daily Record*, 22 December 2008.

19 'Church spokesman claims anti Catholic hostility in Scotland "deep and wide",' *Sunday Times*, 28 November 2010.

20 Peter Kearney, 'Anti-Catholic hostility in Scotland', Part 1 (text supplied by the Scottish Catholic Media Office).

21 Mark Smith, 'Dallas case does the Church a disservice', *Scotsman*, 20 December 2010.

22 Peter Kearney, *Sunday Times*, 28 November 2010.

23 *The Sun*, 21 April 2011.

24 *The Sun*, 21 April 2011.

25 Russell Leadbetter, Sunday Herald, 28 November 2010.

26 Paul O'Hare, Magnus Gardham and Lachlan Mackinnon, 'Old Firm fallout: Police chief vows 'This madness cannot go on', *Daily Record*, 4 March 2011

27 Iain Macwhirter, 'This dumb, unjust law is Salmond's first own goal', *Herald*, 15 December 2011.

28 Alex Massie, 'A Bill That Shames Scotland', *Spectator*, 21 June 2011.

29 Interview with Michael McMahon MSP 2012.

30 Tom Gallagher, 'The danger of letting the police decide what is offensive', *Scottish Review*, 21 December 2011.

31 *Daily Record*, 4 March 2011

32 Stuart Waiton, 'Snob's Law: Criminalising Football Fans in an Age of Intolerance', Dundee: Take a Liberty Scotland, 2012, p.52.

33 Macwhirter, 'This dumb, unjust law'.

34 Michael Kelly, 'Alex Salmond's anti-sectarian purge has gone too far', *Scotsman*, 17 November 2011.

35 *Guardian*, 20 April 2011.

36 Alex Massie, *Spectator*, 24 November 2011

37 Rob Marrs, Left Back In The Changing Room: Scotland's Gordian Knot', 23 April 2011.

38 BBC News, 23 June 2011.

39 *Daily Record*, 21 April 2011.

40 *The Herald*, 13 May 2001.

41 *The Herald*, 31 March 2012.

42 Graham Grant, Victoria Allen, and Grant McCabe, 'Bombers' attack on Scots society', *Daily Mail*, 31 March 2012

43 Peter Kearney. 'Anti-Catholic Hostility in Scotland', Part 2.

44 BBC News, 16 September 2003.

45 Campbell, *Celtic's paranoia*, p. 216-7.

46 BBC News, 30 August 2011.

47 *Scotsman*, 2 September 2011.

48 George Galloway, *Open Season*, Miranda media, 2011, p.p. 196-7.

49 See Scottish Government, www.Scotland.gov.uk/Topics/ustice/law/ sectarianism– action-1/football-violence/bill

50 Alan Pattullo, 'Dignity, not sanctimony, is required at Parkhead-SPL', *Scotsman*, 21 February 2012.

51 Richard Wilson, 'Lennon would be better served if more were revealed than the raw figure on the touchline', *The Herald*, 13 May 2011.

52 Phil Mac Giolla Bhain, 'The Teachable Moment', *Rebel Journalist*, 23 April 2011, www.philmacgiollabhain.com

53 *Scottish Daily Express*, 7 September 2011.

54 Brian Wilson, 'Let the people sing – yes, even football supporters', *Scotsman*, 30 November 2011.

55 Gareth Rose, *Scotsman* 21 September 2011.,

56 *Scotsman*, 19 November 2011.

57 Interview with Michael McMahon, 2012.

58 Joseph Bradley, 'One Scotland Many Cultures', *Irish Studies Review*, Vol. 14, No 2, 2006, p. 192.

59 Bradley, 'One Scotland', p. 192.

60 See Tom Gallagher, 'Famine Song to Dallasgate', *Scottish Review*, 3 March 2011.

61 *Scotsman*, 25 March 2012.

62 Stuart Waiton, 'The rise and rise of intolerant tolerance', Spiked, 5227 December 2011.

63 See Frank Furedi, *On Tolerance: A Defence of Moral Independence*, Continuum, London 2011.

64 Waiton, 'The rise and rise',

65 Jackie Kemp 'The agenda behind the bill: the feminization of Scotland', *Scottish Review*, 20 December 2011.

66 Kemp, 'The agenda behind the bill'.

67 Coffee House, *Spectator*, 18 October 2011.

68 Interview with Michael McMahon MSP, 5 February 2013.

69 Tom Gallagher, 'The danger of letting the police decide what is offensive', *Scottish Review*, 21 December 2011.

70 Minutes of the Scottish parliament, 14 December 2014

71 *Celtic Journal*, 17 February 2013.

72 *The Sun*, 17 February 2013.

73 Editorial, Tackling bigotry must be proportionate', *Herald*, 28 February 2013.

74 *Herald*, 20 February 2012.

75 'Celtic deny Salmond's claims', *Irish Times*, 16 February 2012.

76 'Celtic deny Salmond's claims'.

77 Alan Pattullo, 'Dignity, not sanctimony, is required at Parkhead', *Scotsman*, 20 February 2012.

78 www.rangerstaxcase.wordpress.com/2011/03/page2

79 Stuart Cosgrove, 'Why the Beast of Armageddon failed to show', *Scottish Football Monitor*, www.scottishfootballmonior.blog

80 Alasdair McKillop, 'Rangers were found guilty of cheating on little more than a hope', *Rangers Standard*, 22 November 2012.

81 Mike Small, 'Rangers' starting in the lowest league is a victory for fans over an inept elite', *Guardian*, 16 July 2012.

82 Gerry Hassan, 'The Wave of Democratic Protest that Changed Scottish Football will Change Society', *Scotsman*, 4 August 2012.

83 'Rangers: Why I endorsed Downfall book', Alex Thomson's View, 17 September 2012, www.blogs.channel4.com/alex-thomsons-view.

84 'Rebel Journalist', www.philmacgiollabhain,com

85 Tom Gallagher, 'Famine Song to Dallasgate', *Scottish Review*, 3 March 2011.

86 'The Incubator', 20 April 2012, www.philmacgiollabhain,com.

87 'Blant Urr nights', 19 May 2012, www.philmacgiollabhain,com.

88 Severin Carrell is the Scottish correspondent of *The Guardian*.

89 'La Breithe Shona do Celtic'!, 6 November 2012, www.philmacgiollabhain,com

90 'Hearing Clearly', 5 July 2012, www.philmacgiollabhain,com.

91 'Too cowardly to report, too bigoted to believe', www.philmacgiollabhain,com, 18 February 2012

92 Phil Mac Giolla Bhain, 'Walking Away from North Britain', *Bella Caledonia*, 21 June 2012.

93 *The Sun* (Scottish edition), 1 September 2010.,

94 Paul McConville, 'Playing the Man and Not the Ball' – *The Sun*, Rangers and Downfall by Phil Mac Giolla Bhain, Random Thoughts Re Scots law, 3 September 2012, www.scotslawthoughts.wordpress.com.

95 Roy Greenslade's blog, 'Scottish Sun cancels book serialisation after Rangers fans jam switchboard', *Guardian*, 3 September 2012.

96 'Liquidation day', 12 June 2012, www.philmacgiollabhain,com,

97 *Daily Telegraph*, 21 November 2012. See also Alasdair McKillop, 'Rangers were found guilty of cheating on little more than a hope', *Scottish Review*, 22 November 2012.

98 submitted to the forum after 'The body at the bottom of the stairs', 21 November 2012, www.philmacgiollabhain,com.

99 A cerebral perspective about the sustainability of the Green regime is provided by Paul McConville, 'Charles Green, Lenders Option', Random Thoughts Re Scots law, 21 February 2013, www.scotslawthoughts.wordpress.com.

100 'An amoral victory', 1 March 2013, www.philmacgiollabhain.com

101 Graham Spiers, 'Green consumed in bonfire of his own making', *The Herald*, 20 April 2013.

102 Andrew Sanders, 'Scottish Football: The Season that Was', *Rangers Standard*, 17 April 2013.

CHAPTER 10

Scottish Christianity: from Malaise to Crisis

THE OFFENSIVE BEHAVIOUR at Football Act beamed the spotlight on an assertive state that was determined to impose morality in a sphere of life believed to be disfigured by quasi-religious passions. Perhaps a long-term perspective is required to place the rise of a state-driven morality in Scotland in context.

In his book *The Unintended Reformation: How a Religious Revolution Secularised Society*, Brad Gregory explores some of the crucial consequences of the Reformation down to modern times. It shattered the concept of Christendom as Europe proceeded to exhaust itself in destructive religious wars.[1] A unified system of Christian morals was swept away and the Enlightenment, from the eighteenth century, sought to supersede contending religious absolutisms. The state sought to rein in and manage religions, acting as an honest broker when introspective disputes threatened wider disruption. Its secular design for living in Scotland arguably enjoyed no greater success than religious philosophies, a 'hyper-plural' set of values enjoying an uneasy sway down to the twenty-first century. No ethical foundation for economic activity or social behaviour loomed on the horizon in secular Scotland.

This chapter profiles an increasingly defensive institutional Christian order in Scotland, with the main attention being devoted to the Catholic Church. It argues that a declining religious base means that the main Christian faiths lack the energy and self-confidence to renew themselves or provide a moral design for a rudderless country. A secular establishment has sprung up relatively recently that has filled the vacuum in policies and ideas in the public sphere. Its ascendancy shows no sign of waning even though its vision for a post-industrial country with a clutch of social problems that is contemplating bold political change, often appears to be an insubstantial one.

Beyond Europe in societies with contrasting political systems and levels of economic development, religion retains the very influential place which it has vacated in Scotland. It has been claimed for instance that there are already more people in China attending Christian services on a Sunday than in the whole of Europe.'[2] In Scotland, religious adherence is often associated with national divisiveness. There are no shortage of commentators ready to assert that the origins of the confrontational side of political discourse can be traced back to the divisive hold religious passions have exercised over the minds of men and women.[3] A Catholic online blogger, *Cum Lazaro*, believes that some contemporary comment- ators are using sectarianism to argue that modern Scotland no longer has a place for religion and that a successful passage to a new self-governing modernity cannot occur without religion's final dethronement.[4]

In defence of the Scottish Christian record in modern times, the rival denominations were usually not prepared to push their differences to the point of outright division. There was an uneasy peace based on mutual accommodation over issues like education.

In a firmly secular Scottish state run along rationalist principles will there be the same pragmatism, or will it be that 'shouty' interest groups decide to go for absolute secular primacy along the lines of what happened in post-1789 France? In England, emphasising an agenda of inclusion and good works, that is firmly secular in scope, has been a feature of David Cameron's post-2010 makeshift coalition government. An impatience with the idea of the churches influencing public morality was evident in his 'Big Society' initiative designed to increase the role of citizens and voluntary groups in promoting social cohesion. It had no noticeable religious component which was surely not the only reason why civic engagement in the form of voluntary activities actually fell during the years in which it was promoted.[5]

In his episcopacy Archbishop Winning had already felt the need to issue a warning about a social climate increasingly hostile to religion:

> 'We live in a world where man has acquired a new arrogance, a false independence: he senses a victory over the forces of nature and has pushed the true God into the background of his life and fashioned

new gods to worship. . . the Church today. . . has never had to tread quite the same depth of darkness. . .' [6]

His period at the helm in Glasgow revealed an inexorable decline in the importance of religion for his flock. A poll carried out by Gallup in 1979 showed that of Scotland's 600,000 Catholics, 54% attended Mass, but 58% approved of birth control, but there was also 73% backing for Catholic schools.[7]

The priority that the church gave to development work in the Third World through the Scottish Catholic International Aid Fund (SCIAF) was proof of its commitment to social justice abroad.[8] The Labour Party continued to be seen as the chief guarantor of these kind of policies at home. But in England Labour MPs from an Irish Catholic background, such as Bob Mellish, Michael O'Halloran and Peter Kilfoyle clashed, sometimes very acrimoniously, with left-wing activists convinced that change lay through a rejection of traditional social conventions.

Abortion was probably the primary cause of the discord between a proletarian base and newly assertive middle-class activists. Between 1967 and 2012, seven million foetuses had been aborted in Britain, only 143 of the termination of pregnancies undertaken because the mother's life was at risk.[9] David Alton stood down as a Liberal Democrat MP in 1997 over this issue and later quit the party whose prominent Scottish member, David Steel had ensured that abortion was de-criminalised in 1967.

A record number of Catholics had been elected to parliament in 1997 when Labour began its thirteen years in office – 64 compared with only 32 in 1966 – but the influence of Catholic values on policy during the longest period of Labour rule, would shrink dramatically.

The composer James MacMillan expressed his concern about the shift in labour values:

'My grandfather was part of a Catholic rearguard action in the NUM in the 1930s and 40s to safeguard the union from a far-left takeover. He, and most of the politically active working class in places like Ayrshire throughout the twentieth century, were old-style socialists. . .

'The Labour movement was their vehicle to build the just society that was promised in the gospels; the welfare state and greater access to education were seen as fruits of moral Christian activism in society.

'A new generation appeared, whose interest seemed less in economic inequality and more in confronting the traditional values of people like my grandfather. . .

'The traditional family and education, sexual mores, artistic aspirations, religious belief – all were now seen as coercive strategies of the powerful, designed to enforce conformity and slavish obedience.' [10]

Strikingly, no Scottish Catholic MP (or indeed MSP) ever gave voice to these kind of concerns. Several achieved high office and are now in the House of Lords: John McFall, Tommy McAvoy, Des Browne, and Michael Martin. It is not unreasonable to suspect that their elevation, at least in part, arose because of their willingness to acquiesce (through silence), in the sidelining of traditional working-class perspectives on a range of social issues.

Nearing the end of his life, Winning had few friends in the Labour Party, excepting George Galloway who wrote for many years in his diocesan paper *Flourish* (but even such a relationship that was bound to be a testy one between two patriarchal types, turned sour). When Winning criticised Blair for allegedly going against his conscience and the views of his constituents by voting for abortion, Catholic figures in Scottish Labour rallied around their Prime Minister: the high-profile Lanarkshire MP, Helen Liddell, later Baroness Liddell of Coatdyke, said her constituency was almost 100% Catholic and those attending her surgery were 'outraged' at the cardinal's 'attack'.[11] Similar comments about Cardinal O'Brien having lost touch with many Catholics in the pews over his hostility to gay marriage, would be heard in 2012.

When Pope Benedict XVI came to Britain in 2010, there were no Scottish parliamentarians in Edinburgh or Westminster with a strongly Christian profile ready to defend his visit against opposition, the bulk of which was coming from secularists. Among VIPs who endorsed a petition urging the Pope to call off his visit were two Scottish Labour peers, Martin O'Neill and George Foulkes.[12]

Donald Dewar, one of the main architects of devolved Scotland, found it hard to conceal 'his general distaste for religion'.[13] The main crisis of his eighteen months as First Minister was undoubtedly over the repeal of Section 28 which forbade discussion of homosexuality in school classes. Winning led the campaign to retain clause 28. In a referendum financed by the transport entrepreneur Brian Souter a total of 1,260,846 ballot papers were returned, 86% of those voting favouring the maintenance of the ban.[14] The collapse in relations between Labour and the church was shown by Dewar's refusal to follow the example of education minister David Blunkett in England and agree that the 'importance of marriage' would be taught in classrooms. Dewar made sure that Scottish children would be taught the 'value of a stable family life'. [15] Dewar's closest allies included two young, able MSPs with strongly secular outlooks, Wendy Alexander and Susan Deacon. As health minister, Deacon ensured that condoms and morning after pills became available in Scottish schools (John Deighan, the Catholic church's parliamentary officer seeing her as the chief political driving-force behind a secularist agenda in a devolved Scotland). [16]

A future Scottish First Minister Henry McLeish, in the late 1990s was the last minister who in a government document gave conventional families pride of place as the cornerstone of domestic arrangements encouraging social stability.[17] Thereafter, it was believed that emphasising mothers and fathers might just stigmatise children with looser family backgrounds.

Section 28 was repealed in Scotland in June 2000 with the passing of the Ethical Standards in Public Life bill. In a private interview Winning said of the bill: 'If that is democracy, then I am no longer a democrat.' [18] Having reassured Catholics that they had nothing to fear from a Scottish parliament before 1997, he branded the institution 'an utter failure' within three years.[19]

But the church's voice was strangely muted on the need to uphold Catholic family values against influential voices stating that the time was overdue to legitimise lifestyles that did not only involve a mother and a father at their centre. No influential voice was raised, arguing that for a great many young women, marriage and motherhood are more important than a career. Voices insisting that Scottish women had been led astray by radical feminism and the view that the surest route to happiness was a career that offered financial independence with men and marriage being strictly optional, were absent from the Scottish media (unlike in England or Ireland). The Glasgow-born English Tory Iain Duncan-Smith (a Catholic convert) was almost alone in speaking out about the negative outcomes that could flow from a benefit and tax system that, for people in the bottom fifth of the population, makes traditional marriage disadvantageous.[20] Not one of Scotland's 129 MSPs has been on record saying anything remotely similar.

In 2006, an event occurred which symbolised the arrival in Scotland of a new order where it seemed public workers were obliged to actively identify with the cause of a mobilised minority. John Mitchell, a Catholic, working at Cowcaddens fire-station in Glasgow was one of nine firemen who were ordered against their will to take part in the event, Pride Scotia, in 2006. They were expected to fraternise with marchers dresses as nuns and priests who behaved in a lewd manner in order to ridicule Christianity. The firemen decided instead to hand out fire safety leaflets to members of the public on a nearby street. They were then promptly disciplined by Strathclyde Fire and Rescue. Its chief, Brian Sweeney, declared the men had damaged their careers by their actions. He said: 'This is a strong disciplinary action. . . that is placed on their personal record file and puts them in a very difficult employment position.'

Failing to overturn the disciplinary findings at three internal appeals Mitchell took the matter to an Employment Tribunal. In his defence, it was made clear that, in line with Catholic teaching, he is opposed to homosexual acts without condemning homosexuals themselves. But he had never sought to foist his views on anyone else and felt that others should have shown him that same respect. In 2009, days before the hearing was due, Strathclyde Fire and Rescue admitted they had failed to take account of his religious beliefs. He was awarded damages and also received an apology from his employers. Mike Judge of the Newcastle-based Christian Institute said that 'it is tyrannical to punish someone because they will not take part in a public rally on an issue with which they disagree.'[21]

Chief Fire officer Brian Sweeney, who my researches indicate is (or was) a West of Scotland Catholic, confirms the success of a certain kind of integration for this community. Progress is assured in the state sector for a previously submerged social group if its aspirational members adhere to the rules of the secular state intent on regulating the behavior of its workforce. The tendency to tightly manage, and to enforce conformity, has deep and respectable roots in Scottish society going back at least to the Reformation. A God-centred Protestantism may be on the wane but the state still exhibits the Presbyterian inclination to impose strict rules meant to uphold a guiding doctrine in everyday life. Presbyterianism itself has become more decentralised, often based around congregations which reveal a strong element of participation and openness in their endeavour to perform practical giving in hard-pressed communities. Ironically, it is humanists and liberals at the helm of the Scottish state who are the new enforcers. Some show a rigidity towards people's private feelings which has characterised their backing for the sects that claim to be working for the liberation of gays and lesbians. Perhaps because, unlike hardline Protestants, the secular left has not usually been seen as an overt foe of Catholicism (at least in Britain), upwardly mobile Catholics often have had few qualms about functioning in this decidedly secular environment. Those who harbour qualms about performing work duties that appear to clash with the ethical foundations underpinning their faith find that the state can sometimes be unforgiving if crossed, which may also help to enforce conformity.

Two Catholic midwifery sisters faced a stark choice when in 2008, a new management at Glasgow's Southern General Hospital ruled that from now on they would be forced to supervise the carrying out of abortions. In March 2012, the Court of Session ruled that the 1967 Abortion Act allowed only permitted qualified conscientious objection. The decision is likely to have worrying repercussions for people with pro-life views working in Scotland's health services.[22] It was overturned by the Court of Session as this book was going to press but an appeal from the NHS appears likely.

It remains to be seen if new planned legislation for legalising the concept of gay marriage will require professionals in the teaching profession to give witness for their faith. Hitherto, the spotlight has been on Catholic adoption societies.

The decision, late in 2012, of the Scottish Charities' regulator to withdraw the charitable status of the Catholic adoption agency, the St. Margaret's Children and Family Care Society, is a hardline ruling but one fully in line with its strongly secular outlook. This care society is just one of a number in Britain which face closure because of an ethical clash with the state over the 2010 Equality Act. The belief that 'they have a primary duty to try and ensure the welfare and future happiness of children in their care' means that Catholic adoption societies are sceptical that this can be done by allowing gay couples to adopt them.[23]

Both under Blair and Gordon Brown, Labour's willingness to acquire a reputation as a force for change through re-engineering society, spread disenchantment among some devout Scottish Catholics. In some quarters, it was hoped that the SNP would be more responsive to grassroots concerns about worrying forms of social change. But soon after taking office, there were signs that the SNP was partial towards social engineering. The party's manifesto, issued in 2010, revealed that it wished to broaden the definition of marriage. Disenchantment with each of its Unionist rivals won it an unexpected absolute majority at Holyrood in 2011. The Scottish Social Attitudes survey of 2010 provided figures that suggested support for same-sex marriage has risen from 41% in 2002 to 61% in 2010.[24]

Once again the most forthright opposition to this move would come from Catholic ranks. Cardinal Winning had spelled out his objections to the gay lifestyle as long ago as 2000. He wrote in the *Spectator*, 'Gay sex is wrong because such behaviour is not good for the human person. Far from liberating the person it ensnares them in a lifestyle that can never respond to the deepest longings of the human heart.'[25]

In a letter to the magazine, Sir Elton John retorted: 'Cardinal Winning and his ignorance are totally representative of why people are turning away from the Church. . .' [26]

Cardinal O'Brien repeatedly asserted that allowing gay marriage would be disastrous for the social fabric of Scotland and he demonstrated in front of Holyrood over the issue at the end of in 2011. But he and his allies across the Christian spectrum had a redoubtable opponent in the Equality Network. It was an influential NGO promoting equality across the range of Scottish life that enjoyed close links with the civil service. It worked closely with the Scottish Government Equality Unit's 'Hearts and Minds' division which was open about the need for radical state intervention to make social equality the norm in society. [27]

The Equality Network cooperate closely with Stonewall, a campaigning group of gays prominent in elite occupations and adept at networking. It has devised an award called 'UK Diversity Champions'. Many important national and local bodies have signed up, from the army and the fire service to major local authorities such as Glasgow and Edinburgh. They contribute £2,000 for this merit and they are given tasks to perform in order to fulfil the criteria. The re-education of employees in order to understand equality issues is a central priority. The Scottish government is one of its most vocal backers.

Tom French, the charity's policy co-ordinator, complained of the church's 'anti-gay agenda', one the Equality Network would oppose if promoted in schools.[28] For its part, the church feared that if a lawyer could successfully show that Catholic social teaching, as interpreted in religious education, was hostile to gay marriage, denominational education could face the biggest challenge in its 95-year history. The backing of the Scottish political and media establishment for gay marriage was a given. But in countries where it had been legalised, gays had not rushed to avail of the right and often Stonewall appeared to be talking over their heads. Interestingly, Alan Duncan, the first Conservative MP to come out as gay and who is in a civil partnership, is implacably opposed to gay marriage. So is Labour MP Ben Bradshaw who was the first Cabinet minister to enter into a civil partnership. He has stated that, 'This isn't a priority for the gay community. . . This is pure politics.' [29]

In framing legislation, the SNP decided to endorse the ultra-secular view. At the end of 2012, it was announced that new guidelines for prosecuting opponents of same-sex marriage were to be introduced in the Civil Partnership (Scotland) bill, designed to restrain anyone thought to be using inflammatory or offensive language on the subject. The Scottish Government also planned to forbid parents from removing children from all lessons where gay marriage was discussed from primary school upwards. [30] It remains to be seen what will happen to teachers who refuse to teach their pupils that marriage is what the expanding equality laws says it is. Archbishop Tartaglia of Glasgow had already stated that he could see himself 'going to jail' for speaking out against same-sex marriage.[31]

In Edinburgh and London, two governing parties bitterly at odds over the constitutional future of the UK, were prepared to close ranks to redefine the meaning of marriage and, by extension, the meaning of the marital home and the family. In some eyes, there seemed to be an absence of awareness in political circles of just how hard-won a social construct marriage had been and how it had had to 'fight against polygamy and against the idea that men owned women. It had to establish rules against incest, and against marrying children.'[32]

The social critic Brendan O'Neill saw this elite convergence as an 'intensification of the modern state's desire to get a foot in the door of our private lives and to assume sovereignty over our relationships'. [33] But at Westminster, there was more readiness to heed public unease than seemed to be the case at Holyrood.

154 MPs, about a quarter of the Commons, responded to a survey on voters feelings, 74% saying they would sum up the balance of correspondence they received as negative, with almost half, 47%, saying they were 'strongly negative'. Levels of opposition of well over 50% to David Cameron's plans to fast-track gay marriage into law were reported from each of the main parties.[34]

On 5 February 2013, 175 MPs at Westminster opposed Cameron's plans but at Holyrood, a parliament designed to be representative of the diversity of Scottish opinion, there were no vocal opponents. Instead, it was interest groups drawn from campaigning bodies closely linked to the bureaucracy, the media, and the universities which framed the debate. Tim Hopkins, director of the Equality Network stated his confidence the majority of people in Scotland support same-sex marriage but he opposed the call for a referendum on the issue made by Cardinal O'Brien in July 2012.[35]

Despite the SNP proclaiming that it was leading Scotland towards a new politics, it was secular elites drawn from interest groups close to the state which defined the debate in Scotland. Arguably the SNP, lacking economic remedies to reinforce the case for independence, was instead imbued with the centralising urge to micro-manage the worlds of parenting, the home, and domestic relationships.

Despite the strongest UK opposition coming from Scottish Catholicism, the debate in Scotland lacked the vigour and depth to be found in England and O'Brien's rhetorical vehemence was off-putting to some. Brendan O'Neill characterised gay marriage as a brazen attempt by a metropolitan elite to impose its will on society:

> '. . . an elite rewriting of the meaning of marriage. It elbows aside the central role marriage played for centuries – as an institution through which not only a couple but communities themselves managed the socialisation of children and intergenerational relationships – in favour of decreeing that marriage is simply and definitively 'about two people who love each other making a formal commitment to each other [It is] . . . simply about companionship.'[36]

Such views were rarely reflected in the Scottish print and broadcasting media, arguably the professions where a liberal lifestyle was already most esteemed. It was in the religious press rather than the mainstream media that an eloquent defence of traditional marriage was more easily found. The ex- BBC journalist, David Kerr, writing in a Catholic newspaper in 2011, argued:

> '. . . we now have several generations-worth of hard evidence which clearly re-affirms that children are most likely to flourish within a family based upon a mum and dad who are married to each other. Indeed, the married family is Scottish society's first, best and cheapest department of health, welfare and education. And while it is an ideal which is not always achievable it is still a concept held in high esteem by most Scots and in particular, say polls, by the young. . .'[37]

Aileen Campbell, the SNP's children's minister, defended a template for the raising of children in which references to mothers and fathers was conspicuously absent.[38] David Kerr, as recently as 2009, an SNP parliamentary candidate, continued to hope that Alex Salmond would make 'the correct call' and not 'make us only the 11th nation in the world to re-define marriage.'[39]

Hitherto, the church had been prepared to give the SNP the benefit of the doubt over radical law-making that allowed for civil partnerships and gay adoptions. But its leaders were now openly sceptical about promises, such as that Bishop Tartaglia of Paisley (as he then was) got from Alex Salmond that (in the prelate's words) 'introducing same-sex marriage would not restrict the freedom of Catholics to practice their faith.' A suspicious bishop went on to write:

> 'I am not sure if he understood the difference between freedom of worship and freedom of religion, or if he understood it only too well, and was hedging his bets, knowing full well that once legislation permitting same-sex marriage was on the statute books, zealots would call for sanctions against people who publicly expressed dissent from the new orthodoxy.' [40]

In Scotland the campaign to preserve marriage as essentially a heterosexual institution meant to encourage stable relationships and the socialisation of children was driven by the Catholic hierarchy. This allowed journalists in the media to argue that they were generals without an army owing to dissent in the pews.[41] It may also have been a sign of the fragmented nature of the clergy in Scotland as priests tried to cope with mounting burdens or, in some cases, buckled under the strain. By contrast, in England and Wales, it was a campaign dominated by grassroots clergy in which the bishops only intervened late in the day.

In January 2013, 1,054 priests, accounting for almost a quarter of all Catholic priests in England and Wales, in a joint letter, raised fears that their freedom to practice and speak about their faith will be 'severely' limited and dismissed Government reassurances as 'meaningless'.

David Cameron's moves to redefine marriage was even likened by these priests to those of Henry VIII, whose efforts to secure a divorce from Katherine of Aragon triggered centuries of upheaval between church and state. They warned that, taken in combination with equality laws and other legal restraints, the Coalition's plans would prevent Catholics and other Christians who work in schools, charities and other public bodies speaking freely about their beliefs on the meaning of marriage. Even the freedom to speak from the pulpit could be under threat, they claimed. And they feared that Christians who believe in the traditional meaning of marriage would effectively be excluded from some jobs – just as Catholics were barred from many professions from the Reformation until the nineteenth century.[42]

English MPs, including Labour ones had already indicated they would oppose Cameron's bill. But Scottish Catholic politicians including Willie Bain, MP for Glasgow North, Jackie Bailie, MSP for Dumbarton, Patricia Ferguson, MSP for Glasgow Maryhill and Neil Findlay, MSP for Lothians, have all told the 'equal marriage' campaign that they would vote in favour of the re-definition of marriage.[43] It was notable that in Scotland, the bill's architect, Frank Mulholland, the Lord Advocate, was a Catholic who was prepared to introduce tough sanctions to enforce a radical state-led agenda of secularism.

Cardinal O'Brien had described the gay marriage proposals as 'madness'. He asserted:

> 'The Scottish Government's consultation on redefining marriage had three times more respondents than the consultation on the constitution, demonstrating clearly that far more people are concerned about fundamental matters of morality at the present time.' [44]

The issue caused turmoil in the SNP just when a united front was needed in the run-up to the 2014 independence referendum. In August 2011 when the SNP parliamentarian John Mason put down a motion at Holyrood on the issue of same-sex marriage, he didn't condemn it but 'merely requested that no person or organisation should be forced to be involved in or to approve of same-sex marriages.' According to SNP member David Kerr, 'the torrent of, well, hate that was then showered upon him by numerous nationalists was deeply disturbing to many SNP members on all sides of the debate.' [45]

The SNP Euro MP Alyn Smith retorted that his party colleague's motion 'saddened' him and wrote: 'What is in the small, mean, angry heads of bigots is a matter for them.' [46]

Veteran campaigner Alan Clayton warned of 'the secular liberal whizzkids who have hijacked the party':

'To many like myself, who have spent a lifetime knocking on doors in the west of Scotland, in particular reassuring Catholic residents (that there is nothing to fear from the SNP) it is a personal tragedy. There clearly is something to fear from the SNP.' [47]

Salmond's predecessor as party leader, Gordon Wilson warned about the same-sex proposals at the 2011 SNP conference: 'It will lead to further social disintegration, sexual confusion and greater intolerance, where any in public life or service, who dare to uphold the Christian view of marriage, will be ostracised or discriminated against'.[48] He later became one of the leaders of the 'Scotland for Marriage' organisation which emerged to oppose the plans. Two hundred people took part in the demonstration outside a meeting of the Scottish Cabinet at Renfrew Town Hall on 23 August 2012, an action applauded by Scottish bishops.[49]

Soon afterwards, it was announced by Stonewall that Cardinal O'Brien had won its 'Bigot of the Year' award (against tough international competition).[50] For his part, Alex Salmond expressed regret about Stonewall's move but the Scottish Government ruled out cutting the £100,000 a year that goes to the charity. [51]

Later in the same month, Archbisop Tartaglia declared that the Scottish Government had to face up to the reality that Scotland was and still is an anti-Catholic country: in a secular land 'popular culture is inventing all kinds of new reasons to marginalise and hate Catholics. In the face of this, the Catholic community of Scotland remains steadfast. . . and fully committed to being part of Scottish society.' [52]

Retired teacher John Scott backed Cardinal O'Brien's stance, tracing key social problems to the collapse of traditional marriage. He lived in Drumchapel for many years and taught at St. Andrew's High School in nearby Clydebank from 1975 to 1995. In March 2012, he urged Brian

Fitzpatrick, a Catholic lawyer supporting the change, to take a 10-minute walk from his church in Bearsden to Drumchapel [in Glasgow]:

'Having done so little for the least well-off in the past forty years, the political and media establishment looks to console itself by making Scotland a "beacon of toleration". That it should seek to use marriage to achieve this, is ironic.

'At the heart of the social problems in Drumchapel, and scores of similar areas, in modern Scotland is the collapse of traditional marriage, where people marry and stay married to bring up children. Marriage as Cardinal O'Brien wishes to promote it. Cardinal O'Brien is contesting the positive self-image of the establishment; telling it that its plans will not produce a better society.

'For the modern Scots establishment, the suggestion that it is not progressing, not more moral than every previous generation, not creating a virtuous republic, is extremely unwelcome.'[53]

On social attitudes, polls had shown a greater degree of social conservatism among Scottish Catholics than to be found in the rest of the population. A 2000 poll with a large sample found 36per cent of Catholics supported more opportunities for women compared with 43per cent of the population in general (an indication that the primary role of the woman as a home-maker still enjoys credibility despite the inroads of feminism); 14per cent backed more opportunities for gays and lesbians compared with 19per cent of Scots in general; while 52per cent believed the availability of abortion has gone too far compared with only 33per cent of Scots overall.[54]

With sin becoming an obsolete concept, it was increasingly hard to detect what was the place for religion in official Scotland, other than for the Cardinal and the Kirk Moderator to be ceremonial figures meekly endorsing the ascendant secularism. The Catholic church was firmly outside the patronage networks. A body like the Scottish Catholic Media Office wisely chose to remain apart from media associations where a common position on major issues was informally worked out. Devolved Scotland had become a one-ideology state even before reaching its tenth birthday. Autonomy, equality and rights were the intellectual pillars of the new order. The outspoken Anglican 'Cranmer' has observed: 'These are the values that allow each to be whatever he or she chooses.' [55]

The kind of left-leaning public morality in the ascendant in Scotland might crack down on smoking, or alcohol intake, but essentially it was permissive. It upheld the desire for human beings to acquire omniscience over their own space – children searching for meaning and fulfillment, women enjoying control of their own bodies. Opposition to injustice and inequality was combined with a disregard for authority without which it is hard to see morality enduring. Equality is a slippery concept when, under New Labour the economic form continued to widen. There is enough evidence to suggest that if delivery is left in the hands of large sprawling bureaucracies, often concerned to satisfy their own appetites, then it is hard to prevent new forms of inequality springing up.

Scotland's senior bureaucrats and many of its academics and social experts are committed to a planned society based on scientific and expert reasoning. They are increasingly impatient with moral reasoning based on religion or anything else that is un-scientific. It is a form of positivism, the French doctrine meant to create balance and order after the French revolution. But in practice, it allows a lot of room for disorder in those large parts of Scottish society where its improving values have been rudely rebuffed or only half-heartedly applied.

Someone like Canon James Morrow (1934-2010) was a crank in this new Scotland. Born in Paisley, one of 12 children, he campaigned for much of his priesthood for the rights of the unborn child. There was no room for them in the science of society being practised in positivist Scotland. More than once, he was imprisoned when his protests over the violation of respect for human beings at their earliest stage of life resulted in a court fine.[56] His concern for the unborn was accompanied by increasing nervousness over the fate of the elderly. The former Anglican Bishop of Rochester, Bishop Nazir-Ali asked in 2011: 'If you can dispense with a person at the earliest stage of life why not do it at the later stages. Or in between?' He warned that the prevailing secular worldview was undermining respect for human life and warned of the danger that totalitarianism could easily be the end result of audacious political experiments with untrammeled secularism.[57] Rowan Williams, in his final speech as Archbishop of Canterbury reflected on a society so 'frenetically oriented towards youth. He said that older people are 'tolerated but not valued, while we look impatiently at our watches, waiting for them to be 'off our hands'.[58]

The new social media was a primary outlet for the promotion of youth and it was also one of the chief forms for promoting the edgy new comedy that extolled personal autonomy and social experimentation. One of the most striking exponents of the need to engage in radical self-discovery has been Frankie Boyle, the son of Irish immigrants who, growing up in Glasgow in the 1970s, embraced a new post-modern culture shaped around dissent and doubt. This successful comedian has described how going to Sussex university expanded his horizons: 'Yes, a lot of the people were daft, middle class cunts, but they were often pretty attractive and a relief from the crushing conformity of Scotland.'[59] As a library assistant, he became familiar with the works of Noam Chomsky, a philosopher who has acquired a cult-like status among many young people by depicting the USA as a the principal source of oppression and terror in the contemporary world.[60]

In 2005, Britain's *Prospect Magazine* ran a poll asking readers to vote on the world's top public intellectuals and Chomsky won by a landslide. Many young Catholics embarked upon Boyle's rebellious journey without trashing conventions to the extent that he has done but their arrival in the secular university marked an important staging-post in their abandonment of meaningful religious faith. Boyle's black rage, laced with a modicum of comic wit, appeals to some downscale Catholics, many of whom struggle to meet his ticket prices. According to official figures released in 2013, the percentage of Catholics in Scottish prisons is almost double their percentage in the population and they are affected disproportionately by unemployment and poor health. [61]

Cultural changes meant that a figure like Frankie Boyle was a far more representative and influential Scot from a Catholic background than Canon James Morrow or Peter Kearney of the Scottish Catholic Media Office, increasingly resented in secular circles for some of his outspoken statements. Kearney finds it laughable that the church is still thought to pull strings from behind the scenes. In early 2013 he challenged anyone to name a single piece of legislation in the past decade which the Catholic Church has publicly opposed and which ultimately *failed* to become law.[62]

The sense that politicians were leading society into deepening danger in order to retain relevance in the eyes of the young led Bishop Devine of Motherwell, in 2012, to accuse David Cameron of being a false friend of Christianity, while constantly undermining the family and religious freedom: 'On what basis can you expect anyone – Christians in particular – to trust or respect you?' [63]

Relations between the Scottish bishops and the Conservatives had never been good since the time Cameron became their leader in 2005. Shortly afterwards, he snubbed a request by Cardinal O'Brien for a meeting in London, saying he could make no time in his diary for him.[64] Such lofty disdain from a UK metropolitan politician may help to explain why he moved close to Alex Salmond and the SNP. But in August 2012, the cardinal announced that he was refusing any further direct contacts with the Scottish Government on same sex 'marriage'. According to a sympathetic commentator, it was 'perfectly understandable as a response to his having been banging his head against the brick wall of political indifference to the deeper issues involved here.' [65]

The Catholic church is perhaps bound to come into conflict with a state that had such sweeping ambitions and believes itself to be omni-competent (despite so much evidence to the contrary). By staying outside the state's patronage network, it could not be easily appeased by offering material rewards for good behaviour. Its delinquency in the eyes of ruling liberals placed a growing question-mark over the continuation of its system of denominational schools.

Arguably, the Catholic church could use its limited resources more effectively for instance by taking a more comprehensive stand on the retreat of ethics in state services. The deaths of thousand of hospital patients arising from the neglect of nursing staff is not an issue which has attracted its attention. These nurses were trained on an elitist theoretical basis at universities and exposed to American business school ideology in order to meet targets. How to care for people was lost sight of.[66] An ethical perspective on state treatment of the infirm and vulnerable would have been all the more effective if it had been multi-denominational.

But there were insufficient grounds for inter-church solidarity on many

234

urgent issues. Cardinal Winning perhaps did not help matters when, at a ceremony in Glasgow's City Hall in January 1999 to mark the fiftieth anniversary of his entry to the priesthood, he argued that Catholicism would be Scotland's sole faith in the twenty-first century.[67] But three years later, a church spokesman admitted that Roman Catholic weekly church attendance had declined by 19per cent between 1994 and 2002. Just over 200,000 Catholics attended mass in Scotland at the dawn of the new millennium. The fall of 22per cent was even steeper for the Church of Scotland; between them these denominations still accounted for three-quarters of all Scottish churchgoers, Church of Scotland 40per cent and Catholic 35per cent.[68]

The Catholic Church's authority in many places was already being badly dented by mounting evidence of the sexual abuse of children and young people by clergy which important elements in the Vatican bureaucracy and national churches tried to cover up. But Catholic morale and moral credibility took a battering from the high number of cases in Ireland, the USA and elsewhere and 'the hardly less devastating exposure of a culture of institutional secrecy that often put the interests of the Church before the welfare of the victims'.[69] In the twilight of John Paul II's pontificate, Cardinal Joseph Ratzinger attempted to overcome years of neglect and cover-up after being placed in charge of handling those priestly sexual abuse cases from all over the world that had surfaced. In 2005, he complained in a Good Friday meditation, shortly before he was elected Pope: 'How much filth there is in the Church and even among those who, in the priesthood, ought to belong entirely to him [Jesus Christ].'[70]

As Benedict XVI, he strengthened canon law to compel Church authorities to inform the police of abuse accusations; and he investigated and condemned powerful figures who had managed to escape censure.' But, writes John O'Sullivan, 'though his zeal never weakened, his energy and ability to pursue crime and the criminals through the ecclesiastical machine did.' [71]

No well-publicised claims of clerical sex abuse, involving minors, surfaced in Scotland until the dramatic exit of Cardinal O'Brien. In April 2013, Pat McEwen, now aged 63, claimed that he had been raped as a child, including once at Carfin grotto and that when the issue was placed before

Bishop Devine in 1998, he took no action against the accused priests. Devine stated his belief that McEwen, a recovering alcoholic, was a fantasist but Alex Neil, the SNP politician, currently minister of health and well-being, had written to Cardinal O'Brien about McEwen's claims as early as 2010. [72]

John Haldane, a prominent Catholic philosopher, referred to a gay subculture in parts of the Scottish church.[73] The most serious incident to be made public resulted in the jailing for three years of Fr. Desmond Lynagh in 1996 after he had been found guilty of abusing seminarians at the Catholic seminary at Blairs in Aberdeenshire. [74]

Before the events of 2013, most headlines were instead reserved for the scandal surrounding the Bishop of Argyll, Roderick Wright (1940-2005). Born in Govan in Glasgow to Gaelic-speaking West Highland parents, in 1996 he eloped with his housekeeper whom he had met in Lourdes, it later emerging that he was the father of a son by another parishioner. [75] The loneliness that could often be at the heart of the celibate ministry recently produced a moving memoir by a former Scottish priest, Govan-born Martin Gordon who sought laicisation from Rome in the 1960s.[76] In 2012, Professor Haldane, called on Rome to overturn its ban on ordaining married men so as to ease the shortage of priests and better relate to the faithful (though later appearing to shrink from this step). [77] But 'Cum Lazaro' a convert from Episcopalianism, was doubtful:

> '. . . married priests might solve the numbers issue, but even that isn't a clear gain. In regard to the 'softer' advantages such as resemblance to the laity and plausibility in the issue of child abuse, such advantages, even if they exist are small and doubtful; and there are clear disadvantages. (Ask divorced clergy.) Maybe married priests should be allowed: it's clearly possible in a way that allowing women to be priests isn't. But my own view is that the advantages are so unclear that it's an unwise step.' [78]

Opposition to the 2010 state visit to Britain of Pope Benedict XVI was overwhelmingly drawn from humanists and secularists belonging mainly to the middle-class professions who made much of the church's internal difficulties. Many British anti-clericals were incensed when, prior to his visit, the Pope criticised the Equality Bill. It was an important bill, by Harriet Harman, the Labour deputy leader, and was a consolidation measure bringing different strands of anti-discrimination law together in line with implementing EU directives.

The Pope warned in February 2010 that the equality law imposed 'unjust limitations on the freedom of religious communities to act in accordance with their beliefs'. Under it, the church organisations would be required to hire candidates who do not fit in with their religious doctrine or share their convictions, for instance on homosexuality, when recruiting key staff, such as faith school head teachers or youth workers. Harman had called her legislative package 'an opportunity not only to build a new economic order, but a new social order as well'. But she dropped her plan to force Churches to comply with secular employment law.[79]

No one with traditional Christian views who was prepared to defy the liberal consensus on lifestyle issues, sat around Gordon Brown's cabinet table by 2010. In May 2008, the Catholic Cabinet members Ruth Kelly, Des Browne and Paul Murphy voted for a sharp cut in the upper abortion limit to 12 weeks. All three, subsequently, had either left or been pushed out of government. John Denham, the minister in charge of public policy on faith issues was a humanist who told church leaders that he did 'not believe in god but rather in reason and human rights'. [80]

Opposition to the visit from militant Protestants was almost non-existent. The ranks of protesters were instead dominated by 'New Atheists' who took issue not with specific aspects of the Catholic faith but all religious faith.[81]

Previously a continental phenomenon, anti-religious feeling has increasingly become a British speciality. It was galvanised in 2007 by the appearance of *The God Delusion*, a book that has been consistently in the bestseller lists ever since. Its author, Richard Dawkins, a biologist from Oxford has pursued an online campaign against Catholicism in particular that is as colourful and uninhibited as Ian Paisley's was in his prime. In December 2012, Professor Dawkins declared that raising a child as a Catholic was worse than subjecting it to sexual abuse.[82]

Misgivings existed among other scientists about his style and methods.

Professor Robert Winston, in a 2008 lecture in Dundee observed that that Dawkins's insulting and patronising approach to religion did science a disservice, alienating religious people from it.[83] Madeleine Bunting, the liberal journalist, warned in her turn that streams of angry books from academics and influential journalists flaying religion 'are going to do very little to challenge the appeal of a phenomenon they loathe too much to understand'.[84]

Catholic ability to counter the influence of doctrinaire secularists in various national institutions was hampered by the absence of strong allies elsewhere in the religious sphere. The natural partner for Scottish Catholicism in defending core Christian values would have been the Church of Scotland. Certainly, from Edinburgh to Ayrshire, there were laudable examples of ecumenical activity. In one urban community on each Good Friday a shared afternoon service followed a morning procession to the local supermarket where an ecumenical service took place in its car park.

The 2007 Church of Scotland Yearbook revealed that active membership was down from 1,230,000 (1966) to 504,000 (2006).[85] Innovations like women clergy were unable to prevent growing isolation, with churchgoers an ageing demographic. The tension between the primary aim of preaching the gospel or else concentrating on being a national institution continued to gnaw at the church. Ann Allen, a prominent retired church official stated in 2012: 'If we are not doing the first, we are certain to decay, ending up as a glorified social club.'[86] Harry Reid, a regular commentator on the condition of the Kirk, believes that the Kirk could recover some relevance and halt the erosion of Christian values generally if it returned to the educational sector after having been absent for over 140 years.[87] Not a few Scottish Protestants bitterly regret the retreat of religion from nondenominational schools, believing that the absence of Church of Scotland schools has contributed more to the secularisation of our society than any other single factor.

But it is unlikely whether the Kirk could revive its influence through returning to the educational arena. A bureaucracy based in George Street, Edinburgh is absorbed with managing decline. Historic city centre churches in Edinburgh are being closed or amalgamated due to shrinking congregations. St. George's Tron Church, arguably the most visible Presbyterian church in Glasgow was plunged into crisis when its congregation quit rather than accept gay ministers. The secession of more parishes appears unavoidable if the final decision on this question, due in mid-2013, goes in favour of gay clergy.[88] A recognisable denominational outlook is fading to the detriment of the Kirk. Young people committed to gospel values are impatient with ministers who depart radically from biblical teaching. Trainee ministers are increasingly dominated by young evangelicals. They would claim to be mainly the ones who possess 'a real calling' needed in order to inspire people and build up a durable congregation.

Torrance Parish Church of Scotland is a flourishing 'Bible based, prayer founded gathering of the Lord's people in the village of Torrance' in the commuter-belt north-east of Glasgow. It maintains the strong missionary impulse which is perhaps the Kirk's greatest contribution to global Christianity, supports many missionaries 'who have gone all over the earth to tell about the love of God so that many may come to a living relationship with Him.' [89]

It has an Edinburgh counterpart in St. Catherines-Argyle, a church in the Marchmont district with two often packed Sunday morning services, the later one attracting plenty of students during academic term time.[90] It places strong emphasis on training gospel workers so as to form committed disciples of Jesus Christ. Such churches are a magnet for young people who believe God-centred beliefs should not be an anachronism – people who recoil from a culture based around celebrity, spectacle and consumerism.

Nearby is Mayfield parish church which is described as 'liberal and inclusive'.[91] *Grapevine*, its parish magazine reveals a church rich in activities led by an energetic minister the Rev. Scott McKenna. His sermon of 19 August 2012 centred on Julian Assange, the fugitive online distributor of American diplomatic secrets. Leaders were urged to display wisdom in responding to the challenge that he posed to global centres of power. [92]

But when I attended St. Catherine's several months later, the emphasis was on praying for British soldiers in Afghanistan and other dangerous places. Individual churches are likely to obtain success in offering a Christian vision for some of the acute challenges in Scottish society – drug dependency and other addictions, youngsters unable to find a place in the labour market, children and young people growing up in dysfunctional families and without role models enabling them to avoid harm. But it is unclear whether this work can be done within the parameters of the established Kirk where the spectrum of thought on how to preach Christ's ministry may now be wider than it has ever been in its history.

The defensiveness of the Kirk establishment was shown when the Orange Order passed a resolution in 2012 on 'Our Protestant Heritage'. Part of it read: 'it is a sad reflection that in today's society, many Protestants consider that the Orange Order is more in harmony with their values and aspirations than the Kirk. We as an institution never envisaged nor aspired to such a position, and it is an appalling indication of how far the Kirk has deteriorated...'

The Convenor of the Church and Society Council, Rev. Sally Foster-Fulton hit back. 'The idea that the Orange Order speaks for anyone except its own members is laughable... They stand for an unjust world and the Church of Scotland rejects their beliefs as outdated, outmoded and just plain wrong.'

But according to Ian Wilson, the Order's chief intellectual, examples of Kirk activity which she provided 'only confirmed how far the Kirk had strayed from the Great Commission to preach the gospel... climate change ... zero tolerance on domestic abuse, the tragic plight of the Palestinians... the iniquities of the Budget... and much, much more'.[93] Harry Reid gave cautious backing to the Order on this issue, remarking: 'The Kirk doesn't seem to be able to speak for Scotland, and it hasn't for a generation. The Orange Order are probably quite right about that.' [94]

In time, the Catholic church was able to manage its internal strains no better than its main Protestant counterpart. This was true of the relatively weak Cardinal O'Brien, who faced priests unwilling to obey him, and of his far more assertive predecessor.

Quite early in his episcopate, Winning announced a pastoral plan meant to harness the untapped energy of the laity and encourage the most dedicated among them to relieve priests of some of the burden of parish work as well as pioneering new forms of Catholic engagement. Some priests felt their role as the unquestioned leaders in their parish might come into question. Others feared that the church was simply overextending itself when it needed to husband its resources. The archbishop needed flinty idealists like the early Jesuits to make it work and such dedicated soldiers of Christ were increasingly hard to come by.

Many parish clergy, the bulk of whom are into late middle age or even older, have already been badly stretched creating new parishes on the edges of towns and cities or implementing the liturgical changes of Vatican II and they did not relish fresh challenges. One of the priests entrusted with implementing the plan threatened legal action against Winning after the press was briefed on his alleged role in the worsening financial situation of the Glasgow archdiocese. [95]

Understandably, his own motivation flagged, but it had been a novel endeavour which might have left a greater impact if implemented at a stage when both church and community were in a more vigorous state. The financial strains it led to forced Winning to take a number of painful decisions, such as the closing of inner-city parishes at short notice, a cause of hurt and bewilderment to many. Despite some observers concluding that he had never grown out of being 'a corner boy', the longer-term verdict about his vision for the church may prove to be kinder.

Winning's successor, Mario Conti, a careful diplomat rather than a populist, smoothed his transfer from Aberdeen to Glasgow by telling his priests at his first meeting with them: 'I speak frankly when I say that I have noticed a certain weariness on the part of many of you – and in some circumstances a real frustration in implementing the Pastoral Plan.' [96] His answer to stretched resources was the creation of pastoral co-workers who would assist the clergy in some of their parish duties. His was one of the first British archdioceses to establish 'the Permanent Diaconate, open to married men of more mature years. . . who can offer a good service. . . to the Church.' [97]

Scottish Catholicism remained orthodox by European standards. Most bishops were content to see the era of experimentation ushered in by

Vatican II in the 1960s winding down in some key respects and central authority being re-affirmed under John Paul II in the 1980s. Monsignor John Fitzsimmons who had attended the Vatican Council and later become a rector of the Scots College in Rome found himself sidelined in the 1980s. Instead of being destined to rise to the top of the church, he languished in comfortable exile in a suburban Glasgow parish where he wrote a memoir (currently unpublished) in which he vented his frustration at leading church contemporaries and rather naively depicted the BBC as a friend of the church despite it being in the foreground of attempts to secularise Scotland.[97] Even Archbishop Winning, who Fitzsimmons believed had been promoted beyond his abilities, revolted against Vatican imperialism as in 2001 when he flew to the defence of Bishop Maurice Taylor of Galloway. He headed the international commission on English in the Liturgy whose translation of the Missal was arbitrarily halted by a particularly insensitive Latin American cardinal. 10,000 changes were imposed and, according to a clerical admirer, Maurice Taylor, was hung out to dry but still bore his ordeal with stoicism.[99] Nearly a decade after his retirement, he continues to be an excellent preacher someone inspired by the religious ideals shaping Vatican II and who, aged 87, is still prepared to relieve priests of parish duties when required.

Bishop Taylor's treatment showed that the governance of the church was in danger of falling under the control of well-placed and ruthless clerical bureaucrats. Vatican II had re-affirmed the long-held view that ultimate authority rested with the college of bishops in union with the Pope which perhaps suited the Scottish wing of the church wary of radicalism whether from the right or the left.

In 2003, the choice of Archbishop Keith Patrick O'Brien as the man to succeed Winning as Scotland's cardinal for a time seemed unusual given his reputation as a liberal. As soon as news of his obtaining the cardinal's red hat was out, he said at an impromptu press conference at St. Mary's Cathedral that female priests, married clergy and contraception should now all be up for discussion.

According to a careful observer of church affairs, 'the Papal nuncio in London was immediately instructed by furious Vatican officials to insist that O'Brien make a public statement of his fidelity to the teachings of the

Catholic Church. O'Brien did so quietly at a morning mass the following day.[100]

Both O'Brien and indeed his predecessor Cardinal Gray, protected Fr. Andrew Monaghan who for thirty years had a midnight phone-in programme on Edinburgh's Radio Forth. He specialised in reaching out to people in the pit of despair and managed to talk many out of suicide. But he attracted the ire of ultra-traditional Catholics for advice he gave on contraception and abortion, and whose intercessions with Rome led to him being silenced in 2009.[101] He made a valiant attempt to engage with some of Scotland's vast number of social casualties and he offered a practical example of the church's concern for people in desperate circumstances which was bound to increase its standing even in quarters suspicious of faith.

Cardinal O'Brien actually lacked formal authority over the Scottish Church but for over a decade, he was viewed as not only the premier British Catholic (England lacking a cardinal for much of this time) but Scotland's best known Christian leader. But fame came at a price. Secular elites were thrilled when he condemned nuclear weapons in forthright terms but baffled and upset when he condemned what for many of them was a badge of modernity like same-sex marriage. I clashed with him in 2010 when he assailed the USA for retaining the death penalty in some states which appeared to confirm its violent and unprogressive character. I pointed out that a similarly strong line on law-and-order would probably be shown by Catholics in working-class areas disfigured by high levels of violent crime.[102] The cardinal, by contrast, had extolled the Scottish justice system and given loud backing to the justice minister, Kenny MacAskill for releasing the man convicted of the 1998 Lockerbie bombing on compassionate grounds.[103]

His decision to outspokenly project a Catholic perspective on various issues of the day perhaps unconsciously sprang from resignation about being able to promote Catholic renewal in his archdiocese. It is one that has been particularly hard hit by the crisis in religious vocations. The sprawling new town of Livingston with three parishes, is serviced by just two priests and a mere handful covered ten parishes in the Scottish Borders. The reorganisation of church structures in Edinburgh and the other eastern divisions of the church occurred in 2007 but renewal has proven elusive. Some parishes have inactive priests which causes distress especially to elder members of their parish who remember when it was almost unknown for priests to have such a minimalist approach to their duties. Others remain dedicated pastors but are hard-pressed. But the experience of Winning in Glasgow shows how difficult it is to provide leadership and direction at a time of ebbing religious fervour. He admitted to one priest six months before his death that he was tired and had little energy for new challenges.

O'Brien announced his departure in late 2012. His fate may be to remembered chiefly for a high-profile position on a disparate range of issues, a cheerful and approachable captain of a ship that was holed below the water-line while proposals for renewal from the laity were agreed but usually shelved. His own authority may have been eroded in the eyes of not a few of his own priests due to the way he elevated his own role and neglected day-to-day administration while (some claim) advancing favourites. [104] This was a dangerous stance which would lead him to bow out in ignominious circumstances due to damaging charges from men who rebelled against that frayed authority. The oath O'Brien signed in 2003 required him to vow to uphold the right to life, the 'evils' of contraception and homosexuality, as well as priestly celibacy. Remarkably for some, 48 hours before his resignation, he stated in a press interview: 'I'd be very happy if [priests] had the opportunity of considering whether they should be married. Many priests have found it very difficult to cope with celibacy ... and felt the need of a companion, of a woman, to whom they could get married and raise a family'. [105]

He then quit as archbishop, apparently at the Pope's own request on 25 February 2013 after he had been reported to the Vatican for alleged 'inappropriate acts' with three priests and one ex-priest of his diocese. [106] These allegations had been with the Vatican for some time and it is unclear whether O'Brien's return to unorthodoxy or the danger that they would be made public on the eve of a Papal conclave in which O'Brien was due to participate, brought matters to a head. On 3 March he issued a statement admitting that 'there had been times that his sexual conduct had fallen below what is expected of a priest, archbishop and cardinal.' [107]

After several months absence from Scotland, he had returned by the start of May 2013. He announced his intention to live in retirement in

Dunbar where 90% of mass goers at of Our Lady of the Waves church signed a statement welcoming him among them.[108] By contrast, angry serving bishops were reported to view his unannounced return as a cause of further damage to the church. On 3 May 2013, a phone call from Rome to the cardinal made it clear that his place was no longer in Scotland. Canon John Creanor, said he would be 'horrified' if the Rome move was true as 'the people of Dunbar are keenly awaiting his arrival'.[109] Speaking to a packed church the next evening, he said that the church had been hit by a 'tsunami' in recent times and, given the absence of direction, the only recourse was to seek spiritual solace by praying for the guidance of Jesus Christ. [110]

This personal crisis has led to a crisis of institutional authority. If church figures find it hard themselves to live a life based on Christian ethics, then it is only on a small number of issues, the abortion one to the fore, that their judgment is likely to carry weight. Most Catholics continued to regard abortion with horror (except in defined circumstances) but they have been unwilling to shape their electoral choice around that issue. According to an observant middle-class Catholic, Jim McCormick, a researcher in the third sector, attitudes to same sex marriage were far more varied. He argued in the press that many middle-class Catholics were unimpressed by the strident church approach on the issue. I recall attending a service at Christ the King's in Glasgow on 30 December 2012 and seeing one young professional walking out in the middle of the mass with his child in his arms. He showed irritation over the fact that a wedding service was attached to the mass as part of 'marriage Sunday' and the unhappiness spread to others in the congregation who observed that the photographing of the newly wedded couple was taking up to five minutes. McCormick wrote:

> 'I am still a practising Catholic. . . [but] I've watched all but a handful
> of friends turn away from the Church. A few return when their
> children arrive. At Mass, we're asked to reach out and encourage
> them back. On many issues of economic and social justice, the
> Catholic Church has a strong story to tell. But on same-sex
> relationships – especially when the issue is personalised so
> carelessly – what kind of approach is being offered? . . . The Church
> needs to listen as well as to lead. To recognise diversity within its

own ranks. To atone for its errors. To show respect when it seeks respect. But in the end, a journey of faith is personal not hierarchical. We can make it with or without our Church leaders.'[111]

It remains to be seen how pressing such voices will be in the wake of O'Brien's fall. Much depends on the willingness of the hierarchy to review a role marked by complacency and defensiveness in key respects. It is not even clear to what extent these men were prepared in the past to discuss with one another the challenges bearing down on the church and the shortcomings of some of those preaching the message of Christ.

A new Archbishop of Glasgow, Philip Tartaglia had been consecrated shortly before this crisis erupted. He had made remarks at what he assumed to be a private gathering in Oxford that the early death of David Cairns, the Labour MP for Inverclyde, aged 44, might be linked to his sexual orientation. He prefaced them with the comment that 'society was being very quiet' about reports of the 'physical and mental health of gay men'. The Scottish press sat on these artless comments until the day of his installation as bishop and then pursued him as he left Glasgow's cathedral.[112]

Mr Dermot Kehoe, the MP's partner, said: 'David died of pancreatitis: a gallstone blocked his pancreatic tract. [It] could have happened to anybody. To take a personal tragedy like this and seek to use it to make a political point, it's more than upsetting, it's deeply painful.' Later both agreed to meet privately. [113] However, the archbishop did not retract his observations about the health risks of a homosexual lifestyle. Some might say they were lent force when, later in the year, the leader of Glasgow city council, Gordon Matheson was arrested by police after a passer-by complained about an alleged act of indecency being committed with another man in a car.[114] No charges were brought and the politician stayed on as political leader of the city. Many newspaper readers were contemptuous of him and the political standards prevailing in the city but both the media and even his political opponents in the SNP remained tight-lipped about the matter (in contrast to the anger about a remark by Tartaglia which, however insensitive, had been made in private).

Philip Tartaglia was one of nine children born into an Italian immigrant family in Glasgow's east end (his father being interned in World War II like so many others born in Italy). He will already be aware that a west of Scotland media, very much enmeshed with the secular political elite, is likely to wish to make capital at both his expense and that of the church. His predecessor Mario Conti was handled less roughly by the media even when he asserted the traditional Catholic viewpoint on different moral issues (usually in carefully-worded letters to the press). But on one issue he took a stand which is likely to give him an uncomfortable place in church history.

On 9 September 2009, Scotland's bishops welcomed guests to Columba House in Edinburgh to celebrate its fiftieth anniversary as a repository for Catholic archival records and a centre for historical research.[115] It was seen as having worked for the benefit of the Church. Yet within three years Archbishop Conti declared that a pioneering initiative to unify the religious archives of a nation was no longer capable of fulfilling this task.[116] Instead, plans to break up the archive and move the bulk of the collection, of up to one million items, for the historical period prior to 1878 to Aberdeen (where Conti had been bishop from 1977 to 2001) had been in train from as early as 2002.[117] Conti was intent on creating a centre of Catholic culture and heritage there. It would be centred around Aberdeen University whose offer to accept the archives had been accepted by the bishops in 2008.[118]

Plans for the dispersal of the archives were enacted without the engagement of professional archivists, the Scottish Catholic intellectuals and historians generally. Ninety historians signed a letter of protest in May 2012 opposing what was described as an ill-conceived and arbitrarily-handled move.[119] Mario Conti was able to railroad through the scheme on account of his being President of the Heritage Commission of the Bishops conference, which reports to a trust for which he is chairman, whose recommendations are voted on by the Bishops' conference which he continues to belong to by virtue of being an emeritus archbishop after retiring. Dr. Michael Turnbull, perhaps the most prolific historian on Scottish Catholicism in recent times, who has played a central role in trying to save the unified national archive, asked pointedly in August 2012, 'how can this be good governance?' Tom Devine, perhaps Scotland's most visible historian, requested a meeting with the bishops only to be rebuffed: he and colleagues were informed by a church spokesman in May 2012: 'the bishops are unanimous in their decision that this is the best way forward.'[120]

The flight from dialogue showed a remarkable lack of concern about conciliating intellectuals, many of them Catholic, when the church now finds itself with very few friends and backers in influential Scottish circles. A later letter signed by Devine and two fellow historians bluntly stated: '. . . the Church's high reputation among historians has collapsed. . . Archbishop Conti's . . . attitude has not changed and is unlikely ever to change. We can see no other way forward than to urge that. . . [he] is withdrawn from any further involvement in this affair. This is a matter of utmost urgency if the Church has any regard for a professional interest in its history. . .'[121] On 24 July 2012, four members of the Scottish Catholic Heritage Commission (who included Lady Catherine Gill wife of Brian Gill, Scotland's premier law official) quit in protest at the absence of free debate over 'an ill-conceived scheme. . . that will cause incalculable damage'.

'Having been appointed to the commission for our skills and knowledge about the Catholic heritage, from architecture to printed books and manuscripts, and [having] given our time and energy freely. . . we believe,' they wrote that 'the time has come when we can do more to protect the Catholic heritage of Scotland outwith the commission.' [122]

A former Heritage Trust member claimed that Cardinal O'Brien had remarked in a letter that he did not believe the fate being prepared for the archives was the best solution but he voted in favour in order to support his brother bishop.[123] Such Episcopal amity is refreshing when compared with the situation in the 1930s when the nurse of one ailing archbishop used to shield him from visitors and berate another brother prelate when members of the laity phoned up for advice.[124] But it is still a singular position to hold for a senior church figure who supposedly has a flair for public relations. It shows an inability to be a proper guardian of the church's historical patrimony and, on the part of the bishops in general, it suggests an underlying philistinism (though several retired ones have misgivings about the impact on the church's long-term reputation). If fully accurate, it indicates that the church leadership in Scotland has not learned from painful recent episodes in the life of the church in Ireland and elsewhere, that a lack of transparency and refusal to permit dialogue only brings in its wake considerable discredit. This point may be fully realised when Cardinal O'Brien's successor looks around for intellectual support in order to fend off the attacks of secularists only to find that less is available than was hoped for.

But what many assume to be a desire for a legacy on the part of Mario Conti may not see fruition until after his lifetime if ever. Funding shortfalls may prevent Aberdeen University being able to act as a home for the archives and some are convinced that not just the post-1878 papers but those preceding that year too belong to individual dioceses.

Often seen as tired and introspective as it battles to defend a Catholic ethical perspective in aggressively secular times, the Church cannot afford complacency or compromise in the field of education. Denominational schools are increasingly vital for the transmission of the faith especially with both parents often having demanding work roles or else being increasingly secular in outlook.

But despite the Catholic state system being nearly a century old, it continues to be viewed as an aberration across different parts of the Scottish spectrum. Its schools stand out far more than in England where the denominational religious sector comprises one-third of all schools (involving two large denominations, including the established Church of England). By contrast, the Church of Scotland has run no schools since 1871.

In Scotland, the Catholic schools constitute about 15% of all state schools (there are a few Episcopalian schools and one Jewish school). [125] Perhaps they would be less exposed if other faiths were able to form schools on a similar basis. The fast-growing Muslim community is the prime candidate but nursery and primary schools set up in Glasgow and Dundee after 1999, have been unable to endure, having been criticised by state inspectors on various grounds. [126]

Denominational schools continue to be judged not by their academic performance due to the strongly-held view in different quarters about their role and impact. Opinion polls suggest that many would endorse the view that [they] 'foster estrangement between Catholic and Protestant communities and influence the behaviour of children'.[127]

In June 2011, Borders MSP and Conservative Justice Spokesman John Lamont claimed that dividing children between Catholic and nondenominational schools amounted to'. . . state-sponsored conditioning of sectarian attitudes.'[128] Brought up in Kilwinning, he recalled aggressive inter-school rivalries, leading a sympathetic commentator to suggest that he seemed to be indicating that the problem was not 'the existence of these schools' but hatred bred from others 'borne out of ignorance'.

On the Labour side Sam Galbraith, a former education minister, had argued in 2006 that religious schools were the 'root cause' of divisions and sectarianism and should be 'scrapped'.[129]

Catholic voices contend that inspectors have rarely if ever found examples of divisive attitudes being fostered in the denominational sector and that it is in the home and not the classroom that bigotry is too often incubated.[130] Supporters say that the emphasis on a moral dimension equips many pupils with a sense of citizenship and a willingness to look beyond their own material aspirations in order to empathise with others, even far beyond Scotland.[131] Asylum seekers are a group championed by the official church whose often arduous conditions in Scotland are treated sympathetically in Catholic schools. Claims about these schools encouraging upward mobility among pupils from lower-income groups are also frequently heard. [132]

Donald Gorrie, the architect of the 2003 law which enabled a sectarian dimension to be taken into account in criminal acts, himself stated his desire to see Catholic schools phased out and replaced by a single state tier. He believed that an improved system could emerge by 'merging the best values of Catholic schools with non-denominational schools' despite the fading performances of the secular state educational sector across the UK.[133]

But Catholic educational expert Tom Fitzpatrick was less sanguine. Writing in 1999, he believed that in merged schools, the likelihood that a secular ethos would prevail was a high one.[134] Certainly, there seemed to be little resistance to cultural changes running counter to Christian values in the non-denominational sector. Douglas Osler, a senior inspector of schools, in a 2001 report on schools standards, found that two out of three non-denominational secondary schools failed to follow government advice on the frequency of religious observance.[135]

Enough Catholic students are probably still able to grasp basic biblical concepts, characters and motifs, ones that have helped shape Western culture and were commonly understood throughout Scotland one or two generations ago. Pupils are likely to be taught at some stage, in Catholic schools, one of the key tenets of Christian belief – that human nature is necessarily flawed and that mankind's weaknesses mean that salvation and perfect happiness are unlikely to be encountered on this earth. But this runs counter to the belief of many a modern intellectual or planner that a terrestrial paradise can be created here by adhering to a particular ideology or dutifully complying with a set of targets; and it appears positively medieval to those in business and the entertainment industry who promote a culture of conspicuous consumption and sometimes excess.

The Catholic Church in Scotland is bound to be suspect in these and other quarters because of a message which urges people to think of their duties and restrain their appetites. As distressed laity and gleeful detractors found in 2013, church figures have not always rigorously applied their own teaching but nor has it been repudiated in the church's history. In 2003, the Scottish Catholic Education Service (SCES) was set up in part to strengthen the Catholic voice in educational matters at a time of such flux, not just in central government but at local level also. [136]

In 2013 Peter Kearney, the head of the Scottish Catholic Media Office caused controversy when, in a letter published in the newspaper, he wrote: 'In much the same way as America's black citizens in an earlier era were urged to straighten their hair and whiten their complexions to minimise their differences with the white majority, many will surely urge Scottish Catholics to stop sending their children to Catholic schools or making public or overt declarations of faith.' It was part of a wider argument that this tenacious spokesman had long made that in Scotland the chief remedy for overcoming sectarianism was usually for Catholics to jettison visible parts of their identity. He was strongly criticised by the paper and also by the leading historian Tom Devine for making a direct comparison with American blacks, one that Kearney denied making.[137]

John Downie, the head of public affairs at the Scottish Council for Voluntary Organisations (SCVO) produced the most outspoken criticism from any public official, telling the SNP government in 2010 that 'if they really want to get rid of sectarianism then getting rid of faith schools would be the bold and right action to take.' To outrage from the Catholic Church, this official, who said in his article that he was a Rangers season ticket holder, stating that the government was wrong to look for answers to sectarianism by regulating football. The 'solution' instead was to focus on the real cause of sectarianism, namely the school system. [138]

Growing numbers of young Catholics, especially from the 1980s began to separate themselves from a religious ethos. At university, some were prepared to renounce conventional attachments and even a commitment to learning itself in favour of rebellious counter-cultural voices. The Coatbridge-born former Catholic, Michael Connarty's life story (as related on Wikipedia) reveals his journey away from religious commitment. A successful student politician at the University of Stirling, he went on to become a local government chief and long-serving Labour MP. He is now a humanist and in 2008, he closed ranks with Ulster's Democratic Unionist MPs in condemning the Celtic goalkeeper Artur Boruc for wearing a shirt with the words 'God Bless the Pope'. [139]

An irreverent and humorous counter-cultural voice is provided by the detective novelist Christopher Brookmyre. Raised a Catholic in Barrhead, Glasgow, in early adulthood he renounced this faith in favour of humanism. One of his novels, *A Tale Etched in Blood and Hard Black Pencil* (2006) draws on his childhood memories to present a less-than-nostalgic vision of life in a Catholic primary and secondary school during the 1970s and 1980s.[140]

Thanks to the choices being made by their parents, for growing numbers of Catholics, 'denominational schools', were by the1990s, 'the only regular contact that many Catholics have with religious expressions of Catholicism.'[141] Catholic educational expert Monsignor Joseph Chambers argued in 2007 that many secular Catholic parents still 'want to hand on the values of Catholic home and family life and in many cases they feel inadequate to do that themselves as parents. . . they are expecting the teachers. . . to hand on their faith by what they say and what they do by example.'[142] It placed a considerable responsibility on headteachers and those in the religious education sector and no doubt reinforced the determination of the Church to defend its schools in the face of growing establishment scepticism in Scotland.

There is bound to be uncertainty about the future of Catholic schools in light of the growing isolation for the church produced by the O'Brien affair. The police, higher education and local government have seen amalgamations in the name of efficiency and savings; a Catholic church run by prelates too often willing to duck hard issues and make allowances for poor-quality decision-making within their own ranks, will be ill-placed to shield Catholic schools from secularist politicians or accountants. If, as Tom Devine has claimed, this is the greatest crisis of Scottish Catholicism since the Reformation, it remains to be seen if the Scottish church is capable of revitalising itself as happened in Catholic Europe in the sixteenth century. Or will the instinct be to circle the wagons and ride out the ordeal, hoping that a fitful normality returns?

Archbishop Tartaglia's admitted on on the day that his brother prelate left Scotland for a period of penitential exile that :

'our credibility and moral authority have been undermined. It will take time, perhaps a long time to recover these intangible but important realities. But we cannot be defeatist. The answer to this sad episode is not to throw in the towel. We need, rather, to renew our faithfulness to Jesus Christ and to go about our business humbly.'[143]

Under the Argentinian Jorge Bergoglio, the Pope who took the name of Francis upon being elected by his fellow cardinals in March 2013, the main focus of interest will probably lie beyond Europe. This means that unless the laity steps forward to demand a more direct role in the life of Scottish Catholic church, a narrow clerical establishment will seek to ride out the crisis with minimum change. A secular order will, in turn, be able to entrench its influence, facing only feeble competition in the realm of ideas about the direction Scotland should be taken in. This is highly regrettable when clearly what Scotland needs is voices offering renewal for a society that has few spiritual resources of the kind needed to withstand a twin economic and ethical crisis visible now in many parts of the West.

NOTES

1 See Brad Gregory, *The Unintended Reformation: How a Religious Revolution Secularised Society*, Harvard, Mass, USA: Harvard University Press, 2012.

2 Robert Fulford, 'In China, yes they know it's Christmas time', *National Post*, 22 December 2012

3 See Gerry Hassan, 'Wha's like us Scots who tear each other to pieces', *Scotsman*, 5 November 2011.

4 'Guess Who Won't be Coming to Dinner', Cum Lazaro, 8 November 2011.

5 *Daily Telegraph*, 25 April 2012.

6 McGinty, *The Turbulent Priest*, p. 173.

7 McGinty, *The Turbulent Priest*, p.p. 244-5.

8 Lynch, 'Catholics, the Catholic Church and Political Action', p.p.59-60.'

9 'Time to Challenge The Conspiracy of Silence About Abortion', David Alton, blog, www. Davidalton.net, 6 October 2012

10 James MacMillan, 'Unthinking dogmatism', *The Spectator*, 30 January 2008.

11 Daily Telegraph, 29 October 1996, McGinty, *Turbulent Priest*, p. 350.

12 *Guardian*, 15 September 2010.

13 McGinty, *Turbulent Priest*, p. 389.

14 McGinty, *Turbulent Priest*, p. 417.

15 McGinty, *Turbulent Priest*, p. 414.

16 Interview with John Deighan, 5 December 2012.

17 Interview with Michael McMahon MSP, 5 February 2013.

18 McGinty, *Turbulent Priest*, p. 419.

19 McGinty, *Turbulent Priest*, p. 418.

20 BBC News, 8 February 2011, 13 March 2012.

21 'RC Fireman wins 'landmark' case', *The Christian Institute*, 20 January 2009, www.christianorg.uk

22 Ian Dunn, 'Forced to supervise abortions', *Scottish Catholic Observer*, 2 March 2012.

23 'Leading barrister calls on Scottish Government to aid Catholic Charity', Cum Lazaro, 25 January 2013.

24 Gerry Hassan, 'Same-sex marriage row shows need for equality', *Scotsman*, 15 December 2012.

25 *Spectator*, 6 June 2000.

26 McGinty, *Turbulent Priest*, p. 419.

27 Interview with John Deighan.

28 *Scotsman*, 27 August 2012.

29 October 2012 ResPublica, www.respublica.org.uk

30 *Daily Telegraph*, 13 December 2012.

31 *Scottish Catholic Observer*, 3 August 2012.

32 Charles Moore, 'When Conservatives forget how to be conservative, they lose', *Daily Telegraph*, 15 December 2012

33 Brendan O'Neill 'The iron fist in the velvet glove of gay marriage'. Spiked online,' 12 December 2012.

34 *Scottish Catholic Observer*, 5 October 2011.

35 *Scotland on Sunday*, 15 July 2012.

36 O'Neill 'The iron fist'.

37 David Kerr, 'High stakes on same-sex 'marriage' *SCO*, 12 October 2011

38 Interview with John Deighan.

39 Kerr, 'High stakes'.

40 Cum Lazaro, 'Bishop of Paisley on religious freedom', 28 June 2012.

41 Editorial in the *Scotsman*, 8 October 2011.

42 *Daily Telegraph*, 12 January 2013.

43 *Scottish Catholic Observer*, 16 March 2012.

44 *Scotland on Sunday*, 15 July 2012.

45 Kerr 'High stakes'.

46 *Scotsman*, 12 October 2011.

47 Letter, *Scotsman*, 24 August 2012.

48 *Scotsman*, 12 October 2011.

49 *Scotsman*, 24 August 2012.

50 Cranmer, 'Cardinal Keith O'Brien wins Stonewall's Bigot of the Year 2012', 1 November, 2012, http://archbishop-cranmer.blogspot.com

51 *Scotsman*, 3 November 2012.

52 Ian Dunn, 'Scotland remains an anti-Catholic country', *Scottish Catholic Observer*, 23 November 2012.

53 John Scott, 'In defence of the beleaguered cardinal', *Scottish Review*, 2 April 2012.

54 Michael Rosie and David McCrone, 'The Past is History: Catholics in Modern Scotland', in Devine, *Scotland's Shame*, p. 216.

55 Cranmer, 'Britishness, Christianity and cultural cohesion', 4 April, 2011.

56 *Catholic Directory for Scotland, 2011*, Glasgow: Burns Publications, 2011, p.p. 521-2.

57 The Iona Institute, 'Aggressive secularism undermining UK's Christian

values says Anglican bishop', 26 March 2011 www.ionainstitute.com

58 *Daily Telegraph*, 18 December 2012.

59 Frankie Boyle, *My Shit Life So Far*, London: Harper Collins 2009, p. 123.

60 Boyle, *My Shit Life*, p. 98.

61 *The Sun*, 1 May 2013.

62 Memo written in January 2013 shown to the author.

63 Cranmer, 9 December 2012. www.archbishop-cranmer.blogspot.uk

64 Private information.

65 Cum Lazaro, 'Gerry Hassan, Cardinal O'Brien and the future of Scotland', 21 August 2010.

66 John Bingham, 'Targets and jargon 'prevent generation of nurses stopping abuse', *Daily Telegraph*, 1 January 2013.

67 *Scotsman*, 16 January 1999.

68 Peter Kearney, 'Scottish Church Decline is Not Inevitable', Scottish Catholic Media Office, 15 May 2003.

69 Eamon Duffy, 'A visit that reflects our changing times', *Daily Telegraph*, 11 September 2010.

70 Gerald Renner, 'Scandal: the story of Fr. Maciel', *Tablet*, 27 May 2006.

71 John O'Sullivan, 'Benedict's reformation', *Spectator*, 16 February 2013.

72 *Daily Record*, 29 April 2013 and 2 May 2013.

73 *Sunday Times*, 3 March 2013.

74 *Daily Record*, 25 July 1996.

75 *Daily Telegraph*, 26 May 2005.

76 Martin Gordon, *No Love Here – A Priest's Journey*, Harmony Row Books, Cork 2011.

77 *The Tablet*, 19 October 2012; Sunday Times, 3 March 2013.

78 Cum Lazaro, 23 October 2012, www.cumlazaro.blogspot.com

79 Editorial, 'The Pope, Labour and religious freedom', *Daily Telegraph*, 1 February 2010.

80 *Daily Telegraph*, 20 September 2009.

81 Kevin Rooney, 'What really gets their goat about Catholicism', *Spiked*, 16 September 2010.

82 *Daily Mail*, 23 December 2012.

83 *Guardian*, 12 September 2008.

84 Madeleine Bunting, 'The New Atheists loathe religion far too much to plausibly challenge it', *Guardian*, 7 May 2012.

85 McKinney, *Catholic Schools*, p. 350.

86 Interview with Ann Allen, December 2012.

87 Beyond Belief, BBC Radio 4, 22 August 2011.

88 BBC News, 9 December 2012.

89 www.torranceparishchurch.org.uk

90 See www.stcatherines-argyle.org.uk.

91 www.mayfieldsalisbury.org

92 www.mayfieldsalisbury.org

93 'Order's attack on the Kirk draws blood', *Orange Torch*, September 2012.

94 Ibid.

95 McGinty, *Turbulent Priest*, p. 281.

96 Mario Conti, *Oh Help!: the Making of an Archbishop*, Edinburgh: Black and White, 2003, p. 200.

97 Conti, *Oh Help!*, p. 200.

98 Memoir seen by the author.

99 Private information.

100 Stephen McGinty, 'Cardinal Keith O'Brien's legacy destroyed', *Scotsman*, 4 March 2013.

101 Deadline News, 12 June 2009, www.deadline news.co.uk

102 See Tom Gallagher, 'Cardinal Error: forgetting the main task', *Scotsman*, 14 September 2010.

103 Michael Holden, 'Cardinal says Scots fed up with U.S. over Lockerbie', Reuters, 8 August 2010.

104 Private information.

105 *Daily Telegraph*, 24 February 2013.

106 Catherine Deveney, 'UK's top cardinal accused of "inappropriate acts" by priests', *Observer*, 23 February 2013.

107 BBC News, 3 March 2013.

108 *Scotsman*, 2 May 2013.

109 *Guardian*, 4 May 2013.

110 The author was in the congregation.

111 Jim McCormick: 'The ability to listen marks great leadership', *Scotsman*, 28 July 2012.

112 *Scotsman*, 25 July 2012.

113 *Scotsman*, 26 July 2012.

114 *Scotland on Sunday*, 20 January 2013.

115 Scottish Catholic Historical Association, *Newsletter* 3, September 2009, p.2.

116 Letter, *Herald*, 26 July 2012.

117 Letter from Prof Tom Devine and others, *Tablet*, 15 September 2012.

118 'Fears over Catholic archive fate', BBC News, 2 May 2008.

119 *Herald*, 18 May 2012.

120 Private source.

121 Published in the *Herald*, 3 August 2012

122 Letter, *Scotsman*, 24 July 2012.

123 Private information.

124 Information from the late Dr. John Durkan.

125 McKinney, *Catholic Schools*, p. 90.

126 McKinney, *Catholic Schools*, p.p. 92-3.

127 Paul Hutcheon, 'Catholic church fury as charity boss blames faith schools for sectarianism', *Sunday Herald*, 5 February 2012.

128 Hamish Macdonnell, 'Sectarianism and Catholic Schools – The Taboo we are afraid to discuss', *Caledonian Mercury*, 24 June 2011.

129 Jason Allardyce, 'Galbraith: Scrap faith schools', *Sunday Times*, 24 December 2006.

130 Peter Kearney, 'Bigotry taught in the home not the classroom', *Edinburgh Evening News*, 24 February 2002.

131 McKinney, *Catholic Schools*, p. 210.

132 See Lindsay Paterson, 'Catholic Education and Scottish Democracy', *Journal of Education and Christian Belief*, Vol. 4 No 1, 2000.

133 BBC News, 6 February 2002.

134 Tom Fitzpatrick, 'Catholic Education in Scotland', in T.G.K. Bryce and W.M.Humes, *Scottish Education*, Edinburgh University Press 1999, p. 264.

135 Kearney, 'Bigotry taught in the home'.

136 McKinney, *Catholic Schools*, p.89.

137 Gerry Braiden, 'Likening sectarianism to US racism "beggars belief" ', *Herald*, 9 January 2013, 'Civil Rites', *Sunday Herald*, 13 January 2013.

138 Hutcheon, 'Catholic church fury'.

139 *Daily Record*, 30 April 2008.

140 Mark Fisher, 'These are Human matters', *Humanitie*, Scottish Humanist Society, Spring 2008.

141 McKinney, *Catholic Schools*, p. 152.

142 McKinney, *Catholic Schools*, p. 153.

143 *Scotsman*, 5 March 2013.

Conclusion

THE POSITION of the Catholic church during the first century of the Irish Catholic presence in Scotland was similar to that of the church in Western Europe in 'the Dark Ages' that followed the collapse of the Roman Empire. It was the only strong institution left in the community, exercising a range of functions not all of them strictly religious ones. In many ways, the church insulated a community that sometimes felt under siege and tried to impose boundaries that would ensure it had it a trans-generational character in Scotland.

Often, it was greatly assisted by organised anti-Catholicism which strengthened the inclination of its own adherents to close ranks. It enjoyed prestige and was reluctant to surrender power when the civil state increasingly intruded in the lives of the Catholic poor. A major victory had been won by preserving a separate Catholic educational settlement that, by the second quarter of the twentieth century, was funded by the state. But this concession was always contested by forces in society which were not invariably crudely anti-Catholic and the church could obtain no further outposts of influence.

A church rooted among Irish immigrants and their descendants instilled identity and helped reinforce solidarity in sometimes desperately tough economic conditions. But it was probably organised suspicion and hostility from some Protestant ranks which deserve to be singled out for preserving an enclave outlook that spanned generations. A collision could have occurred after 1918 if clerical leaders had encouraged the laity to assert a Catholic identity in the wider society. But usually being suspicious of lay autonomy, this was never on the cards. Priests who were at ease with working alongside the laity rarely achieved promotion and the Catholic community stagnated in the post-1945 years; arguably this was the time when it had both the inner strength and a favourable national context that could have enabled it to break out of an identity based on traditional clerics and deferential lay folk.

At the time of writing (in Spring 2013) the Catholic church is on the defensive and indeed in disarray. Leading figures have found it difficult to live up to, and enforce, what is a tough moral code, at least by contemporary standards. The inability of some clerics to resist libidinous impulses has reduced the level of threat that the church once represented in the eyes of those who feared or resented its power. The profile of self-confident power that has attracted the wrath of sundry radicals who wish to implant a new order in society was on display in Winning's years as archbishop of Glasgow. But it is one that Scottish Catholicism appears to be fast shedding. The church's weekly newspaper insisted in 2013 that 'we are still a force to be reckoned with'.[1] But arguably, the poor quality of church leadership on display has corroded Scottish opposition to secular causes like same-sex marriage. Paris witnessed successive mass protests early in 2013 against this proposal. 270,000 protested, many in their late teens and early twenties on 21 April 2013 just before the proposal became law. [2] In Scotland, such mobilisations are rare for any issue. Only Celtic supporters protesting against a mass-round-up by police on 16 March, succeeded in filling Glasgow's George Square with several thousand irate fans several weeks later.

The church is inhibited by its own organisational crisis. It has lost many of the dedicated priests who wanted to marry through laicisation under Paul VI and the numbers did not diminish when John Paul II withheld this right. Lay participation has not been encouraged by unimaginative bureaucracies with which some prelates have been content to surround themselves and priests often find that their dedication wanes and frustrations mount due to the rigidly hierarchical (or else disorderly manner) in which dioceses are organised. It is hard to see the current administrative structures remaining intact in Scotland if the number of priests remains so low.

Of course, it still has considerable resources; it is a spiritual alliance which has a special appeal in times of material hardship and social confusion and it has usually thrived on persecution. Overall, it has outlasted most other institutions whose prowess depends on human ability and motivation.

Within living memory, anti-clericalism was the basis of a militant reaction to Catholicism from agitators based in inter-war Edinburgh and Glasgow. But it waned in the post-war period and, rather unusually, church troubles in Scotland stem from infighting among clerics. Infighting around more substantial issues, specifically the direction which Western Christianity should take, much earlier lay behind the Reformation. There were deep-seated disagreements about doctrine and rituals and the manner in which the church exercised temporal power. The dissension in Scottish church ranks, by contrast, owes more to a particularly fevered episode of *Father Ted*, the perennially popular satire on priestly foibles (located on an Irish island but that could have also been set in a Scottish housing scheme).

Some priests find it beyond their powers to live up to the standards which they preach, ones which are increasingly out-of-fashion in popular culture. This is perhaps the culmination of a long process whereby clerics are no longer viewed as figures possessing an authority which demanded respect. Their standing gradually diminished as the Catholic community grew more multi-layered in the last third of the twentieth century. Catholics advanced economically through education, an arena of socialisation which explained reality in a firmly secular way: the world was human-centred rather than an entity which had been moulded by divine intervention. Modern education focussed on the material world and sometimes mocked the spiritual realm. This humanistic view of the world underscored the ability of individuals to achieve fulfilment through their own efforts rather than being part of a wider religiously-inspired community.

But irrespective of the values and beliefs being promoted in the educational sphere, an increasingly independent-minded laity was bound to look more sceptically at clerical authority.

> Its assertion that its hierarchy is both divinely instituted and vested with a unique power of infallibility on matters of faith and morals – runs so deeply counter to the democratic, pragmatic and questioning spirit of the modern world: in an age when people doubt authority, the Church claims to embody authority. [3]

In 2013, it is hard to see how such a claim can be taken seriously at least for some time to come. The revelation that Scotland's premier Catholic had allowed double standards to shape his approach to the ministry came as a tremendous shock (and not just to Catholics). Cardinal O'Brien had appeared to be the most approachable and least hidebound Catholic leader of modern times. Perhaps on closer inspection, his conduct towards several of his own priests might not have seemed so strange to anyone familiar with some of the ways that authority figures in Scotland have exploited their power and influence. His advances towards them might have remained permanently hidden but for the willingness of several clerics to denounce him to Rome at the very end of his period of leadership. No other Scottish public figure has had his private life exposed to such searing examination possibly since the disgrace of General Sir Hector MacDonald, the archetypal Scottish war hero, one followed by his suicide in 1901.

Dante, in his epic work the *Divine Comedy* describes the different circles of hell in which are to be found numerous top church figures, Popes among them. In Latin countries, clerical vice and double-standards ('Tartuffery') have long been seen, even by believers, as recurring maladies undermining the church but not its message. In Scotland, for a long time, the faithful appear to have been more trusting, or else naive. Trust in the integrity of church leaders was high perhaps because the need for solidarity in a hostile environment buried critical perspectives about authority even when it was poorly exercised. In 2013, some prominent Catholics like the journalist Kevin McKenna were ready to hang O'Brien out to dry while other personalities, such as the London-based Baroness Helena Kennedy advocated a more charitable response to his shortcomings. On 18 May, Richard Holloway, former Episcopalian Bishop of Edinburgh, even compared Vatican efforts to silence O'Brien to a CIA rendition. The letters pages of the *Scottish Catholic Observer* in the weeks after the crisis erupted reveal a surprising number of Catholics prepared to treat O'Brien in the same charitable manner that many people adopted towards John F. Kennedy when news of his promiscuity, while American President, post-humously became public knowledge. This must be un-nerving to his former colleagues on the bench of bishops whose calls for him to depart Scotland became increasingly shrill when it became known that he was back in the country and planning to stay. On 15 May Rome announced that he was leaving Scotland to undertake a period of spiritual renewal, prayer and penance and that any return would have to be agreed with the Vatican.

However lacking in self-knowledge Cardinal O'Brien may have been, he appears to have had a sound grasp of popular psychology. He may have seen through his long ministry that the faithful are very comfortable with the 'compassion culture' that became the trademark of his role. He championed various causes, often secular ones which involved him projecting emotional empathy for sometimes unpopular issues such as immigration and the early release of a man convicted of blowing up a plane over Scotland. Politics in Britain has, in its turn, evolved from a sometimes stern defence of core values to the championing of sentimental causes by politicians who often have no other way of showing that they are still in touch with the voters. This has often been seen as fake sincerity on their part which only creates future difficulties.

Politicians who betray popular trust through personal wrong-doing can expect little quarter from the media and scorn from a public whose low estimation of their profession has once again been confirmed. But by his actions and statements since stepping down from high office, it appears that Cardinal Keith O'Brien thinks that he can cheat such a fate. He stated that, 'If Christianity is about anything at all, it's about forgiveness,' and expressed the hope that his Church would help him to put the scandal behind him. [4] This brought a rebuke from some readers of the Catholic weekly carrying his remarks, one writing:

> 'Forgiveness is a gift of God to those WHO REPENT. In order to repent, you first need to examine and fully understand the sin.'[5]

This is a defence of 'the authority' culture' which had previously animated the church. Clerical authority was legitimised by dedication and service. It is a conception of the church ministry which Pope Francis sought to reaffirm in May 2013. He said:

> '. . . authority is always synonymous with service, humility, love. It means to enter into Jesus' logic, who bends down to wash the feet of the Apostles.'

He then condemned the opposite:

'We think of the harm inflicted on the People of God by men and women of the Church who are careerists, social climbers, who "use" the people, the Church, brothers and sisters – those they should serve – as trampolines for their own personal interests and ambitions. But these do great harm to the Church.'[6]

From these remarks, it would appear that the new Pope is likely to be unmoved by the plea of one of his errant cardinals for compassion. It would not be unreasonable to expect that if the disorderly affairs of the Scottish church required the two men to meet, Francis would ask Cardinal Keith why he fails to see the need for any retribution for his worldly behaviour. Having acquired a profile on Third World issues, he could at least spend a year or two doing light charity work abroad before settling down in Dunbar. Bishop Casey of Galway quietly performed such penitence for thirteen years after his disgrace in 1994.

A Church struggling to apply its own doctrines to a leading figure who admits defying them, will find it hard to avoid sliding into crisis. It's a gift for politicians who wish to be left alone to devise a public morality that will make their plans easier to accomplish.

While attending the funeral of Margaret Thatcher on 17 April 2013, Scotland's own assertive political leader Alex Salmond brushed aside the problems of the Catholic Church and expressed his confidence in its strength and relevance.[7] He helpfully exposed another danger which this and indeed other churches face – that of becoming political props of elite forces with whom they become entangled in relations of mutual dependency.

The O'Brien saga highlights the failure to make Christian ethics a guide for living for a generation of Scottish Catholics. Ironically, its failure to project its values within society enables it to stand alongside some of its secular foes. Arguably, much the same charge could be levelled at them. Secularists have been unable to ensure that their liberal approach to sexuality, marriage and child-rearing has been followed by beneficial social results. The declining traditional family has not been supplanted by dynamic alternatives whose vitality has been shown in positive social ways.

An intrusive church ,enforcing a set of norms base around moderation in personal conduct, has been replaced by an activist state which has acquired far more power over people's everyday lives in a much shorter time period. It has encroached on many aspects of family life and presided over 'the expropriation of the child. . . by the health and welfare profess-ionals'.[8]

Christopher Lasch (1932-1994) was an American social critic who warned about the harm being done by powerful social institutions as they snatched much of the autonomy enjoyed by individuals and wider family groups. He criticised both the political left and right for their headlong promotion of untrammelled capitalism or else the big state as frameworks for organising humanity. He argued that the outcome was problematic for society as whatever degree of freedom and autonomy existed in commun-ities was gradually extinguished. [9] He argued that people were falling prey to harmful dependencies, those linked with corporate capitalism on the one hand and a heavy-handed bureaucracy with a controlling agenda on the other.

Scotland, perhaps in an even more concentrated form than America, has witnessed the rise of these poles of authority. They appear to be rivals but often in fact complement one another. People's capacity to resist has been fainter than in America because of the long-term dominance of hierarchical and often authoritarian forms of power. Restless Scots dissatisfied with the established order have more often than not concluded that it is preferable simply to leave rather than to try to alter things from within.

In Scotland, there is plenty of evidence pointing to how human autonomy was constrained first by industrial capitalism which took production away from the family household, and much later by the state which, through a growing number of agencies, regulated private life. Many improvements resulted but 'a culture of narcissism' increasingly also took hold. People became increasingly self-obsessed, shunning long-term commitments and active social engagement. The nuclear family buckled under these pressures. Democracy, in its turn, grew impaired because of the shrinking number of people anchored in stable relationships who were prepared to be actively involved in public affairs: the sense of social obligation and confidence in the future which brought ordinary folk into politics, began to shrivel.

Young people availed of education more than in any previous epoch. But they encountered few intellectuals with a mission to educate them or the nation. So it is hardly surprising that many of the values underpinning education have turned out not to be transformative ones that decisively alter the interior lives of those who reach university. A lot of people simply enjoy the opportunities to relax and socialise. The exposure of over one-third of young people to higher education has not had a catalytic effect, creating a more engaged and responsible group of citizens intent on reshaping society on a liberal and humanistic basis. Instead,a superficial conformism to a range of external norms and values prevails. Materialism has been the primary beneficiary of educational expansion and no new set of cultural values have been pioneered with a clearly spiritual dimension.

Perhaps it was impossible for the Catholic church to be unaffected by the narcissistic values pressing in on it. Lasch criticised a lot of American intellectuals who, by their rejection of the obligations of family and community, confronted inner emptiness and promoted often destructive social experimentation.[10] Some of these observations may be relevant for Cardinal O'Brien, part of whose conduct suggested that he may also have possessed such an inner emptiness. .He appeared to act as if he could defy political gravity by condemning gay marriage in virulent terms after having violated his own priestly vows by indulging in same-sex behaviour. A number of priests, in their turn, broke ranks due to perhaps personal slights and humiliations and sought his downfall , something that it is hard to imagine happening in earlier times.

It might almost be seen as Scottish Catholicism's own belated 1968 moment when insiders decided to be guided by sentiment and feelings and stage a revolt against a power centre whose authority they no longer believed in. But it is hard to see how this revolt against discredited structures will revitalise the life of the church anymore than the generation of 1968 succeeded in renewing democratic politics in the West. If there is one consolation it is that this mini-clerical revolt may be a sign that of the church belatedly becoming more integrated in Scottish life. Its internal tremors reflect the uncertainties and frustrations of a country currently lacking any guiding values capable of being used to overcome debilitating problems that have given it some of the worst social indicators in the developed West.

Christopher Lasch believed that a stagnant society could only renew itself from within through utilising 'the traditions of localism, self-help and community action'. In this way people build their own 'communities of competence', often enabling them to stand up to powerful interests ready to take them down harmful paths.[11] But the times when Scotland has played host to community-led initiatives have been fleeting ones. It is perhaps through such loosely structured grassroots initiatives that Christians stand the best chance of influencing the direction of society. The potential has existed within Protestant ranks for gospel values to resonate with large numbers of people. Conventional church-going may be in sharp decline but innovate forms of religious ministry are still capable of galvanising individuals and this happens in a range of communities. But it is hard to see either religious or state establishments promoting a sense of social renewal driven forward by the enthusiasm of ordinary Scots. It is bound to generate insecurity as the necessity for elite dominance is inevitably thrown into question. The late Cardinal Winning, although sometimes deeply insensitive in his conduct , was comfortable with a degree of 'people's power'. But his own priests blocked him from going in this direction.

The far more influential Left is also nervous about popular mobilisations that might question its own formulas for modernisation. Those intellectuals who adopt progressive stances around the need to follow various secular paths towards emancipation have platforms in the media but, frustratingly for some of them, lack any conspicuous following. Their scornful approach to towards elements of the fan-base who were trying to save Rangers FC from years of misrule, may help to explain why. It betrayed a mindset that suggested these activist fans simply did not know what was in their own interests and it was better if Rangers simply vanished from the face of Scotland and a new progressive era for the 'national game' was allowed to get underway. But it turns out that Scottish football in general is afflicted by a major financial crisis and there are no easy ways of preventing big clubs in Scotland's two largest cities becoming defunct. Perhaps the readiness of groups of supporters to defy prevailing apathy and passivity and to try and rescue something permanent from the debris is something to be admired rather than disparaged.

Doomsayers in the media were warning that it could be the Church of Scotland's turn to be rent asunder by divisions. The 2013 General Assembly was due to decide whether to allow gay and lesbian clergy in relationships to practice as ministers. There was no shortage of passionate speeches but a compromise was skillfully engineered by the outgoing Moderator Albert Bogle and his successor Lorna Hood, based on ideas from Professor David Fergusson of the Divinity school at Edinburgh University (New College). A motion was passed affirming that a ban on gay clergy was still the default position but that liberal congregations could opt out under a 'conscience clause'. This was a deft manoeuvre but it is far from easy to spot the capable people behind it in the sphere of conventional Scottish politics.

Observing the Kirk's General Assembly (GA) in session is a useful reminder that Scots have been making their own choices about how they should be governed in the religious realm for a very long time. But this experience is not channelled into the work of the Scottish Parliament. It still appears to be an apprentice assembly uncertain of its own voice. Before its formation in 1999, Scottish politicians used to be spotted in the visitors gallery of the GA because there was a genuine interest in what the Kirk was thinking about particular issues. But now they rarely come and few seem troubled by it. The legislation being passed would indicate that morality is increasingly seen as a secular concern with the state having a predominant role.

The new Convenor of the Church and Society Council (the successor to the Church and Nation committee) appeared to be comfortable about ceding a lot of ground to Caesar. The holder of this office pays an annual visit to Westminster and the Rev Sally Foster-Fulton declared after two days of engagements with Scottish MPs in 2012 that:

'the politicians that represent us in London work hard, care passionately and love the people they have been asked to serve'.[12]

This claim runs counter to numerous polling surveys which show a deepening disconnect between those in the political world and ordinary citizens in every corner of Britain. The Convenor, a passionate and energetic advocate of global justice, originally from South Carolina in the USA, is not reticent about offering theological and ethical perspectives on a range of political concerns at home and abroad. In February 2013, hackles were raised in some corners of the Kirk when she claimed that on Palm Sunday, Jesus's entry into Jerusalem, riding a donkey, was one directed 'against the power and might of the Roman Empire'.[13] On her Commission's blog, traditionalists quickly protested over what was seen as a politicisation of the Gospel story. One wrote:

> 'Are you honestly suggesting that Jesus was leading a demo against the might of the Roman Empire? Jesus's entry into Jerusalem was the preparation for his death and resurrection, his death for our sins so that we might be put right with God and receive salvation rather than the death we deserve'.[14]

The Convenor had only recently returned from a visit to Israel and the occupied West Bank where she had expressed her shock 'at the dangerous inhumanity of the checkpoint' constructed by Israel in order to thwart suicide bombing. [15] A report entitled 'The Inheritance of Israel: A Report on the Promised land' followed in April 2013 . It brought the Kirk an unusual amount of attention beyond Scotland. This sprung from its claim that promises made to the Israelites in the Old Testament of the Bible were never intended to be taken literally and that 'Christians should not be supporting any claims by Jewish or any other people to an exclusive or even privileged divine right to possess particular territory.'[16]

The 2012 General Assembly had already agreed that the Church of Scotland would no longer consider the Israeli perspective when campaigning on the Israeli-Palestinian conflict. [17] In the face of strong international criticism, including from the Israeli government, the Kirk retreated somewhat on the eve of the 2013 General Assembly. On 9 May a joint statement was issued with the Scottish Council of Jewish Communities that stated:

> 'We agreed that the drafting of the report has given cause for concern and misunderstanding of [the Church's] position and requires a new introduction to give clarity about some of the language used. There is no change in the Church of Scotland's long-held position of the rights of Israel to exist; the Church condemns all violence and acts of terrorism; the Church condemns all things that create a culture of anti-Semitism'.[18]

The media in Scotland, one of its most secular professions, appeared increasingly unsure how to handle the Kirk. The life story of the new Moderator Rev Lorna Hood was interesting and uplifting but she got surprisingly little media attention. A working-class woman who overcame early adversity, including the death of both her parents before the age of 20, she was the first member of her family to gain a place at university. [19] For the last 33 years, she has been parish minister in Renfrew North, and is candid about the fact that the Church is managing decline but also that it can still bring hope to communities by the preaching of God's word. Such individuals are no longer prominent in politics and less visible even in the Kirk's own ranks where dynasties and husband-and-wife combinations sometimes wield substantial influence .

In different ways, the liberal and evangelical wings of the Kirk are engaged in practical projects, either nationally or at parish level which seek to affirm a moral community. There is currently no Catholic articulation of what a moral community should consist of in Scotland other than obeying the ten commandments and being charitable to the needy. This is surprising since, arguably, there continues to be a case for attributing moral value to religion. The emphasis, not just of Christian faiths ,on the importance of showing gratitude for the gifts of life and forbearance of its disappointments, will always surely enjoy a resonance in Scotland which remains as faraway as ever from any earthly promised land. [12] Very sketchy blueprints for national salvation, show even less signs of being realised than the ones previously unfurled to celebrate or sweep away industrial capitalism.

Christian intellectuals are now are only to be found in tiny parts of Scottish academia and they only surface at times of crisis in religious ranks. The Catholic church remains suspicious of intellectuals who belong, however uneasily at times, to a Catholic tradition, and does not know how to engage with them. Incredibly, the brazen attempt of an overmighty archbishop emeritus to privatise a millennium of archival history continues unabated in the post-O'Brien era.

A re-configuration of Catholicism, if the existing model is stretched to breaking-point, seems increasingly likely. And it might not be so calamitous: An institution centred around a series of church figureheads could make way for a far more decentralised one with the boundaries between clergy and laity diminishing in importance. In the face of crisis, a revival in knowledge about the faith and how to apply it in a challenging human environment could help renew Catholicism and enable durable partnerships to be forged with other decentralised Christian groups.

Magnus McFarlane-Barrow was a fish-farmer in the Scottish Highlands whose faith was re-energised in the 1990s thanks to orientating his life towards helping children in poor countries to get regular meals while in school. Mary's Meals was the result. Unless a church currently built around unavoidably fallible figureheads radically re-assesses how to perform its spiritual mission, then it is other Christian faiths or else inspiring lay members like McFarlane-Barrow who are more likely to fill the Christian vacuum that has opened up .

It remains to be seen whether a Christian renewal, not confined to any denomination and with ordinary church-adherents at its centre, is capable of challenging an ascendant but insubstantial secular blueprint for organising society. The currently near-monolithic humanist establishment badly needs competition in the realm of ideas and policies. If there is religious renewal, it should advance through the value of its remedies for some of the collective ills which cast a dark shadow over Scotland; if it is a top-down affair, seeking to win authority through manipulating institutions and information channels, it is likely to fizzle out.

In Scotland, an entire year after this book's appearance will be dedicated to argument among the political class in Scotland about what kind of territorial politics suit the country. It appears to be a vast intellectual distraction at a time when pressing social problems exist which arguably deserve to be far more of a priority for the politicians obsessed by the referendum being held in September 2014. If Christian forces are genuine about wishing to be good shepherds at a time of growing national uncertainty, then opportunistic relationships with the Caesars of Scotland need to be spurned. The crisis which suddenly overtook the Catholic Church could still prove to be a good crisis if it encourages autonomous thinking in which established power structures have to account for their conduct . Secular institutions need to be held to account in just this way, arguably to an even greater extent.

Political independence might be a welcome development if it encouraged genuinely independent-minded people. But forceful personalities and appealing soundbites are no substitute for a democracy that escapes from the manipulative designs of the ruling few. Alienation and disengagement usually follow such un-inspired elitism. In the absence of any original designs for managing some of the deepest social and economic ills of the country, unsettling symptoms like sectarianism appear likely to be features of the Scottish landscape into the future. The country is sufficiently insular to be unmoved by communal quarrels manipulating religion that have produce a grim litany of misery from Pakistan to Burma and right across the Middle East. This is the kind of internecine strife Scotland has had closes brushes with in the past. Whatever the political future for Scotland, it will surely be brighter if there is an inclination to learn lessons from the durability of sectarianism and understand that its staying power does not stem from religious factors alone.

NOTES

1 *Scottish Catholic Observer*, Editorial, 26 April 2013.

2 John Laughland 'France's revolutionary road', *Spectator*, 27 April 2013.

3 Walter Russell Mead, 'Benedict's Choice and the Crisis of the Western Church', *Via Meadia*, 24 February 2013.

4 Elena Kurti, 'Does Cardinal O'Brien deserve banishment or pardon?', *Tablet*, (blog by the deputy-editor), 10 April 2013.

5 Ibid.

6 Jeff Mirus,'Christ Loved the Church: Francis Throws Down the Gauntlet to Religious', *Catholic Culture*, 9 May 2013, www.catholicculture.org

7 Scottish Catholic Media Office, 18 April 2013.

8 See Norman Birnbaum, 'Gratitude and Forbearance: On Christopher Lasch', *The Nation*, 13 September 2011.

9 Sean Collins, 'Scourge of the elites', *Spiked Review of Books*, March 2013, www.spiked-Online.com,

10 Birnbaum, 'Gratitude and Forbearance'.

11 Jeremy Beer, 'The Radical Lasch', *American Conservative*, 27 March 2007.

12 Sally Foster-Fulton, 'A Westminster Visit', 12 December 2012, www.churchsociety.blogspot.co.uk

13 Sally Foster-Fulton, 'Easter witness for peace at Faslane', 22 March 2013, www.churchsociety.blogspot.co.uk

14 'Gordon','Easter witness for peace at Faslane'

15 Sally Foster-Fulton, Fences make good neighbours? I don't think so', 21 February 2013. www.churchsociety.blogspot.co.uk

16 *Haaretz*, (Israeli daily newspaper), 3 May 2013.

17 *Jewish Chronicle* (London), 31 May 2012.

18 *Scotsman*, 10 May 2013.

19 *Life and Work*, May 2013.

20 Birnbaum, 'Gratitude and Forbearance'.

DIVIDED SCOTLAND

274

Index

Carlyle, Thomas 22, 39
Carnochan, John 13
Carrell, Severin 208
Casey, Bishop Eamon 264
Catholic Church, Scottish Pre-1800
    18-20
    19th Century 22-3, 26-7, 40,
        41-2, 259
    1900-1945 51, 67-9, 73, 89-
        90
    1945-2000 103-6, 122-4,
        240-2, 135-9
    21st century 190-1, 224-5,
        228, 234-49
Catholic schools 45-7, 64-5 73,
    80-1, 108-9, 142-3, 152, 181-
    2, 249-52, 253
Catholic Truth Society 42, 93
Catholic Union 47, 48, 65, 66, 70,
    72
Catholic Young Men's Society 42,
    88
Celtic FC 10, 43, 62, 110, 111,
    119, 154, 156, 157, 158, 159,
    185, 186, 194, 195, 197
Celtic fans 152, 155, 156, 157,
    159, 194, 200, 201, 203, 260
Chalmers, Rev. Thomas 27
Chambers, Fr. Joseph 179, 252
Charleson, Robert 27
Chomsky, Noam 233
Church of Scotland 25-6, 32, 78-9,
    81-3, 91, 115-8, 119, 139,
    144, 162, 191, 223, 238-40,
    268-70
Clayton, Alan 230
Clerical sex issues 234-5, 244-5,
    253, 262-4, 266
Co-operative Society 71, 91
Communist Party 41, 66, 71, 136
Conan Doyle, Sir Arthur 41
Condon, Fr. Michael 27, 28
Connolly, James 49, 58
Connolly, Dr. Patrick 53, 99
Conservative Party 108

Conti, Archbishop Mario 161, 167,
    241, 247, 249
Cormack, John 15, 87-90, 92-4
Cosgrove, Stuart 205
Coull, Dave 187, 188
Creanor, Canon John 245
Cunningham, Roseanna MSP 194,
    202

D
Daiches, Lionel 98
Dalglish, Kenny 158
Dalrymple, Fr. J.H. 116
Dalton, Feargal 176
Daly, Lawrence 66
Daniel, Canon Joseph 104
Darragh, James 107
Dawkins, Richard 12, 192, 237
de Valera, Eamon 60
Deacon, Susan 221
Deighan, John 221
Dempsey, James 120
Denham, John MP 237
Denvir, John 29
Devine, Bishop Joseph 35, 55, 125,
    140
Devine, Tom 153, 167, 172, 177,
    247, 252, 253
Devlin, Joseph 49
devolution 148-9, 150
Dewar, First Minister Donald 168,
    221
Dewar Gibb, Andrew 95
Diamond, Charles 43, 51, 57, 58
Dickie, Rev. J.M. 82
Dinwiddie, Rev. Melville 115
distributism 69
Dollan, Agnes 53
Dollan, Patrick 53, 63, 71
Doogan, Mary 189
Downie, John 252
Duff, Lyall 188
Duffy, Judith 170
Duncan, Alan MP 225
Duncan-Smith, Iain MP 222
Dunn, Fr. Stephen 161

Pope John Paul II 138, 146
Protestant Action Society 15, 87-90, 92-4
Protestantism, militant 20, 85-90, 92-3, 114-5, 119, 161, 261

R

Rangers FC 119, 155, 171, 174, 204, 205, 207, 267
Ratcliffe, Alexander 85, 114
Reid, Harry 170, 238, 240
Reid Miller, Major 84
Renewal Movement 123
Rosie, Michael 10, 14, 173
Ross, Fr. Anthony 36, 75, 125
Roy, Frank MP 161

S

Salmond, First Minister Alex 151, 182, 186, 187, 188, 189, 194, 196, 204, 228, 230, 234, 264
Scanlan, Archbishop Donald 105, 118, 124, 125, 127
Scott, John 230
Scott, Mark 159, 176
Scottish Catholic Archives 247-9
Scottish Catholic International Aid Fund 219
Scottish National Party 14, 95, 121, 140, 151, 152, 176, 182, 185, 186, 187, 188, 189, 190, 193, 195, 199, 200, 202, 203, 224, 225, 227, 228, 229, 230, 234, 236, 246, 252
Scottish Protestant League 85, 107
secularism 11-12, 192, 217-28, 233, 236-8, 252, 261
Sewell, Dennis 159, 171
Shanks, Rev. Norman 15
Sinn Fein 49, 58, 59, 60, 87
Slavin, Fr. Willy 146
Small, Mike 206, 214
Smith, Alyn MEP 230
Smith, Mark 193, 212
Smith, Walter 158

Society for the Protection of the Unborn Child 105
Souness, Graeme 158
Souter, Brian 221
Steel, Lord David 219
Stein, Jock 119, 156
Stirling, Colonel A.C. 62
Stonewall 225, 230
Storrar, Rev. William 191
Struth, Bill 207
Sullivan, Joseph MP 61
Sweeney, Brian 222, 223

T

Tartaglia, Archbishop Philip 226, 228, 230, 246, 253
Taylor, Bishop Maurice 242
Templeton, William MP 85
Terken, Fr. Peter 49
Thatcher, Prime Minister Margaret 109, 141, 264
Thomson, Alex 207, 208, 209
Thomson, George Malcolm 81, 94
Torley, John 48
Tracey, Fr. Bernard 30
trade unions 31, 112-4, 200
Turnbull, Michael 90, 247

U

universities 45, 69-70, 78, 83, 105-106, 122-3, 124, 171, 233, 252, 266, 270

V

Vatican 26, 33, 121-2, 241-3
Vincent de Paul Society, St. 42

W

Waiton, Stuart 195, 201, 203
Wallace, Jim MSP 177
Walls, Patricia 152, 154, 174, 180
Watson, Rev. F.E. 80
Wheatley, John 49, 51, 58, 63, 71, 84
Whitley, Rev. Henry C. 83
Whyte, Craig 203, 210

INDEX